First World War
and Army of Occupation
War Diary
France, Belgium and Germany

24 DIVISION
17 Infantry Brigade
Queen's (Royal West Surrey Regiment)
8th Battalion
1 February 1918 - 30 April 1919

WO95/2208/2

The Naval & Military Press Ltd
www.nmarchive.com
Published in association with The National Archives

Published by

The Naval & Military Press Ltd

Unit 10 Ridgewood Industrial Park,

Uckfield, East Sussex,

TN22 5QE England

Tel: +44 (0) 1825 749494

www.naval-military-press.com

www.nmarchive.com

This diary has been reprinted in facsimile from the original. Any imperfections are inevitably reproduced and the quality may fall short of modern type and cartographic standards.

Contents

Document type	Place/Title	Date From	Date To
Heading	WO95/2208 8 Btn Queens (RW Surrey)		
Heading	8th Bn Roy. West Surrey Regt (The Queen's) Feb 1918-Apr 1919		
Heading	8th Bn "The Queens" RWS Regt War Diary Volume XXXI February 1918		
War Diary	Trenches	01/02/1918	02/02/1918
War Diary	Templeux Quarries	03/02/1918	06/02/1918
War Diary	Trenches	07/02/1918	11/02/1918
War Diary	Bernes	12/02/1918	18/02/1918
War Diary	Trenches	19/02/1918	23/02/1918
War Diary	Montigny	24/02/1918	27/02/1918
War Diary	Montigny-Hancourt	28/02/1918	28/02/1918
Operation(al) Order(s)	8th Bn The Queen's R.W.S. Regt Operation Order. No. 6 Appendix I	01/02/1918	01/02/1918
Operation(al) Order(s)	8th (S) Battn The Queen's R.W.S. Regt Operation Order No. 7 Appendix II	04/02/1918	04/02/1918
Operation(al) Order(s)	72nd Infantry Brigade Operation Order No. 6. Appendix III	04/02/1918	04/02/1918
Miscellaneous	Table	04/02/1918	04/02/1918
Miscellaneous	Amendment No 1 To Operation Order Nos. 5 & 6.	04/02/1918	04/02/1918
Operation(al) Order(s)	72nd Infantry Brigade Operation Order No. 8	03/02/1918	03/02/1918
Miscellaneous	Amendment to 17th Infantry Brigade O.O. No 221. Appendix III	04/02/1918	04/02/1918
Operation(al) Order(s)	17th Infantry Brigade Operation Order No 221	03/02/1918	03/02/1918
Miscellaneous	Table "A". Issued with 17th Inf: Bde O.O. No 215		
Miscellaneous		04/02/1918	04/02/1918
Operation(al) Order(s)	8th Bn. The Queen's. R.W.S. Regt. Operation Order No. 8 Appendix III	06/02/1918	06/02/1918
Operation(al) Order(s)	17th Infantry Brigade Operation Order No 222 Appendix IV	09/02/1918	09/02/1918
Miscellaneous	Table "A"		
Operation(al) Order(s)	8th Bn. The Queen's R.W.S. Regt Operation Order No. 9 Appendix IV	10/02/1918	10/02/1918
Operation(al) Order(s)	17th Infantry Brigade Order No. 224 Appendix V	17/02/1918	17/02/1918
Operation(al) Order(s)	8th Bn. The Queens. R.W.S. Regt. Operation Order No. 10 Appendix V	18/02/1918	18/02/1918
Operation(al) Order(s)	8th Battn The Queen's. R.W.S. Regt. Operation Order. No 11. Appendix VI	19/02/1918	19/02/1918
Operation(al) Order(s)	17th Infantry Brigade Order No 225 Appendix VII	21/02/1918	21/02/1918
Miscellaneous	Distribution of 17th I. Bde Order No 225		
Miscellaneous	Table "A" issued with 17th I. Bde Order No 225		
Operation(al) Order(s)	8th Battn The Queen's. R.W.S. Regt. Operation Order No 12. Appendix VII	21/02/1918	21/02/1918
Operation(al) Order(s)	73rd. Infantry Brigade Order No. 180	21/02/1918	21/02/1918
Miscellaneous	Amendment To 73rd Infantry Brigade Order No. 160 Appendix IV		
Miscellaneous			
Operation(al) Order(s)	8th Bn. The Queen's R.W.S. Regt.Operation Order No. 13 Appendix VIII	22/02/1918	22/02/1918

Operation(al) Order(s)	8th The Queens. R.W.S. Regt Operation Order No. 14 Appendix IX	27/02/1918	27/02/1918
Operation(al) Order(s)	8th Bn The Queen's R.W.S. Regt. Operation Order No. 15. Appendix IX	28/02/1918	28/02/1918
Miscellaneous	C Form Messages And Signals.	28/02/1918	28/02/1918
Miscellaneous	Corrigenda To 17th I. Bde O. No 227 Appendix IX	27/02/1918	27/02/1918
Operation(al) Order(s)	17th Infantry Brigade Order No 227	26/02/1918	26/02/1918
Miscellaneous	Table "C"		
Miscellaneous	Table "A" issued with 17th I. Bde Order No 227 dated 26/2/18	26/02/1918	26/02/1918
Miscellaneous	Table "B"		
Heading	8th Battalion Royal West Surrey Regiment March 1918		
Heading	8th Bn "The Queens" R.W.S Regt War Diary Volume 31 March 1918		
War Diary	Hancourt Montecourt	01/03/1918	01/03/1918
War Diary	Montecourt	02/03/1918	11/03/1918
War Diary	Montecourt Vendelles	12/03/1918	12/03/1918
War Diary	Vendelles	13/03/1918	17/03/1918
War Diary	Vendelles-Le Verguier	18/03/1918	18/03/1918
War Diary	Le Verguier	19/03/1918	22/03/1918
War Diary	Le Verguier-Montecourt	22/03/1918	22/03/1918
War Diary	Montecourt-Li Court	23/03/1918	23/03/1918
War Diary	St. Christ	23/03/1918	23/03/1918
War Diary	Licourt-Chaulnes-Omiecourt	24/03/1918	24/03/1918
War Diary	Omiecourt	25/03/1918	25/03/1918
War Diary	Omiecourt-Chaulnes	25/03/1918	25/03/1918
War Diary	Chaulnes-Vrely	26/03/1918	26/03/1918
War Diary	Vrely	27/03/1918	27/03/1918
War Diary	Vrely-Castel	28/03/1918	28/03/1918
War Diary	Hailles	29/03/1918	30/03/1918
War Diary	Thezy-Fouencamps	31/03/1918	31/03/1918
Miscellaneous	C Form. Messages And Signals. Appendix I	21/03/1918	21/03/1918
Miscellaneous	A Form. Messages And Signals. Appendix II	23/03/1918	23/03/1918
Miscellaneous	A Form. Messages And Signals.	23/03/1918	23/03/1918
Miscellaneous	A Form. Messages And Signals.		
Miscellaneous	A Form. Messages And Signals.	23/03/1918	23/03/1918
Miscellaneous	Appendix III	24/03/1918	24/03/1918
Miscellaneous	Messages And Signals. Appendix IV	25/03/1918	25/03/1918
Miscellaneous	A Form. Messages And Signals.		
Miscellaneous	A Form. Messages And Signals. Appendix IV	25/03/1918	25/03/1918
Miscellaneous	A Form. Messages And Signals. Appendix V	27/03/1918	27/03/1918
Miscellaneous		27/03/1918	27/03/1918
Miscellaneous	S. A.	27/03/1918	27/03/1918
Miscellaneous	OC. "C". Coy	27/03/1918	27/03/1918
Miscellaneous	To J.A.	27/03/1918	27/03/1918
Miscellaneous	To The Adjutant	27/03/1918	27/03/1918
Miscellaneous	ED K C	17/01/1918	17/01/1918
Miscellaneous	To The Adjutant E D	27/03/1918	27/03/1918
Miscellaneous	OC.D Coy.	27/03/1918	27/03/1918
Miscellaneous	The Adjutant E.D	27/03/1918	27/03/1918
Miscellaneous	To The Adjutant from O/C. C. Coy.		
Miscellaneous	A Form. Messages And Signals. Appendix VI	29/03/1918	29/03/1918
Miscellaneous	A Form. Messages And Signals. Appendix VI	30/03/1918	30/03/1918
Miscellaneous	Messages And Signals. Appendix VII	30/03/1918	30/03/1918
Miscellaneous	Messages And Signals.	30/03/1918	30/03/1918
Miscellaneous	8th Queens Appendix VIII	31/03/1918	31/03/1918

Miscellaneous	8th Queens	31/03/1918	31/03/1918
Miscellaneous	C Form Messages And Signals.		
Miscellaneous	8th Queens Appendix IX	02/04/1918	02/04/1918
Map			
Heading	Appendix I 8 Queens Mar/18		
Heading	8th Battn. The Queen's (Royal West Surrey Regiment). April 1918.		
Heading	8th Bn The Queen's R.W.S. Regt War Diary Volume XXXII Vol 32		
War Diary	Fouencamps	01/04/1918	02/04/1918
War Diary	Fouencamps-Boves	03/04/1918	03/04/1918
War Diary	Gentelles	04/04/1918	05/04/1918
War Diary	Gentelles-Longeau	05/04/1918	05/04/1918
War Diary	Saleux-St Valery	06/04/1918	06/04/1918
War Diary	St Valery-Pende	07/04/1918	07/04/1918
War Diary	Pende	08/04/1918	16/04/1918
War Diary	Pende-Woincourt	17/04/1918	17/04/1918
War Diary	Pernes-Magnicourt	18/04/1918	18/04/1918
War Diary	Magnicourt	19/04/1918	30/04/1918
Heading	Appendices I to IX.		
Miscellaneous	Copy of Telegram Appendix I	01/04/1918	01/04/1918
Miscellaneous	Appendix II	03/04/1918	03/04/1918
Miscellaneous	Appendix III	04/04/1918	04/04/1918
Miscellaneous		04/04/1918	04/04/1918
Miscellaneous	To The Adjutant E.D. From O.C. No.2 Coy	04/04/1918	04/04/1918
Miscellaneous	Messages And Signals.	04/04/1918	04/04/1918
Miscellaneous	To The Adjt E D From O.C.No. 2 Coy	04/04/1918	04/04/1918
Miscellaneous		04/04/1918	04/04/1918
Miscellaneous	Messages And Signals.	04/04/1918	04/04/1918
Miscellaneous		04/04/1918	04/04/1918
Miscellaneous	Appendix IV	05/04/1918	05/04/1918
Miscellaneous		05/04/1918	05/04/1918
Miscellaneous	Appendix V	06/03/1918	06/03/1918
Miscellaneous	Appendix V A.	08/04/1918	08/04/1918
Miscellaneous	Appendix VI	09/04/1918	09/04/1918
Miscellaneous	Amendment to 17th Inf: Bde Order No. 231 Appendix VII	16/04/1918	16/04/1918
Operation(al) Order(s)	17th Infantry Brigade Order No. 231	16/04/1918	16/04/1918
Miscellaneous			
Miscellaneous		16/04/1918	16/04/1918
Miscellaneous		17/04/1918	17/04/1918
Operation(al) Order(s)	8th Bn The Queens R.W.S. Regt Operation Order No. A. 1. Appendix VII	16/04/1918	16/04/1918
Miscellaneous	Administrative Instructions For The Entrainment Of The 24th Division, (Less Artillery). Appendix VII	16/04/1918	16/04/1918
Miscellaneous	24th Division	16/04/1918	16/04/1918
Miscellaneous			
Miscellaneous	8th Queens	16/04/1918	16/04/1918
Miscellaneous	24th Division No. A.199/445 Appendix VIII	20/04/1918	20/04/1918
Miscellaneous	Appendix IX	22/04/1918	22/04/1918
Heading	8th Bn The Queen's R.W.S. Regt War Diary for May 1918 Volume XXXIII June 7th 1918		
War Diary	Magnicourt-Houdain	01/05/1918	01/05/1918
War Diary	Les Brebis-Maroc	02/05/1918	02/05/1918
War Diary	Maroc	03/05/1918	11/05/1918
War Diary	Maroc Trenches	12/05/1918	12/05/1918

War Diary	Trenches	12/05/1918	17/05/1918
War Diary	Trenches-Les Brebis	18/05/1918	18/05/1918
War Diary	Les Brebis	19/05/1918	24/05/1918
War Diary	Trenches	24/05/1918	31/05/1918
Operation(al) Order(s)	17th Infantry Brigade Order No. 232. Appendix I	30/04/1918	30/04/1918
Miscellaneous	March Table "A" to accompany 17th Infantry Brigade Order No. 232.		
Miscellaneous	March Table "B" to accompany 17th Infantry Brigade Order No. 232. dated 30/4/18	01/05/1918	01/05/1918
Miscellaneous	Reference March Table "B" dated 1st May 1918.	02/05/1918	02/05/1918
Miscellaneous	8th Queens	01/05/1918	01/05/1918
Operation(al) Order(s)	8th Bn The Queens R.W.S. Regt. Operation Order No. A.2 Appendix I	30/04/1918	30/04/1918
Operation(al) Order(s)	17th Infantry Brigade Order No. 232 Appendix II	11/05/1918	11/05/1918
Miscellaneous	Relief Table "A" (issued with 17th Inf: Bde Order 233 dated 11th May)		
Operation(al) Order(s)	8th Bn The Queen's R.W.S. Regt. Operation Order. No. A.4. Appendix II	12/05/1918	12/05/1918
Operation(al) Order(s)	8th Bn The Queen's R.W.S. Regt Operation Order No. A.S Appendix III		
Miscellaneous	To.O.C. Company From Adjutant.		
Operation(al) Order(s)	17th Infantry Brigade Order No. 234 Appendix III	15/05/1918	15/05/1918
Operation(al) Order(s)	8th Bn. The Queens. R.W.S. Regt Operation Order. No. A.6. Appendix IV	00/05/1918	00/05/1918
Operation(al) Order(s)	8th Bn.The Queens. R.W.S. Regt. Operation Order. No.A.7. Appendix V	25/05/1918	25/05/1918
Operation(al) Order(s)	8th Bn. The Queens. R.W.S. Regt. Operation Order. No. A. 8. Appendix VI	29/05/1918	29/05/1918
Heading	8th Bn The Queen's R.W.S. Regt War Diary Volume XXXIV June 1918 Vol 34		
War Diary	Trenches	01/06/1918	05/06/1918
War Diary	Les Brebis	06/06/1918	11/06/1918
War Diary	Trenches	12/06/1918	23/06/1918
War Diary	Les Brebis	24/06/1918	29/06/1918
War Diary	Trenches	30/06/1918	30/06/1918
Operation(al) Order(s)	8th Bn. Queens. R.W.S. Regt Operation Order. No. A. a Appendix I	04/06/1918	04/06/1918
Operation(al) Order(s)	8th Bn. The Queen's Regt Operation Order. No. A. 10. Appendix II	10/06/1918	10/06/1918
Operation(al) Order(s)	8th Bn The Queen's R.W.S. Regt Operation Order No A 11. Appendix III	16/06/1918	16/06/1918
Miscellaneous	C.O.		
Operation(al) Order(s)	8th Battn The Queen's Regt. Operation Order No. A. 12. Appendix IV	22/06/1918	22/06/1918
Operation(al) Order(s)	8th Bn. The Queen's. Regt. Operation Order. No. A. 13. Appendix V	28/06/1918	28/06/1918
Heading	8th Bn. The Queens R.W.S Regt War Diary Volume XXXV for July 1918. August 9th 1918		
War Diary	Trenches	01/07/1918	12/07/1918
War Diary	Trenches-Les Brebis	13/07/1918	13/07/1918
War Diary	Les Brebis	14/07/1918	17/07/1918
War Diary	Trenches	18/07/1918	30/07/1918
War Diary	Les Brebis	31/07/1918	31/07/1918
Operation(al) Order(s)	Operation Order No. A.14 By Lieut. Col. H.J.C. Peirs. D.S.O. Thursday July 4th 1918 Appendix I	04/07/1918	04/07/1918

Operation(al) Order(s)	8th Bn The Queens Rgt. Operation-Order No. A. 16. By Major M.J.C. Peirs D.S.O. Appendix II	11/07/1918	11/07/1918
Operation(al) Order(s)	8th Bn. The Queens R.W.S. Regt Operation Order. No A. 17 By Lieut. Colonel H.T.C. Peirs. D.S.O. Appendix III	17/07/1918	17/07/1918
Miscellaneous	17th Infantry Brigade. G.20/2. Appendix IV	19/07/1918	19/07/1918
Miscellaneous	8th Queens Centre Group. 24th Division "G" Appendix V	23/07/1918	23/07/1918
Operation(al) Order(s)	8th The Queens. Regt. Operation Order. No. A. 18 By Lt. Col. H.J.C. Peirs D.S.O. Appendix V	23/07/1918	23/07/1918
Operation(al) Order(s)	8th Bn. The Queens Regt Operation Order. No. A. 10. by Lieut Col. H.J.C. Peirs. D.S.O. Appendix A. 19	23/07/1918	23/07/1918
Miscellaneous	17th Inf. Bde. No. G.2/131 Appendix VII	25/07/1918	25/07/1918
Miscellaneous	C Form. Messages And Signals.	26/07/1918	26/07/1918
Operation(al) Order(s)	Operation Order No. 26 by Lt. Col. J.C. Walch, D.S.O., R.F.A. Commanding Centre Group 24th D.A.	00/07/1918	00/07/1918
Miscellaneous	8th S. Battn. The Queens	29/07/1918	29/07/1918
Operation(al) Order(s)	8th Bn. The Queen's R.W.S. Regt. Operation Order No. A. 10 by Major R.H. Rowland.	20/07/1918	20/07/1918
Miscellaneous			
Heading	8th Bn The Queen's R.W.S. Regt War Diary Volume XXXVI August 1918		
War Diary	Les Brebis	01/08/1918	04/08/1918
War Diary	Trenches	05/08/1918	16/08/1918
War Diary	Trenches Les Brebis	17/08/1918	17/08/1918
War Diary	Les Brebis	18/08/1918	22/08/1918
War Diary	Les Brebis Trenches	23/08/1918	23/08/1918
War Diary	Trenches	24/08/1918	31/08/1918
Operation(al) Order(s)	8th Bn. The Queens Regt. Operation Order No. A. 21 By Lieut. Colonel H.J.C. Piers. D.S.O., Appendix T	04/08/1918	04/08/1918
Operation(al) Order(s)	8th Bn. The Queen's Regt. Operation Order No. A. 22 by Major. R.H.Rowland Appendix 2	10/08/1918	10/08/1918
Miscellaneous	C Form. Messages And Signals. Appendix III	09/08/1918	09/08/1918
Operation(al) Order(s)	8th Bn The Queen's Regt. Operation Order No. A. 23 Lieut. Colonel H.J.C. Piers D.S.O. Appendix IV	16/08/1918	16/08/1918
Operation(al) Order(s)	8th Bn The Queen's Regt. Operation Order No. A. 24 by Lieut. Colonel H.J.C. Piers D.S.O. Appendix V	22/08/1918	22/08/1918
Operation(al) Order(s)	8th Bn. The Queen's Regt. Operation Order No. A. 25 Appendix 6	28/08/1918	28/08/1918
Miscellaneous	Patrol Orders for night 29th/30th Aug. 1918 Appendix 7	29/08/1918	29/08/1918
Heading	8th Bn The Queens R W S Regt War Diary Volume XXXVII September 1918		
War Diary	Trenches	01/09/1918	04/09/1918
War Diary	Les Brebis	05/09/1918	10/09/1918
War Diary	Les Brebis-Trenches	11/09/1918	11/09/1918
War Diary	Trenches	12/09/1918	22/09/1918
War Diary	Trenches-Les Brebis	23/09/1918	23/09/1918
War Diary	Les Brebis	24/09/1918	29/09/1918
War Diary	Les Brebis-Maisnil-Les-Ruitz	30/09/1918	30/09/1918
Operation(al) Order(s)	8th Bn The Queens Regt Operation Order No. A. 26. Appendix I	31/08/1918	31/08/1918
Operation(al) Order(s)	8th Bn. The Queens Regt Operation Order No. A. 27. Appendix A 28	04/09/1918	04/09/1918
Operation(al) Order(s)	8th Bn. The Queens Regt. Operation Order No. A. 28 Appendix III	10/09/1918	10/09/1918

Operation(al) Order(s)	8th Bn The Queens Regt. Operation Order No. A. 29 Appendix IV	15/09/1918	15/09/1918
Operation(al) Order(s)	8th Bn. The Queen's Regt. Operation Order No. A. 30 Appendix V	16/09/1918	16/09/1918
Operation(al) Order(s)	8th Bn. The Queens Regt. Operation Order No. A. 31 Appendix VI	22/09/1918	22/09/1918
Operation(al) Order(s)	8th Bn. The Queens Regt. Operation Order No. A. 32 Appendix VII	29/09/1918	29/09/1918
Heading	8th Bn The Queen's R.W.S. Regt War Diary Volume XXXVIII October 1918		
War Diary	Maisnil-Les-Ruitz Le Souich	01/10/1918	01/10/1918
War Diary	Le Souich	02/10/1918	05/10/1918
War Diary	Le Souich Graincourt	06/10/1918	06/10/1918
War Diary	Graincourt	06/10/1918	06/10/1918
War Diary	Graincourt-Anneux	07/10/1918	07/10/1918
War Diary	Anneux-Rumilly Trench	08/10/1918	08/10/1918
War Diary	Rumilly Trench-Niergnies	09/10/1918	09/10/1918
War Diary	Niergnies	09/10/1918	09/10/1918
War Diary	Niergnies-Cagnoncles	10/10/1918	10/10/1918
War Diary	Cagnoncles-Rieux	11/10/1918	11/10/1918
War Diary	Rieux	11/10/1918	12/10/1918
War Diary	Rieux-Montrecourt	12/10/1918	12/10/1918
War Diary	Rieux	11/10/1918	11/10/1918
War Diary	Montrecourt	12/10/1918	12/10/1918
War Diary	Montrecourt-Rieux	13/10/1918	13/10/1918
War Diary	Rieux	14/10/1918	14/10/1918
War Diary	Rieux-Cagnoncles	15/10/1918	16/10/1918
War Diary	Cagnoncles	16/10/1918	18/10/1918
War Diary	Cagnoncles-Cambrai	19/10/1918	19/10/1918
War Diary	Cambrai	20/10/1918	25/10/1918
War Diary	Cambrai-Cagnoncles	26/10/1918	26/10/1918
War Diary	Cagnoncles-St. Aubert	27/10/1918	27/10/1918
War Diary	St. Aubert	28/10/1918	31/10/1918
Operation(al) Order(s)	8th Bn. The Queen's Regt. Operation Order No. A. 33 Appendix I	30/09/1918	30/09/1918
Miscellaneous	24th Division No. A. 845 Appendix II	30/09/1918	30/09/1918
Operation(al) Order(s)	8th Bn. The Queens Regt. Operation Order No. A. 34 Appendix III	04/10/1918	04/10/1918
Operation(al) Order(s)	8th Bn. The Queens Regt. Operation Order No. A. 35 Appendix IV	05/10/1918	05/10/1918
Operation(al) Order(s)	8th Bn. The Queens Regt. Operation Order No. A. 36 Appendix V	07/10/1918	07/10/1918
Operation(al) Order(s)	17th Infantry Brigade Order No. 254 Appendix VI	07/10/1918	07/10/1918
Operation(al) Order(s)	17th Infantry Brigade Order No. 256 Appendix VIII	07/10/1918	07/10/1918
Miscellaneous	Operation Order No. A 38 Appendix IX	09/10/1918	09/10/1918
Operation(al) Order(s)	8th Bn The Queens Regt Operation Order No. A. 39 Appendix X	10/10/1918	10/10/1918
Operation(al) Order(s)	8th Bn The Queens Regt Operation Order No. A. 37 Appendix VII	08/10/1918	08/10/1918
Operation(al) Order(s)	17th Infantry Brigade Order No. 253 Appendix XI	12/10/1918	12/10/1918
Miscellaneous	A Form Messages And Signals. App. XII	10/10/1918	10/10/1918
Miscellaneous	A Form. Messages And Signals. App. XIII	11/10/1918	11/10/1918
Miscellaneous	A Form. Messages And Signals. App. XV	11/10/1918	11/10/1918
Miscellaneous	A Form. Messages And Signals. App. XIV	11/10/1918	11/10/1918

Miscellaneous	Special Order Of The Day by Brigadier General G. Thorpe C.M.G. D.S.O. Commanding 17th Infantry Brigade. Appendix XVI	14/10/1918	14/10/1918
Operation(al) Order(s)	17th Infantry Brigade Order No. 254 Appendix XVII	15/10/1918	15/10/1918
Operation(al) Order(s)	8th Bn The Queens Regt Operation Order No. A. 39 Appendix XVIII	16/10/1918	16/10/1918
Miscellaneous	Amendment to 17th Infantry Brigade Order No. 255 Appendix XIX		
Operation(al) Order(s)	17th Infantry Brigade Order No. 255	18/10/1918	18/10/1918
Miscellaneous	8th Bn The Queens Regt. Operation Order No. A. 40 Appendix XX	19/10/1918	19/10/1918
Operation(al) Order(s)	8th Bn The Queen's Regt. Operation Order. No. A. 41 Appendix XXI	23/10/1918	23/10/1918
Miscellaneous	Scheme in conjunction with 104 Coy. R.E.	23/10/1918	23/10/1918
Operation(al) Order(s)	17th Infantry Brigade Order No. 256 Appendix XXII	25/10/1918	25/10/1918
Miscellaneous	March Table to accompany 17th Infantry Brigade Order No. 256		
Operation(al) Order(s)	17th Infantry Brigade Order No. 257 Appendix XXIII	25/10/1918	25/10/1918
Miscellaneous	Table "A"		
Miscellaneous	Table "B"		
Miscellaneous	App. XXIV	16/10/1918	16/10/1918
Miscellaneous	17th Inf. Bde. No. G. 7/11 Appendix XXV	28/10/1918	28/10/1918
Miscellaneous	General Idea		
Miscellaneous	Special Idea	28/10/1918	28/10/1918
Heading	8th Bn The Queen's (R W S Regt) War Diary Volume XXXIX November 1918		
War Diary	St. Aubert	01/11/1918	02/11/1918
War Diary	St Aubert-Bermerain	03/11/1918	03/11/1918
War Diary	Bermerain-Villers Pol	04/11/1918	04/11/1918
War Diary	Villers Pol	04/11/1918	04/11/1918
War Diary	Villers Pol-Le Pissotiau	05/11/1918	05/11/1918
War Diary	Le Pissotiau	05/11/1918	07/11/1918
War Diary	Le Pissotiau-Bavai	08/11/1918	08/11/1918
War Diary	Bavai	08/11/1918	16/11/1918
War Diary	Bavai-Jenlain	17/11/1918	17/11/1918
War Diary	Jewlain-Aubry	18/11/1918	18/11/1918
War Diary	Aubry-Somain	19/11/1918	19/11/1918
War Diary	Somain	20/11/1918	25/11/1918
War Diary	Somain-Lecelles	26/11/1918	26/11/1918
War Diary	Lecelles	27/11/1918	29/11/1918
War Diary	Lecelles-Baisieux	30/11/1918	30/11/1918
War Diary	Baisieux	30/11/1918	30/11/1918
Operation(al) Order(s)	8th Bn The Queens Regt Operation Order No. A. 42 App I	02/11/1918	02/11/1918
Miscellaneous	Reference 24th Divisional Order No. 262 App. II	01/11/1918	01/11/1918
Miscellaneous	Rough Plan Of Attack.		
Operation(al) Order(s)	17th Infantry Brigade Order No. 259 App III	02/11/1918	02/11/1918
Miscellaneous	17th Infantry Brigade No. 259/1	03/11/1918	03/11/1918
Miscellaneous		05/11/1918	05/11/1918
Operation(al) Order(s)	17th Infy Bde Order No. 262 App V		
Operation(al) Order(s)	17th Infy Bde Order No. 261 App IV	06/11/1918	06/11/1918
Operation(al) Order(s)	8th Bn. The Queens Regt. Operation Order No. A.43 App VI	16/11/1918	16/11/1918
Operation(al) Order(s)	17th Infantry Brigade Order No. 264 App VII	16/10/1918	16/10/1918
Operation(al) Order(s)	17th Infantry Brigade Order No. 266 App VIII	16/11/1918	16/11/1918

Operation(al) Order(s)	8th Bn The Queens Regt Operation Order No. A. 44 App IX	17/11/1918	17/11/1918
Operation(al) Order(s)	8th Bn The Queens Regt Operation Order No. A. 45 App X	18/11/1918	18/11/1918
Miscellaneous	24th Division No. A. 196/71 App XI	19/11/1918	19/11/1918
Miscellaneous	8th Bn The Queens Regt Operation Order No. A.46 App XI	26/11/1918	26/11/1918
Operation(al) Order(s)	17th Infantry Brigade Order No. 267 App XIII	25/11/1918	25/11/1918
Miscellaneous	Table 'A' to accompany 17th Infantry Brigade Order No. 267		
Operation(al) Order(s)	8th Bn The Queens Regt Operation Order No. A. 47 App XIV	29/11/1918	29/11/1918
Operation(al) Order(s)	17th Infantry Brigade Order No. 268 App XV	29/11/1918	29/11/1918
Miscellaneous	Table 'A' Issued with 17th Inf. Bde. Order No. 268		
Heading	8th Bn The Queens R W S Regt War Diary Volume XXXX December 1918		
War Diary	Baisieux	01/12/1918	31/12/1918
Heading	8th Bn The Queen's (R.W.S.) Regt War Diary Vol. XLI January 1919		
War Diary	Baisieux	01/01/1919	21/01/1919
Heading	8th Bn The Queen's R W S Regt War Diary Volume XLII February 1919		
War Diary	Baisieux	01/02/1919	28/02/1919
Heading	8th Bn The Queen's R W S Regt War Diary Volume XLIII March 1919		
Heading	This Map Belong To 8th Queens Diary March 1918		
War Diary	Baisieux	01/03/1919	31/03/1919
Heading	8th Bn The Queens RWS Regt War Diary Volume XLIV April 1919		
War Diary	Baisieux	01/04/1919	30/04/1919

WO95/2208

8 BTN QUEENS (RW SURREY)

24TH DIVISION
17TH INFY BDE

8TH BN ROY. WEST SURREY REGT
(THE QUEEN'S)
FEB 1918-APR 1919

FROM 72 BDE
24 DIV

24

8th Bn "THE QUEEN'S" R.W.S REGT

WAR DIARY

VOLUME XXXI

FEBRUARY 1918

H. J. C. Peirs
Major
Commanding
8th Bn THE QUEENS RWS REGT

4/3/18

Feb 18
1
Pp. 49

Vol. XXXI

Page 1.

Army Form C. 2118

WAR DIARY
or
INTELLIGENCE SUMMARY
(Erase heading not required.)

Instructions regarding War Diaries and Intelligence Summaries are contained in F. S. Regs., Part II. and the Staff Manual respectively. Title Pages will be prepared in manuscript.

February 1918

Place	Date	Hour	Summary of Events and Information	Remarks and references to Appendices
Trenches	1.		Day and night very quiet; this was probably owing to heavy mist. Lt. SWAINE was wounded in the arm.	
"	2.		The night was quiet. In the morning our own and enemy artillery and T. Ms. were more active. In the afternoon the enemy shelled the Left Company rather heavily with 5.9 cms. 1 man being killed and 4 wounded. The Battn. was relieved by the 1st North Staffordshire Regiment in the Right Sub. Sector. Relief was complete at 7.30 p.m. On completion of relief the Battn. was disposed as follows:- "A" "B" and Battn. H.Q. at TEMPLEUX QUARRIES "D" Coy " L.10.a.05.50 "C" " " L.5.b.3.3. under the C.O. 1st North Staffordshire Regt. The total casualties for the 4 days in the front line were 1 officer wounded, 1 man killed and 11 wounded.	Appendix I. Bn O.O No 6
TEMPLEUX QUARRIES	3.		In Brigade Support at TEMPLEUX QUARRIES and 1 Coy. at L.10.a.05.50 and 1 Coy. at L.5.b.3.3. Large Brigade Working Parties were found. Between 9 p.m. and 10.30 p.m. the Quarries were shelled with 4.2 cms. and Whizz Bangs. Casualties 1 O.R. wounded.	
"	4		Brigade Working Parties as on the 3rd inst. The Quarries were intermittently shelled throughout the day, salvoes of 6 coming over about every hour. The night was quiet.	
"	5.		Working Parties as before. A draft of 6 officers and 114 O.Rs. joined the Battn. from the 3/4 Queens. The officers were:- Capt. H.G. GARBETT, Lt. R.B. SPARKES, 2/Lt. J. HOWELLS, E.P. PHELPS, S. HALL, E.B. HOGBIN.	[initials]

1875 Wt. W593/826 1,000,000 4/15 J.B.C. & A. A.D.S.S./Forms/C. 2118.

Page 2.

Army Form C. 2118

Instructions regarding War Diaries and Intelligence Summaries are contained in F. S. Regs., Part II. and the Staff Manual respectively. Title Pages will be prepared in manuscript.

WAR DIARY
or
INTELLIGENCE SUMMARY

(Erase heading not required.)

February 1918

Place	Date	Hour	Summary of Events and Information	Remarks and references to Appendices
TEMPLEUX QUARRIES	6.		Working Parties as before. "C" Coy. withdrew from L.5.b.3.3 and came back to dug-outs at L.10.a.	Appendix II Bn OO No 7.
Trenches	7		The Battn. relieved the 8th Royal West Kent Regiment in the Right Sub-Sector of the Divisional front. Relief was complete at 7.10p.m. On completion of relief Coys. were disposed as follows:- In the front line "D" Coy. on the Left "C" " " " Right "A" and "B" Coys. in Support at L.10.a. Battn. HQ. at LEICESTER LOUNGE. Under the new organisation by which Brigades were reduced to three Battalions and owing to the fact that the 12th Royal Fusiliers and the 8th East Kent Regiment (The Buffs) were disbanded, the Battn. was transferred from the 72nd I.B. to the 17th I.B; the transfer taking place at 6 p.m. on the 7th inst. Nothing unusual happened during the night, the enemy being exceptionally quiet. 1 officer and 12 O.Rs. joined the Battn.; Lt. P. HEVERS being the officer.	Appendix III 72 I.B. OO Nos 5 & 6 17 I.B. OO 221 Bn OO No 8
"	8		During the night and day the enemy were comparatively quiet. At about 9 p.m. a few shells fell near Battn. HQ. Casualties: one man died, cause unknown.	
"	9.		Hostile attitude both by night and day fairly quiet. In the early part of the evening enemy machine guns were fairly active; our Lewis Guns replied and quietened the enemy considerably. Our aeroplanes were active during the day.	
"	10		The night was quiet. At 4.30p.m. the enemy put up a heavy barrage on the Battn. on our left. Our artillery replied immediately and no action followed. 2/Lt. C.F. OLLEY and 12 O.Rs. joined the Battn. from the 3/4th Queens.	
"	11.		A quiet night and day. A patrol consisting of 1 officer and 4 ORs went out from our Right Coy. front at 12.30 a.m. They came to an enemy strong point and were heavily bombed. The officer and 1 Sgt. being wounded and 1 L/Cpl. missing. The Battn. was relieved by the 7th Northamptonshire Regiment, relief being complete at 8 p.m. On completion of relief the Battn. proceeded by train from TEMPLEUX to BERNES. Battn. HQs. and 3 Coys. being accommodated in huts at BERNES and 1 Coy. at MONTIGNY. The Battn. came under the orders of the 73rd I.B.	Appendix IV 17 I.B. OO Nos 222 & 223 73 I.B. OO 180 Bn OO No 9.

1875 Wt. W593/826 1,000,000 4/15 J.B.C. & A. A.D.S.S./Forms/C. 2118.

Page 3

Instructions regarding War Diaries and Intelligence Summaries are contained in F. S. Regs., Part II. and the Staff Manual respectively. Title Pages will be prepared in manuscript.

WAR DIARY
or
INTELLIGENCE SUMMARY
(Erase heading not required.)

Army Form C. 2118

February 1918

Place	Date	Hour	Summary of Events and Information	Remarks and references to Appendices
BERNES	12.		The day was spent in cleaning up.	
"	13		The Battalion was employed on Working Parties, 3 full Companys being used. "B" Coy. moved from MONTIGNY to HANCOURT and were accomodated in huts there. 10 O.Rs. joined the Battn from the 3/4th Queens.	
"	14.		Bde. Working Parties as before.	
"	15.		Bde. Working Parties as before. The C. in Chief Field Marshall Sir Douglas Haig, accompanied by the Vth Army Commander General Sir Hubert Gough visited the Bde. area and passed through BERNES. The Battn was complimented on the smart turn-out of the Guard. 4 O.Rs. joined the Battn from the 3/4th Queens. At 6 p.m. the Battn came under the orders of the 17th I.B. again.	
"	16		Bde. Working Parties as before. 5 O.Rs joined the Battn from the 3/4th Queens.	
"	17		Bde Working Parties as before.	
"	18		Bde. Working Parties as before.	
Trenches	19.		The Battn relieved the 7th Northamptonshire Regt. in the Right sub-sector of the Divisional front, E. of HARGICOURT, relief being complete at 7.50 p.m. On completion of relief the Battn was disposed as follows:- Battn HQ. and 2 sections of "D" Coy. at LEICESTER LOUNGE. "D" Coy. on the Left "C" " " " Right "A" & "B" Coys. at L.10.a.	Appendix V 17 I.B.O.O. No 221 Bn O.O. No 10
"	20		The night was comparatively quiet. The following interchange of Coys. took place:- "A" Coy. took over the front held by "C" Coy. "B" " " " " " " "D" " Relief was complete by 8 p.m. At 3.30 p.m. our artillery bombarded the enemy front line trenches and support trenches in the vicinity of RUBY WOOD. The enemy artillery retaliated violently and our front line, support line and Battn HQ. were heavily shelled for 2 hours. Very little damage was done.	Appendix VI Bn O.O. No 11

[illegible initials]

1875 Wt. W593/826 1,000,000 4/15 J.B.C. & A. A.D.S.S./Forms/C. 2118.

Page 4

Army Form C. 2118

WAR DIARY
or
INTELLIGENCE SUMMARY

(Erase heading not required.)

Instructions regarding War Diaries and Intelligence Summaries are contained in F. S. Regs., Part II. and the Staff Manual respectively. Title Pages will be prepared in manuscript.

February 1918

Place	Date	Hour	Summary of Events and Information	Remarks and references to Appendices
Trenches	21.		Comparatively quiet on our front. At 4.30 a.m. there was a heavy bombardment by both sides to the N. of our front. From 5 p.m. until 9 p.m. our 18 pdrs. fired harassing fire as an enemy relief was expected.	
"	22.		Comparatively quiet on our front. The following change of dispositions took place on the Divisional front:- The front was held with the three Brigades in and a Batt.n from each Bde. in the front line or outpost zone. In consequence of this the Right Sub Sector became the Centre Sub. Sector. In order to accomplish this change "C" Coy. (Queens) relieved "A" Coy (West Kents) on the Right, with its Southern boundary at SPADE LANE; "C" Coy. also took over 4 posts from A" Coy. (Queens) which then became the centre Coy. "A" Coy (Queens) took over the Right Group (BAIT TRENCH) from "B" Coy (QUEENS) and "B" Coy (QUEENS) took over the Right Post from the 9th Royal Sussex Regt in FERRET LEFT TRENCH. "D" Coy moved from L.10.a. 2 platoons relieved 2 platoons of the 9th Royal Sussex in HARGICOURT and 2 platoons came to LEICESTER LOUNGE. The relief was complete by 12 noon. On completion of relief the Batt.n was disposed as follows:- Batt.n HQ. at LEICESTER LOUNGE. "C" Coy. on the right with Coy. HQ. in RAILWAY SUPPORT Trench and 2 Sections in SLAG Trench "A" " in " centre " " " " LAKE TRENCH. "B" " on " left " " " " COLOGNE RESERVE LEFT. "D" " in Support " " " and 2 platoons at LEICESTER LOUNGE and 2 platoons in HARGICOURT.	Appendix VII Bde O.O No 12 1/1 E B O.O No 205 1/3 E B O.O No 180
	23		Comparative quiet on our front. The Battalion was relieved by the 3rd Rifle Bde in the Centre sector, relief being complete at 7-40 P.M. On completion of relief the Batt.n proceeded to the camp at MONTIGNY. The Batt.n again came under the orders of the 17th Bde.	Appendix VIII Bde O.O No 13
MONTIGNY	24		Lieut-General Sir C. T. McM. Kavanagh, K.C.B., C.V.O., D.S.O., commanding the Cavalry Corps presented medals to N.C.O's & men of the Batt.n at a Divisional parade nr MONTIGNY at which N.C.O's and men	RW

1875 Wt. W593/826 1,000,000 4/15 J.B.C. & A. A.D.S.S./Forms/C. 2118.

Instructions regarding War Diaries and Intelligence Summaries are contained in F. S. Regs., Part II. and the Staff Manual respectively. Title Pages will be prepared in manuscript.

WAR DIARY
or
INTELLIGENCE SUMMARY
(Erase heading not required.)

Army Form C. 2118

February 1918

Place	Date	Hour	Summary of Events and Information	Remarks and references to Appendices
			of the Battn wearing the '1914 star' ribbon attended. The following received medal ribbons:– D.C.M. and M.M., L/Cpl W. R. Clayden; D.C.M., Sergt C. E. Howe; M.M., L/Cpl S. L. Holman, Pte V. G. Everest, Pte S. H. Swann; Croix de Guerre, Sergt Holloway and Sergt Feist. The Battn found Bde working parties.	
MONTIGNY	25.		Bde Working Parties as before. ~~NCOs + men available fired on HERVILLY range~~	
"	26.		Bde Working Parties as before. NCOs + men available fired on HERVILLY range.	
"	27.		Bde Working Parties as before. NCOs + men available fired on HERVILLY range + parties were detailed for salvage work in the area.	
MONTIGNY – HANCOURT	28		Bde Working Parties as before. NCOs + men available fired on HERVILLY miniature range. Salvage parties as before. In accordance with operation orders the Battn first line transport was to move to the VILLERS BRETTONEUX training area (AMIENS 62) by road, and pass the crucifix BERNES (34 C 3.1 Sheet 62c) at 9-20 A.M. to proceed via FRAMERVILLE-VAUVILLERS. Transport left in accordance with these arrangements and the Battn was under orders to proceed by train from ROISEL the following morning; the 4th East Lancs Regt relieving it at MONTIGNY. All preparations for moving to the rest area were cancelled at 4-30 P.M. In view of an anticipated offensive on the part of the enemy round CAMBRAI and ST QUENTIN the Battn was ordered to proceed at once to MONTECOURT via HANCOURT. (Sheet 62c. 28 a 8.2) Transport was recalled and the Battn arrived at HANCOURT at 7 PM where it spent the night. The 3rd Rifle Bde took over billets at MONTIGNY. Instructions were received to prepare for ALARM ACTION.	Appendix IX 14 I B 00 [illegible] Bn OO No 15 + No 11

R. [illegible] 2nd Lieut
for O.C. 8th Queens Regt

Appendix I.

SECRET

COPY No 14.

8th Bn The Queen's. R.W.S. Regt

OPERATION ORDER. No. 6

Map Ref. 62c 1/40000

1st Feby. 1918.

1. The Battn will be relieved in the Right Sub. Sector by the 1st Bn. NORTH STAFFORDSHIRE REGT. on the 2nd inst.

2.

'A' Coy	(1st N. STAFFS)	will relieve	'B' Coy	(Queen's) at about	5.45 p.m.
'B'	---	---	'A'	---	4.45 ---
'C'	---	---	'D'	---	3.45 ---
'D'	---	---	'C'	---	2.15 ---

3. On completion of relief 'A' & 'B' Coys will proceed to Templeux Quarries, and take over same accommodation as before. 'D' Coy will take over dug-outs near L.10.A central and 'C' Coy. dugouts near Battn. H.Q. at L.5.B.3.3.

4. Guides:- No guides will be required.

5. With the exception of 'D' Coy. O.C. Coys will arrange to send 1 Off and 1 N.C.O. on in advance in the morning to take over their respective dug-outs. The officer detailed by 'A' Coy will also take over Battn H.Q. TEMPLEUX QUARRIES. 'D' Coy will send 1 N.C.O. and 1 man.

6. O.C. 'A' and 'B' Coys will detail 1 man each to report to TOWN MAJOR, TEMPLEUX QUARRIES after relief to act as runners to O.C. 'A' & 'C' Zones respectively.
O.C. 'C' Coy will detail parties of 1 N.C.O. and 2 men and 1 N.C.O. and 3 men for the Bomb and Gum Boot Stores, HARGICOURT respectively.
The parties will relieve similar parties of the 1st N. STAFFS. Regt. Relief to be completed by 11.30 A.m.
O.C. 'B' Coy will detail 1 N.C.O. and 2 men for Bde Bomb Store.
H.Q. Coy will detail 3 men for Traffic Control. HARGICOURT.

7. Officers Kits, mess Kits, cooking dixies, etc of 'A' & 'D' Coys will be dumped at R. Aid Post. ready for loading by 6.30 p.m. Those of H.Q. Coy & 'B' Coy at their respective dumps at the same time. One man to be left in charge of Kits, etc.

There will be no Transport for 'C' Coy.

8. Lewis Guns, Magazines, etc, will be carried.

9. Gum Boots will be returned to Gum Boot Store, HARGICOURT and a receipt obtained for numbers handed in.

10. The Q.M. will arrange for rations for all guards mentioned in para. 6.

11 All Trench Stores, work in hand and proped will be carefully handed over and receipt taken, also a separate receipt will be obtained for reserve rations and water. Certificates of stores etc handed over to reach O.R. by 12 noon. 3rd inst.

12. Completion of relief will be reported by wire or runner using the code word "CHEVALIER".

ACKNOWLEDGE. O.O. No 6.

Issued at 9.30 pm.

E. D. Donnell.
Captain & Adjutant
8th Bn Queen's Regt.

Copies issued to

No 1.	H. Q. Mess.	No 8.	Q. M.
2	O.C. A Coy	9.	M. O.
3.	O.C. B ---	10.	1st North Staffs. Regt
4.	O.C. C ---	11.	R. S. M.
5.	O.C. D ---	12.	Sigs.
6	O.C. H.Q---	13.	File.
7.	T.O.	14.	War Diary.

SECRET   *Appendix II*   Copy No. *4*

8th (S) Battn The Queen's R.W.S. Regt

OPERATION ORDER NO.7.

Map Ref 62c 1/40,000.   February 4th 1918.

(1) "C" Company (The Queen's) will withdraw to L.10.a. tomorrow as soon as the Right Company of the 1st North Staffordshire Regt has been relieved by a Company of the 8th Bn The Royal West Kent Regt.

(2) O.C"C" Company will arrange with Commanding Officer 1st Bn The North Staffordshire Regt as to when he is to move .

(3)O.C. "C" Company will arrange to relieve the following guards at present found by 8th Bn The Royal West Kent Regt :-

R.E. Dump.   HARGICOURT.
Bomb Store   do.

Relief to be complete by 12 noon.
He will also find the following :-

A.A. Guard.   at   L.10.a.
Gas Guard   "   L.10.a.

(4) Blankets etc not for trenches will be brought back by Transport tomorrow night.
Cooking dixies etc will be brought from present Company H.Q. to L.10.a by ration limber.

(5) Completion of Relief will be by wire using Code Word "WALLOPO".

ACKNOWLEDGE:- O.O. 7.

E.D. Donnell
Captain & Adjutant
4/2/18.   8th (S) Bn The Queen's R.W.S. Regt

Copies issued to:-   Issued at *6.0/c* pm.

No.1. O.C. 8th Royal West Kents.
2. O.C. 1st North Staffs.
3. O.C. "C" Company.
4. War Diary.
5. Quartermaster.

Appendix III

SECRET.

COPY NO. 10

72nd INFANTRY BRIGADE OPERATION ORDER NO. 6.

4th February 1918.

1. The 72nd Infantry Brigade (less 8th The Queens (R.W.S.) Regt.) will be relieved by 17th Infantry Brigade (Composed of 1st Royal Fusiliers, 3rd Rifle Brigade and 8th The Queens (R.W.S.) Regt.) on 6th and 7th February 1918. Relief to be complete by 6.0 a.m. on 8th February 1918.
   On relief 72nd Infantry Brigade will become Brigade in Reserve.

2. The 8th The Queens (R.W.S.) Regt. from TEMPLEUX QUARRIES and L.10.a. will relieve 8th Royal West Kent Regt. on night 7/8th and will come under orders of 17th Infantry Brigade after 6.0 p.m. 7th February 1918.

3. All Defence Schemes, Aeroplane Photographs, Work in Hand and proposed and Trench Stores will be handed over on relief and receipts obtained.

4. The command of the present 72nd Infantry Brigade Front will pass to B.G.C. 17th Infantry Brigade at 6 p.m. on 7th February 1918 at which hour B.G.C. 72nd Infantry Brigade will assume command of the Brigade in Reserve.

5. All other details not provided for in these orders will be arranged between C.O's concerned.

6. Completion of reliefs will be wired to Brigade Headquarters stating simply the time the relief was completed.

7. ACKNOWLEDGE.

ISSUED AT 2. 0 p.m.

E.G. Fellowes
Captain.
for Brigade Major.
72nd Infantry Brigade.

COPIES TO :-

1. B.G.C., 72nd Infantry Brigade.
2. FILE.
3. WAR DIARY.
4. 24th Division "G".
5. 24th Division "Q".
6. 4th Dismounted Division.
7. 17th Infantry Brigade.
8. 73rd Infantry Brigade.
9. 47th Infantry Brigade.
10. 8th The Queens (R.W.S.) Regt.
11. 9th East Surrey Regt.
12. 8th Royal West Kent Regt.
13. 1st North Staffordshire Regt.
14. 72nd Machine Gun Company.
15. 72nd Trench Mortar Battery.
16. 24th Div. Artillery.
17. Left Group R.A.
18. Right Group R.A.
19. 24th Div. Train.
20. A.D.M.S.
21. Staff Captain.
22. B.T.O., 72nd Inf. Bde.
23. Signals, 72nd Inf. Bde.
24. 104th Field Coy. R.E.

TABLE.

DATE	UNIT RELIEVED	FROM	TO	UNIT RELIEVING	FROM
Feb. 6th	1st North Staffordshire Regt.	Centre Sub-Section	VRAIGNES CAMP	3rd Rifle Brigade	VRAIGNES CAMP
Feb. 6th	72nd Machine Gun Company	Line	VRAIGNES	17th Machine Gun Coy.	
Feb. 7th	9th East Surrey Regt.	Left Sub-Section	HANCOURT CAMP	1st Royal Fusiliers	HANCOURT CAMP
Feb. 7th	8th Royal West Kent Regt.	Right Sub-Section	∅ VRAIGNES ? or HANCOURT	8th The Queens (R.W.S.) Regt.	TEMPLEUX QUARRIES and L.10.a.
Feb. 7th	72nd Trench Mortar Battery	Line	HANCOURT	17th Trench Mortar Bty.	
Feb 7th	72nd Infantry Brigade Headquarters.	Line	VRAIGNES	17th Infantry Brigade Headquarters	

Train arrangements for move back to VRAIGNES Area will be notified later.

∅ It is not decided whether VRAIGNES or HANCOURT CAMPS will be given up.

4th February 1918.

SECRET.

72nd Infantry Brigade.

O.C. 8th Queens

AMENDMENT NO 1 TO OPERATION ORDER Nos. 5 & 6.

In continuation of Operation Order Nos. 5 & 6.

1. Cancel para (4) of Operation Order No.5. and substitute
The following shows dispositions of Battalions after the change on night 5/6th

8th Royal West Kent Regt.

Right Company CLUB LANE excl. to FISH LANE excl.
Left Company FISH LANE incl. to RUBY LANE incl.
Support Company POND SUPPORT.
Reserve Company LEICESTER LOUNGE.

1st North Staffordshire Regt.

1 Company RUBY LANE excl to F.30.d.95.30 incl. disposed as follows :-
Posts in (a) BOWER LANE Locality
(b) SUGAR TRENCH
COLOGNE RESERVE
(3 platoons less in (a) and (b) above posts)
1 Platoon (L.5.b.3.3. vicinity of present Battalion Headquarters)
Company Headquarters - SUGAR TRENCH.
1 Company F.30.d.95.30 (excl.) to CARBINE TRENCH incl. disposed as follows :-
Posts in (a) CARBINE TRENCH Locality.
(b) MALAKOFF SUPPORT
REDAN LANE. Company Headquarters and 3 platoons less above posts in (a) and (b)
VALLEY POST - 1 Platoon
Remaining 2 Companies will withdraw to MONTIGNY FARM and move to VRAIGNE Camp on afternoon of 6th inst.
Battalion Headquarters will remain in present position

9th East Surrey Regt.

Right Company (a) HUSSAR POST.
(b) RIFLEMAN POST.
ARTAXERXES Company Headquarters and remainder of men not in posts (a) and (b)
Left Company (a) BIG BENJAMIN
(b) LITTLE BENJAMIN
(c) NEW POST
Company Headquarters ARTAXERXES. Remainder of Company not in posts (a), (b) and (c) to be accommodated in HUSSAR ROAD and man BENJAMIN SWITCH in case of alarm
Remaining two Companies disposed as far as possible

(a) HUSSAR ROAD.
TOINE POST.
Company Headquarters - HUSSAR ROAD.
(b) ORCHARD POST
HARDY BANKS
Company Headquarters - HARDY BANKS.
Battalion Headquarters - HARDY BANKS

8th The Queens (R.W.S.) Regt.

3 Companies L.10.a. (1 Company to take over accommodation at present occupied by Cavalry at old 73rd Infantry Brigade Headquarters).
Battalion Headquarters - TEMPLEUX QUARRIES

Cancel para.6. of Operation Order No.5 and substitute.

6. Battalions of 17th Infantry Brigade will take over as follows :-

February 6th. 2 Companies 3rd Rifle Brigade relieve 2 Companies 1st North Staffordshire Regt in Outpost Zone.
2 Companies 3rd Rifle Brigade to TEMPLEUX QUARRIES.
3rd Rifle Brigade Battalion Headquarters relieves 1st North Staffordshire Regt. Headquarters at L.5.b.3.3.

February 7th 8th The Queens (R.W.S.) Regt. relieve 8th Royal West Kent Regt.
On relief 8th Royal West Kent Regt will proceed to HANCOURT
2 Companies 8th The Queens (R.W.S.) Regt. relieve 4 Companies 8th Royal West Kent Regt. in Outpost Zone
x distributed as follows.
1 Company Front Line. CLUB LANE excl. to FISH LANE excl
POND SUPPORT - Company Headquarters and 3 platoons less posts in Front Line.
1 Platoon - LEICESTER LOUNGE (alarm post BOBBY FARM)
1 Company Front Line - FISH LANE incl. to RUBY LANE in
FERRET TRENCH - Company Headquarters and 3 platoon less posts in Front Line
1 Platoon-[illegible] - LEICESTER LOUNGE (alarm post SLAG TRENCH)
Remaining 2 Companies at L.10.a.
Battalion Headquarters relieve 8th Royal West Kent Regt Headquarters LEICESTER LOUNGE and will remain there till accommodation is improved at L.10.a.

February 7th 1st Royal Fusiliers relieves 9th East Surrey Regt.

February 7th 3rd Rifle Brigade Headquarters move back to TEMPLEUX QUARRIES after 8th The Queens (R.W.S.) Regt have moved forward.

[signature]
Captain.
Brigade Major.
72nd Infantry Brigade.

4th February 1918.

S E C R E T.   COPY NO.

72nd INFANTRY BRIGADE OPERATION ORDER No. 8

HARGICOURT
/10000

3rd February 1918.

1. As the 17th Infantry Brigade will be taking over from this Brigade with only 3 Battalions, the Boundaries between Battalions will be altered as follows :-
(a) Boundary between Centre and Right Battalion
E. end of RUBY LANE (excl. to Centre Battalion) - HARGICOURT - UNNAMED FARM - RUBY FARM ROAD (incl. to Centre Battalion)(including COLOGNE Left) - X roads L.5.c.2.3. - point where HARGICOURT TRENCH cuts TEMPLEUX - HARGICOURT ROAD (Road incl. to CENTRE BATTALION)
(b) Boundary between centre and left Battalion
CARBINE TRENCH (incl. to Centre Battalion) - F.29.d.3.3. (Valley Posts incl. to Centre Battalion) - X roads F.28.d.1.2. (PIMPLE Locality excl. to Centre Battalion) - F.27.d.0.0.

2. The re-distribution will take place on the night 5/6th as follows :-
(a) 8th Royal West Kent Regt. will take over the Right Company front from 1st North Staffordshire Regt.
(b) 1st North Staffordshire Regt. will take over Valley Posts from 9th East Surrey Regt
(c) 1 Company of 8th The Queens (R.W.S.) Regt. at present accommodated at L.5.b.3.3. under O.C. 1st North Staffordshire Regt. will withdraw to L.10.a. after the Right Front Company 1st North Staffordshire Regt. has been relieved by 8th Royal West Kent Regt.
(d) The Reserve Company 8th Royal West Kent Regt. will move to LEICESTER LOUNGE to make room for company 8th The Queens (R.W.S.) Regt. mentioned in para. (c) above.

3. Arrangements for this re-distribution to be made between C.O's. concerned.

4. On completion of the change, Battalions will be distributed as follows :-

Right Battalion.	2 Companies Front Line. 1 Company POND SUPPORT. COLOGNE RIGHT. 1 Company LEICESTER LOUNGE.
Centre Battalion	2 Companies Front Line 1 Company COLOGNE LEFT. & VALLEY POSTS. 1 Company vicinity Battalion H.Q. (L.5.b.3.3.)
Left Battalion	As before except that garrison of VALLEY POSTS will move to ARTAXERXES.
Support Battalion.	2 Companies TEMPLEUX QUARRIES. 2 Companies L.10.a.

5. The 3 front Battalions will forward to Brigade Headquarters sketch map showing their new dispositions to reach this office 4.0 p.m. 6th inst.

6. The 17th Infantry Brigade will probably take over as follows :-

(a) Right Battalion 2 Companies Outpost Zone
2 Companies L.10.a.
Battalion H.Q. L.10.a.

(b) Centre Battalion 2 Companies Outpost Zone.
2 Companies TEMPLEUX QUARRIES.
Battalion H.Q. TEMPLEUX QUARRIES.

(c) Left Battalion. as at present.

7. ACKNOWLEDGE.

ISSUED AT 8.30 p.m.

E.G. Fellowes
Captain.
for Brigade Major.
72nd Infantry Brigade.

COPIES TO. -

1. B.G.C., 72nd Infantry Brigade.
2. WAR DIARY.
3. FILE.
4. 24th Division "G".
5. 17th Infantry Brigade.
6. 73rd Infantry Brigade.
7. 8th The Queens (R.W.S.) Regt.
8t 9th East Surrey Regt.
9. 8th Royal West Kent Regt.
10. 1st North Staffordshire Regt.
11. 72nd Machine Gun Company.
12. 72nd Trench Mortar Battery.
13. Left Group, R.A.
14. Right Group, R.A.

Appendix III.

SECRET.

8th Queen

Copy No 7

AMENDMENT to 17th Infantry Brigade O.O.No 221.

Reference para 6, 17th Inf: Bde, O.O.221 dated 3/2/1918.

For L.6.b. read L.6.a. For L.5.c.75.99 read L.5.c.99.15

[signature]

Captain,

4/2/1918. A/Brigade Major, 17th Inf: Bde.

S E C R E T.

Copy No. 7

17th INFANTRY BRIGADE OPERATION ORDER No ~~215~~ 221.

Ref: Map 62c 1/40,000
HARGICOURT Special Sheet.
Ed. 1a. 1/10,000.

1. The 17th Infantry Brigade will relieve the 72nd Infantry Brigade in the Line on the 6th/7th and 7th/8th February 1918.
Relief to be complete by 6 a.m. 8th February.

2. The 17th Infantry Brigade will take over the Line with three Battalions arranged in depth :-

Right Sector......8th Bn. The Queens. (From 72nd I.Bde)
Centre Sector......3rd Bn. The Rifle Brigade.
Left Sector......1st Bn. Royal Fusiliers.

3. In accordance with the re-organisation of Infantry Brigades i.e, the withdrawal of one Battalion per Brigade, the dispositions of the Battalions in the Line will be changed as follows:-

Each Sub-Sector will be held with two companies in the Outpost Zone.
Battalion H.Qrs and two companies West of the Red Line

4. The Battalion H.Qrs of the Right, Centre and Left Sub-Sectors will be respectively at

The QUARRIES in L.10.a.36

The TEMPLEUX QUARRIES (old Support Battalion H.Qrs).
HARDY LANE.

5. The Map locations of the various Company H.Qrs will be issued later together with dispositions of companies.

6. The Boundary Line between the Right and Centre Sub-Sectors will be:-
Front Line at G.1.b.40.46 - RUBY LANE (inclusive to Right Sub-Sector) - junction of RUBY LANE and SUGAR Trench (L.6.a.75.22) thence along road to fork road at L.5.c.~~75.88~~ 99.75 (inclusive to Right Sub-Sector).

7. VALLEY POST (L.5.b.14.95) will be taken over by the Centre Sub-Sector and the Boundary Line between the Centre and Left Sub-Sectors altered accordingly.

8. Until further accommodation West of the Red Line is provided the dispositions of troops of the Left Sub-Sector (except as stated in 7 above) will not be altered.

9. All moves will be in accordance with Table "A" attached.

10. The following intervals will be maintained on the march:-
Between Platoons 200 yards, and
Between 6 Transport vehicles 200 yards.

11. C.Os concerned will make arrangements for dinners to be issued at ROISEL . The available accommodation at ROISEL will be notified later to all concerned.

Continued.

12. A representative from Brigade H.Qrs will be at the detrain-point ROISEL on the 6th and 7th instant.

13. All details of Lookout Posts, Camp Defences, A.A.Lewis Gun positions, and details regarding bombproof defences round hutments in the Reserve Area will be handed over.

14. All Trench Stores, Aeroplane photographs, Defence Schemes, Tables of Work in hand and proposed, Lists of Pass-Words etc will be taken over and receipts sent to Brigade H.Qrs as soon as possible after relief.

15. Completion of relief will be notified to Brigade H.Qrs by wiring the time at which relief is complete.

16. All other details will be arranged by C.Os direct.

17. Command of the Front Line Sector will pass to the B.G.C., 17th Infantry Brigade at 6 p.m. 7th February at which time the Brigade Office will close at VRAIGNES and open at HAUTE WOOD.

18. ACKNOWLEDGE.

[signature]

Captain,

3/2/1918. A/Brigade Major, 17th Infantry Brigade.

Issued to Sigs:
at [illegible]

Copy No 1 to	B.G.C.	Copy No 2 to	Brigade Major.
3.	Staff Captain.	4	8th Buffs.
5.	1st Royal Fus.	6.	3rd Rifle Brigade.
7.	8th Queens.	8.	17th M.G.Coy.
9.	17th L.T.M.Batty.	10.	Sigs: 17th I.Bde.
11.	B.T.O.	12.	B.S.O.
13.	72nd I.Bde.	14.	73rd I.Bde.
15.	49th I.Bde.	16.	"G" 24th Divn:
17.	"Q" 24th Divn:	18.	2nd Dis. Cav. Div:
19.	C.R.E.	20.	C.R.A.
21.	Left Group.	22.	104 Fd Coy, R.E.
23.	129 Coy, R.E.	24.	D.M.G.O.
25.	24th Div. Train.	26.	S.S.O.
27.	A.D.M.S.	28.	73rd Fd Ambce.
29.	74th Fd Ambce.	30.	A.P.M.
31.	Div: Gas Officer.	32.	12th Sherwood Fors
33.	258th Tunlg Co, R.E.	34.	War Diary.
35.	File.		

Table "A". Issued with 17th Inf: Bde O.O.No 215.

Serial No.	Date.	Unit.	From.	To.	Route.	In relief of	Remarks.
1.	6th Feby.	3rd Rifle Bde.	VRAIGNES Camp.	Centre Sub-Sector.	by Light Railway from VRAIGNES or HANCOURT to ROISEL thence by Route March.	1st N.Staff.	Times of entrainment will be notified later.
2.	6th Feby.	17th M.G.Coy.	VRAIGNES&	LINE		72nd M.G.Coy.	
3.	7th Feby.	1st Roy. Fus.	HANCOURT. (Camp "A")	Left Sub-Sector.		9th E.Surreys.	
4.	7th Feby.	8th Bn. The Queens.	TEMPLEUX QUARRIES.	Right Sub-Sector.		8th R.W.Kents.	
5.	7th Febry.	17th L.T.M.Btty.	HANCOURT.	LINE.		72nd L.T.M.Batty.	

---- ------------ O.O.221/2

17th I.Bde Operation Order No 215 issued 3/2/18 should be amended to read No " 221".

4/2/18 Captain.

To all recipients of O.O. 215

A/Brigade Major 17th Infantry Bde.

Appendix III

SECRET.   COPY No. 14

8th Bn. The Queen's. R.W.S.Regt.
OPERATION ORDER. No. 8.

MAP REF. 62c 1/40.000.   6th Feby. 1918.

1 The Battn will relieve the 8th ROYAL WEST KENT REGT. in the Right Sub-Sector on the 7th inst.

2. 'D' Coy (Queens) will relieve 'B' Coy (R.W.KENTS) Left Coy.
'C' -"- -"- -"- 'C' -"- -"- RIGHT -"-.
'A' & 'B' Coys (Queens) will move to L.10.a. and take over dugouts at present occupied by 'C' & 'D' Coys respectively.
Battn. H.Q. will be at LEICESTER LOUNGE.

3 'D' Coy will move from L.10.A. at 5.30. p.m.
'C' -"- will meet guides from 8th R.W.KENTS. at LEICESTER LOUNGE at 4. p.m.
'A' Coy will move from TEMPLEUX QUARRIES at 4.30. p.m. and 'B' -"- at 5.15. p.m.
200 yards interval between platoons.

4 Blankets of H.Q, A & B. Coy will be stacked in bundles of 10. outside O.R. by 10.30. a.m.
Those of 'C' & 'D' Coys will be brought back by the returning ration limbers, 2 men to be left in charge of each kit.

5. Officers kits, Cooking Dixies, Canteens, etc., of H.Q., 'A' & 'B' will be collected at 4.30. p.m in TEMPLEUX QUARRIES.

6. Cooking for 'D' Coy will be done at the R.A. Post. HARGICOURT, that of 'C' Coy at LEICESTER LOUNGE.

7 Rations and all meals etc for the front line Coys will be carried by the two Support Coys.

8 'C' & 'D' Coys will arrange to carry Cooking Dixies, Lewis Guns, etc. tomorrow.

9 Gum-Boots:- Gumboots will be drawn as follows:-
'D' Coy. from Gumboot Store. HARGICOURT.
C -"- -"- -"- -"- LEICESTER LOUNGE.

10 1 Officer & 1 N.C.O per Coy will proceed in advance to take over Trench Stores etc.

11 Trench Stores, work in hand and proposed will be carefully taken over. List of Stores taken & handed over to reach O.R. by 12 NOON 8th INST.

"2"

8. Completion of relief will be by runner or by wire using Code Word. "SABA".

● ACKNOWLEDGE O.O. No. 8.

[illegible]
Capt & Adjutant
8th Queens. Regt.

Issued at. 8.30 p.m.

Copies to.

No 1. H.Q. Mess.
2. O.C. A. Coy.
3. O.C. B. --
4. O.C. C --
5. O.C. D --
6. O.C. H.Q. --
7. T.O.
No. 8. M.O.
9. Q.M.
10. 8th R.W. Kents.
11. R.S.M.
12. Sigs.
13. File.
14. War Diary.

S E C R E T   *Appendix IV*   Copy ....4..

17th INFANTRY BRIGADE OPERATION ORDER No 222

Ref Map HARGICOURT Special Sheet
1/10,000 Ed. 1.a and
62.c. 1/40,000

1. The 8th Bn The Queens(R.W.S) will be relieved in the Right Sub-Sector by the 7th Bn the Northamptonshire Regt on the night 11/12th Feby.

2. On relief the 8th Bn The Queens(R.W.S) will move to BERNES and come under the orders of the B.G.C. 73rd I.Bde & the 7th Bn the Northamptonshire Regt will come under the orders of the B.G.C. 17th I.Bde.

3. The moves will be carried out in accordance with Table "A"(on reverse).

4. The following intervals will be maintained on the march :-
   Between each platoon 200 yards.
   Between 6 transport vehicles 200 yards.

5. A representative from Bde H.Qrs will be at entraining point.

6. All Trench Stores, aeroplane photographs, defence schemes, tables of work in hand and proposed, lists of pass words etc., will be handed over.

7. All details of look-out posts, camp defences, A.A Lewis Gun positions and details regarding Bomb-proof defences round hutments will be taken over.

8. Completion of relief will be notified to Brigade H.Qrs by wiring the time at which relief is complete.

9. All other details will be arranged by C.O's direct.

10. ACKNOWLEDGE.

W H J [signature]
Captain.
A/Brigade Major 17th Infantry Bde.

9/2/18
Issued to Sigs
at ..1.p.m....

Copy No		Copy No	
1	B.G.C	2	Bde Major
3	Staff Captain	4	8th Queens
5	1st Royal Fus	6	3rd Rifle Bde
7	7th Northamptons (*For info*)	8	17th M.G.Coy
9	17th L.T.M.Btty	10	"G" 24th Div.
11	"Q" 24th Division.	12	73rd Infy. Bde.
13	Right Infy. Bde	14	Left Infy Bde.
15	Right Group R.F.A	16	Left Group R.F.A.
17	25th D.A.	18	Office
19	War Diary	20	

Table "A"

Date.	Unit.	From	To	Route	Relieved by	Remarks.
11th Feb.	8th Queens (R.W.S.).	Line	BERNES.	By Light Railway from TEMPLEUX to DZ 205(Q.4.a.2.6) approx.	7th Northamptonshire Regt.	Train arrangements will be notified later.

Appendix IV

SECRET. COPY No. 14.

8th BN. The Queen's. R.W.S. Regt.

OPERATION ORDER. No. 9.

MAP REF. 62c 1/40.000. FEBY. 10th 1918.

1. The Battn will be relieved in the RIGHT SUB-SECTOR by the 7th BN NORTHAMPTONSHIRE REGT on the night of the 11/12th Feby.

2. 'D' Coy (Queen's) will be relieved by 'B' Coy (Northants) @ about 6.30. p.m.
'C' — — — — 'D' — — — 5.30. —
'A' — — — — 'A' — — — 5.0. —
'B' — — — — 'C' — — — 5.15. —

It is probable that the platoon of 'D' Coy in Cologne Reserve will not be relieved; in that case they will move out as soon as 'D' Coy's relief is complete.

3. Guides:- O.C. 'D' Coy will arrange to have 1 Guide per post and 1 for Coy. H.Q. at R.A. Post, HARGICOURT. @ 6.0.p.m.
O.C. 'C' Coy will have guides for each post and 1 for Coy. H.Q. at Batt. H.Q. @ 5.p.m.
No guides will be required for 'A' & 'B' Coys.

4. The Battn will proceed by train from Templeux to Bernes. Time of entraining will be notified later.

5. Transport. 1 Limber per Coy will be at the respective dumps at the following times:-

A & B. Coy.	@	5.30. p.m.
C. Coy.	—	6.0. —
D. —	—	7.0. —

These limbers will carry Lewis Guns, Surplus Kits &c. 1 N.C.O. and 2 men per Coy must be left in charge.
Transport for H.Q. will be at forward dump at 6.p.m.

6. Gum boots:- These will be returned to Gumboot Store, Hargicourt and a receipt obtained for numbers handed in.

7. All Trench Stores, aeroplane photographs, defence scheme, tables of work in hand and proposed, lists of passwords etc, will be handed over.
List of Stores etc handed over to reach O.R. by 12 noon 12th inst.

8. Completion of relief to be reported by runner or wire, using the Code Word, "Couronne"

Acknowledge. O.O. No. 9.

Issued @ .9. p.m.

E. D. Dowell.
Capt & Adjutant.
8 Queens Regt

Copies to.

No. 1.	H.Q. Mess	No. 8.	M.O.
2.	O.C. 'A' Coy	9	7th Northants
3.	— B —	10.	Q.M.
4	— C —	11.	R.S.M.
5	— D —	12.	Sigs.
6	— H.Q. —	13.	File.
7	— T.O	14.	War Diary.

Appendix V

S E C R E T   Copy No ...1.......

17th INFANTRY BRIGADE ORDER No.224

Ref. Trench Map
and Map 62.c. 1/40,000

1. 8th Queens will relieve the 7th Northamptonshires in the Right Sub-sector(73rd I.Bde front) on the night 19th/20th Feby and will come under the Command of B.G.C., 73rd I.Bde.

2. On relief the 7th Northamptonshire Regt will move to and be accommodated in BERNES and will come under the orders of the B.G.C 17th Infantry Bde.

3. The normal intervals between platoons and transport vehicles will be maintained on the march.

4. All trench stores, aeroplane photographs, defence schemes, tables of work in hand and proposed, list of pass words etc., will be carefully taken over. Receipts will be forwarded to these H.Qrs 24 hours after completion of relief.

5. Completion of relief will be notified to Bde H.Qrs by wiring the time at which relief is complete.

6. All other details will be arranged by C.O's direct.

7. ACKNOWLEDGE.

Issued to Sigs at
8 p.m.

17/2/18

L.S.A. Mackenzie Major.

Brigade Major 17th Infantry Bde.

Copy No		Copy No	
1	to 8th Queens	2	to 1st Roy. Fus.
3	3rd Rifle Bde	4	17th M.G.Coy
5	17th L.T.M.Btty	6	"G" 24th Div.
7	"Q" 24th Div.	8	73rd Inf. Bde.
9	72nd Inf. Bde	10	Right Group R.F.A
11	File	12	War Diary.

Appendix V

SECRET. COPY No. 14

8th Bn. The Queens. R.W.S. Regt.

OPERATION ORDER No. 10.

MAP REF. 62c 1/40.000. 18th Feby. 1918.

1. The Battn. will relieve the 7th NORTHAMPTONSHIRE REGT, in the RIGHT SUB-SECTOR on the night of the 19th/20th Feby, and will come under the Command of the B.G.C. 73rd I.B.

2. On completion of relief Coys. will be disposed as follows:-
Bn. H.Q., Leicester Lounge.
'D' Coy (Queen's) on the Left will relieve 'C' Coy (Northants)
'C' — — — Right — " — 'A' — — " —
'B' — — — L.10.A — " — 'B' — — " —
'A' — — — " — — " — 'D' — — " —

3 Coys will proceed via daylight route from Hesbicourt to Hargicourt and will move off from Bernes at the following times.
'A' Coy. 2. pm.
'B' — 2. " — from Hancourt.
H.Q. — 3.0. —
'C' — 3.30 —
'D' — 4.0. —
Normal intervals to be kept between platoons etc.

4 Transport:- One limber for Lewis Guns, Mess Kits, etc will follow each Coy. All material of H.Q. Coy for the trenches will be ready for collection by 2.30 pm.

5 Blankets etc not for the trenches to be returned to Q.M. Stores by 1.30. pm.

6. Guides for 'D' Coy will be at R.A. Post, HARGICOURT at 6.30. pm as follows.
1 for Coy H.Q., 1 for Ferret Group, 1 for Right Group and 1 for Left Group.

7 GUARDS:- O/c A Coy will detail the following.
1. N.C.O. & 2 men Gum Boot Store.
1. N.C.O. & 1 man T.M. Store.
They will report to o/c D Coy (Northants) at L.10.a by 11. am. 19th inst
o/c 'B' Coy will detail the following.
1. N.C.O. & man Bomb Store.
They will report to o/c 'B' Coy (Northants) at L.10.a by 11 am. 19th inst.

8 Trench Stores, work in hand and proposed, reserve rations and water etc will be carefully taken over.
Certificates of Stores &c taken over to reach O.R. by 9 am 20th inst.

9 Completion of relief will be reported by runner or wire using the Code Word "Thus".

Acknowledge.

Issued at 6 p.m.

E. D. Dowell
Captain & Adjutant
8th Queen's Regt.

Copies to.

No 1	H.Q. Mess	No. 8.	M.O.
2	O.C. A. Coy	9.	Sig Off
3	— B. —	10.	Q.M.
4	— C —	11.	7th Northants.
5	— D —	12	R.S.M.
6	— H.Q. —	13.	File
7.	— T.O.	14.	WAR DIARY.

Appendix VI

8th Battn The Queen's. R.W.S. Regt. SECRET.

O P E R A T I O N   O R D E R.   No 11.   No

Map Ref 62.C.   19/2/18.

1. "A" & "B" Coys (Queen's) will relieve "C" & "D" Coys respectively in the Right Sub-sector to-morrow 20th instant.

2. "A" Coy will relieve by day and "B" Coy after dark and "C" & "D" Coys will take over their respective dug-outs.

3. Arrangements for relief will be made between O.C Coys concerned.

4. The Respective fronts will be thoroughly reconnoitred before relief. O.C "B" Coy will arrange to do this before 6 am 20th inst.

5. The inter-change of Cooking arrangements will be arranged by the Master Cook

6. The Quarter Master will arrange with the C.Q.M.Sgts as regards rations, the rations for "B" Coy will not arrive at the R.I Post HARGICOURT before 7 pm.

7. O.C "C" & "D" Coys will arrange to send 2 men to look after their rations at L.10.A. until Coys arrive.

8. O.C "C" Coy will arrange to take over the following Guards :-
1 N.C.O & 1 Other Rank for T.M Store HARGICOURT. at present found by "A" Coy.
1 N.C.O & 1 Other Rank for Bomb Store HARGICOURT at present found by "B" Coy.

9. Trench Stores will be carefully handed and taken over.

10. Completion of relief will be reported by runner, or wire, using CODE word "YAH"

11. A C K N O W L E D G E :- O.O. No 11.

Issued at 11 pm.

Nos 1 "A" Coy.
2 "B" "
3 "C" "
4 "D" "
5 Q.M.
6 T.O.
7 War Diary.
8 File.
9 Sgt Mstr Cook.

E. S. Dowell.
Captain & Adjutant.
8th Battn The Queen's. R.W.S. Regt.

N.B. "A" Coys relief to be complete by 2.30 p.m.

S E C R E T   Appendix VII   Copy No ....

17th INFANTRY BRIGADE ORDER No 225
Ref. HARGICOURT Special Sheet 1/10,000.
62.c. 1/40,000

1. On 22/23rd Feby the Front of the 24th Division will be adjusted so as to be held by 3 Brigades in the line.
Each Brigade will be disposed in depth as under :-
1 Battalion .... OUTPOST ZONE
1 Battalion .... BATTLE ZONE.
1 Battalion .... Reserve.

2. 17th Infantry Brigade will hold the Centre Brigade Sector with boundaries as under :-
Northern(Between 17th I.Bde and 73rd I.Bde).
RUBY LANE(inclusive)-~~FERRET LEFT(inclusive)~~-ENFILADE TRENCH (inclusive)-UNNAMED FARM- HARGICOURT ROAD to junction L.5.d.2.8 (inclusive)-~~PIMPLE LOCALITY~~ Northern end of HARGICOURT to F.26.d. 10.15- PIMPLE LOCALITY (exclusive)- thence track running S.W. through L.4.a., L.3.b., L.3.c. to CRUCIFIX L.3.c.7.7.

Southern(between 17th I.Bde and 72nd I.Bde).
G.7.b.65.10-SPADE LANE(inclusive)-L.12.central-L.11.b.5.2-L.11. central-L.11.c.0.6-L.10.d.2.6-L.10.c.0.6 (accommodation at THE EGG is made available to 72nd Inf. Bde).

Boundaries between Brigades are shewn on attached sketch(issued to Units 17th I.Bde only).

3. To carry out this re-adjustment the following moves and reliefs as per Table "A" attached will take place:-

22nd Feby.(a) 8th Queens under orders of 73rd I.Bde will take over OUTPOST ZONE SPADE LANE G.7.b.65.10 to ENFILADE TRENCH G.1.b.3.7, both inclusive, from Units of 72nd and 73rd I.Bde.
Relief to be completed by 12 Noon.

(b) 1st Royal Fusiliers will move into Brigade Support.

(c) 3rd Rifle Bde will move into Bde Reserve, MONTIGNY FARM.

23/24th Feby. 3rd Rifle Bde will relieve 8th Queens in Brigade Sector. On relief 8th Queens will move to MONTIGNY FARM and will be in Bde Reserve.

4. Details of M.G.Coy and L.T.M.Btty reliefs will be arranged between O&C concerned.
Reliefs to be completed by 6 a.m. on 23rd Feby.

5. Aeroplane photographs, sunprints, trench stores, details of work in hand and proposed will be carefully taken over.

6. The normal intervals between Platoons and Transport Vehicles will be maintained on the march.

7. Completion of relief will be wired to Brigade Headquarters stating time of relief.

8. All other details will be arranged between O&C concerned.

9. H.Qrs 17th I.Bde will close at BERNES 12 Noon 22nd Feby and re-open at HERVILLY at same hour, at which time the Command of the Centre Sub-sector will pass to B.G.C., 17th Inf. Bde.

10. ACKNOWLEDGE.

Issued to Sigs
at 5 p.m.
21/2/18

Wa Mackenzie
Major.
Brigade Major 17th Infantry Bde.

DISTRIBUTION of 17th I.Bde Order No 225

Copy No 1	8th Queens	Copy No 2	1st Royal Fus.
3	3rd Rifle Bde	4	17th M.G.Coy
5	17th T.M. Btty	6	17th I.Bde Sigs.
7	24th Div "G"	8	24th Div "Q"
9	72nd I.Bde	10	73rd I.Bde
11	Right Group R.F.A.	12	104th Field Coy.
13	War Diary	14	File.

Table "A" issued with 17th I.Bde Order No 225

Date	Unit	From	To	Relieving.	Remarks.
Feby. 22/23rd.	8th Queens	Centre Sub-sector 73rd I.Bde Front.	17th I.Bde Sector (New dispositions)	Left Coy 8th R.W.Kents Regt (72nd I.Bde). * 2 Posts 9th R.Sussex Regt (73rd I.Bde).	Under orders of 73rd I.B. * LAKE LEFT & FERRET LEFT
"	1st Roy. Fus.	HERVILLY	Brigade Support 3 Coys. L.10.a. 1 Coy HESBECOURT Bn H.Qrs HESBECOURT	(2 Coys 8th Queens (1 Coy "C" Coy (9th E.Surreys 72nd I.Bde.	1. Relief of 2 Coys 8th Queens to be completed by 12 Noon. 2. To be clear of HERVILLY by 4 p.m.
"	3rd Rifle Bde.	VENDELLES	Brigade Reserve MONTIGNY FARM	1st N.Staffs Regt	To be clear of VENDELLES by 3 p.m. Accommodation being taken over by 8th R.W.Kents.
"	17th M.G.Coy	HERVILLY	LINE	73rd M.G.Coy 6 Guns in OUTPOST ZONE.	Support Guns Nos 3,4,5 will be handed over to 73rd M.G.Coy.
"	17th L.T.M.Btty	HERVILLY	LINE (H.Qrs L.10.a)	73rd T.M.Btty 2 Guns POND SUPPORT 1 Gun FERRET LEFT 72nd T.M.Btty 1 Gun RAILWAY SUPPORT	1. Accommodation in L.10.a. will be provided for by 1st R.Fus. 2. 4 Guns will be in Reserve and will be prepared to take up defensive positions covering RED LINE.
23/24th	3rd Rifle Bde	MONTIGNY FARM	Line	8th Queens	Details to be arranged between C.O's concerned.
"	8th Queens	LINE	MONTIGNY FARM	3rd Rifle Bde.	

Appendix VII

8th Battn The Queen's. R.W.S. Regt.

O P E R A T I O N   O R D E R   No 12.

Map ref 62.c.   21/2/18.

1. The following relief and change of dispositions will take place to-morrow 22nd instant.

(a) "C" Coy (Queen's) will relieve "A" Coy (R.W.Kent Regt) as previously arranged and will also take over No 1 Post, No 2 Post and Post at junction of CLUB LANE and POND SUPPORT TRENCH from "A" Coy (Queen's).
Coy H.Q. will be in RAILWAY SUPPORT TRENCH.
They will also have 2 sections in SLAG TRENCH.
This relief to be complete by 12 noon.

(b) "D" Coy (Queen's) will send 2 platoons to take over A.D Station HARGICOURT and relieve 2 platoons of - Coy 9th R Sussex Regt. They will send the 2 L.G teams of these 2 platoons to L.6.b.50.20. COLOGNE RESERVE TRENCH. One of these teams will relieve the team of the 9th R Sussex Regt there. The other will be guided from there to L.G Post in FERRET LEFT TRENCH.
Coy H.Q. and the remainder of "D" Coy will move to dug-outs at LEICESTER LOUNGE. This relief to be complet by 12 noon and reported to Battn H.Q by runner.

(c) "A" Coy (Queen's) will take over the BAIT TRENCH Group from "B" Coy (Queen's) as soon after dusk as possible and will take over Coy H.Q at present occupied by "B" Coy (Queen's) leaving a small garrison at their present Coy H.Q in POND SUPPORT TRENCH.

(d) As soon as "A" Coy have taken over the BAIT TRENCH Group and the Coy H.Q of "B" Coy., "B" Coy will move their Coy H.Q to L.6.b.50.20. COLOGNE RESERVE. They will also take over the L.G Post there and the one in FERRET LEFT from "D" Coy.

2. O.C "D" Coy will arrange to relieve the T.M and Bomb Store Guards in HARGICOURT at present found by "C" Coy at 10 am.

3. Trench Stores, Work in hand and proposed will be carefully taken over.

4. Completion of relief to be reported by runner or wire using the code word "KELB"

5. A C K N O W L E D G E:- O.O. No 12.

Issued at 11.30 pm.

E. D. Donnell.
Captain & Adjutant.
8th Battn The Queen's. Regt.

21/2/18.

Copies to
"A" Coy.
"B" "
"C" "
"D" "
R.W. Kent Regt.
9th R.Sussex Regt.

Transport Officer.
Quarter Master.
War Diary.
File.
H.Q. Mess.

S E C R E T. COPY NO:- 17

Ref Map 62C, 1/40,000 & Trench Map.

73rd. INFANTRY BRIGADE ORDER NO.180.

H.Q., 73rd. I.B., February 21st.1918.

1. The front as now held by the 24th. Division will be adjusted to form a three Brigade front on the 22nd. and night 22/23rd. February 1918.
Each Brigade will then be disposed in depth as under:-

1 Battn. - Outpost Zone.
1 Battn. - Battle Zone.
1 Battn. - Rearward Zone. (Rest billets).

2. Consequent on above, the Southern Boundary of the Brigade will be altered to run as follows:-

RUBY LANE (exclusive) - FERRET LEFT (exclusive) - ENFILADE TRENCH (exclusive) - UNNAMED FARM HARGICOURT ROAD to junction L.5.d.2.8.(exclusive) - North East edge of HARGICOURT (exclusive) - PIMPLE locality (inclusive) - track running South West through L.4.a., L.3.b. and c to Crucifix L.3.c.7.7.

3. In order to carry this adjustment into effect reliefs and moves will be carried out as under:-

A. The 8th. Queens Regiment will take over the Sector from ENFILADE TRENCH to SPADE LANE - G.7.b.65.10. (both inclusive) relieving:-
(i). 1 coy. 8th.R.W.Kent Regt. on the right.
(ii). 9th. Royal Sussex Regt. in such posts as are included within the boundary detailed in para 2.
Relief to be complete by 12 noon at which hour the command of the Sector will pass to B.G.C., 17th. Infantry Brigade.

B. The 9th. Royal Sussex Regiment will extend their front to the Northern Boundary of the Brigade relieving the 13th. Middlesex Regiment in the present Left Sub-section.

C. The 7th. Northamptonshire Regiment at present located in BERNES, will move to HERVILLY - leading company will not arrive at HERVILLY before 3 p.m.

D. The 73rd. Machine Gun Company will be relieved by 6 guns of 17th. Machine Gun Company in the following positions:-
BOBBY FARM - L.11.b.08.38.
" " - do.
COLOGNE FARM - L.6.c.42.32.
LAKE LEFT POST - L.6.a.55.20.
COTE TRENCH - L.10.b.09.53.
HARGICOURT TR. - L.4.c.90.19.

and relieve 17th. Machine Gun Company in positions as under:-
No.3. - F.28.c.6.5.
No.4. - F.28.d.2.6.
No.5. - F.28.d.2.1.

Company Headquarters and the remaining 5 guns will be located at TEMPLEUX QUARRIES.
Battle Positions for 2 guns will be selected in SHERWOOD TRENCH at approx. F.27.d.4.0. and L.3.b.5.7. and the other three guns will remain in reserve.

E. The 73rd. Light Trench Mortar Battery will be relieved by 3 guns of 17th. Light Trench Mortar Battery in positions at:-

POND SUPPORT - 2 guns.
FERRET RIGHT - 1 gun.

The following positions will then be occupied:-
SUNKEN ROAD - L.5.b.99.93.
BENJAMIN SWITCH-F.29.b.1.7. (approx).
TOINE POST x
ORCHARD POST.

The remaining two guns will be located at Battery Headquarters L.2.b.85.10. with Battle Positions at points selected in HARGICOURT TRENCH.

4. On completion of reliefs on 22nd. and night 22/23rd. February 1918 the 73rd. Infantry Brigade will be disposed as follows:-

A. Outpost Zone. - 9th. Royal Sussex Regiment.

Right front company. Southern Brigade Boundary to CARBINE (incl).	1 pl.3 sects.	- COCOA locality.
	1 pl.	- SUGAR "
	1 pl.1 sect.	- INDIAN POST.
	Coy.H.Q.	- L.5.b.3.2.
Left front coy. CARBINE (excl). to Northern Brigade Boundary.	1 coy. (less 1 pl.)	- 9 posts front line.
	2 sects.	- HUSSAR POST. (anti-raiding).
	2 sects.	- BENJAMIN POST. (anti-raiding).
	Coy. H.Q.	- ARTAXERXES POST.
Support coy.	1 pl.	- VALLEY POST.
	$1\frac{1}{2}$ pl.	- ARATXERXES POST.
	$1\frac{1}{2}$ pl.	- HUSSAR ROAD, F.29.a.99.50.
	Coy. H.Q.	- do.
Reserve Coy.	$1\frac{1}{2}$ pl.	- HILL POST
	$2\frac{1}{2}$ pl.	- HUSSAR ROAD, F.22.d.70.95.
	Coy. H.Q.	- do.

Battalion Headquarters - HARDY LANE.

Advanced Battn. " - L.5.b.3.2.
(2nd.in command)

B. Battle Zone. - 13th. Middlesex Regiment.

1 company - HUSSAR, TOINE and ORCHARD POSTS, and HARDY BANKS.
2 coys. & Battn.H.Q. - TEMPLEUX QUARRIES.
1 coy. - ROISEL.

C. Rearward Zone - 7th. Northamptonshire Regiment (Rest billets).
4 coys. and H.Q. - HERVILLY.

D. 73rd. M.G.Coy. - as detailed in para 3 (d).

E. 73rd. Light T.M.Battery - as detailed in para 3 (e).

5. ....

Appendix XVIII

AMENDMENT TO 73rd. INFANTRY BRIGADE ORDER NO.180.

Cancel Line 2, para 4 (b). and substitute:-

1 coy. - TOINE and ORCHARD POSTS and HARDY BANKS.

[signature]
Captain,
for Brigade Major, 73rd. Infantry Brigade.

H.Q. 73rd. I.B.
21. 2. 18.

Copies to all recipients of 73rd I.B. order 180.

5. All other details will be arranged direct between O's.C. concerned.

6. All Trench Stores, details of Reserve Rations and Water, Defence Schemes, Maps, Aeroplane Photographs, Schemes of work in hand and proposed, L.G. A.A. positions, etc. will be carefully taken/over and handed details forwarded to this office within 36 hours of relief.

7. Details of Look-out Posts - Camp Defences with Map, A.A., L.G. positions - details as regards Bomb proof defences round hutments will be taken over at HERVILLY.

8. Completion of reliefs will be wired to this office - Code Word"PONG".

9. Acknowledge.

[signature]

Issued at 4 p.m.

Captain,
for Brigade Major, 73rd. Infantry Brigade.

Copy No.1. War Diary.
2. File.
3. "G" 24 Div.
4. "Q" 24 Div.
5. 17th. I.B.
6. 72nd. I.B.
7. Left Flank Bde.
8. 9th. Royal Sussex Regt.
9. 7th. Northamptonshire Regt.
10. 13th. Middlesex Regt.
11. 73rd. M.G.Coy.
12. 73rd. Light T.M.Battery.
13. 129th. Fd. Coy. R.E.
14. 73rd. Fd. Amb.
15. Area Comdt. HERVILLY.
16. " " BERNES.
17. 8th Queens.

SECRET. Appendix VIII Copy No. 14.

8th Bn. The Queen's R.W.S. Regt.

OPERATION ORDER. No. 13.

Map Ref. 02C. 22nd Feb. 1918.

1 The Battn will be relieved by the 3rd RIFLE BRIGADE in the CENTRE SUB-SECTOR on the 23rd inst.

2 'A' Coy (Queens) will be relieved by 'C' Coy (R.B.) at about 6 pm.
'B' — " — 'B' — " — 6.30 pm
'C' — " — 'A' — " — 5.0 pm.
'D' — " — 'D' — " — 4.0 pm.

3 On completion of relief the Battn will proceed to the camp at Montigny.

4 O.C. Coys will ensure that their men move off in properly formed parties either under an Officer or an N.C.O. according to the strength of the party.

5 Transport for H.Q., 'A', 'C' and 'D' Coys will be at the CRATER dump at the following times:-

H.Q. Coy at 6 pm.
'A' — " 6.30 —
'C' — " 6. —
'D' — " 6. —

Transport for 'B' Coy will be at the R.A. Post. HARGICOURT at 7 pm.
O.C. Coys will leave 1 N.C.O. and 2 men to look after Lewis Guns, kits etc., and hold them responsible for their safe arrival at Montigny.

6 O.C. 'C' Coy will detail the following guides to be at Battn. H.Q. L.11.b.45.85 at 4.15 pm.
1 Guide for the posts South of CLUB TRENCH
1 — " — — NORTH — " —
— " — — Coy. H.Q.
1 — " — — SLAG TRENCH.

7 Trench Stores, work in hand and proposed, etc will be carefully handed over. Certificates for Stores handed over to reach O.R. 9 am 24th inst. Certificates for Iron Rations and Reserve Water to be sent to Battn H.Q. by special runner immediately these have been taken over by the incoming unit.

8. All Petrol Cans will be returned to Transport Lines.

9. All Gum Boots will be returned to Gum Boot Store, HARGICOURT and a receipt obtained for numbers handed in.

10 Completion of relief will be reported by runner or wire using Code word "YALLAH".

11 Acknowledge: O.O. 13.

Issued at 9.15 pm.

Captain & Adjutant
8th Bn Queens Regt.

Copies to.

No 1. 2. Q. Mess.	No 6. O.C. HQ. Coy	
2. O.C. 'A' Coy	7. T.O.	No. 11. R.S.M.
3. O.C. 'B' —	8. Q.M.	12. SIGS.
4. O.C. 'C' —	9. M.O.	13. FILE.
5. O.C. 'D' —	10. 3rd R. Bde.	14. WAR DIARY.

Appendix IX

SECRET

Copy No. 13

8th The Queens. RWS Regt

OPERATION ORDER No. 14

27th Feby. 1918.

Map Ref. 62c & Amiens.

1. The first line Transport, with the exception of 4 Lewis Gun limbers will move to VILLERS. BRETONNEUX, Area by road on Feby 28th under command of B.T.O of 17th I.B.

2. Convoy will pass Crucifix, BERNES Q4c51 at 9.20 am and X Roads HANCOURT Q8d29 at 10.17 am.

3. The 8th Queens transport will follow 17th M.G. Coy at interval of 200 yards.

4. Convoy will stop the night of the 28th at FRAMERVILLE-VAUVILLERS and reach VILLERS BRETONNEUX March 1st.

5. Guides will be at X Roads 1200 yds E of VILLERS BRETONNEUX at 10. am 1st March.

6. The four Lewis gun limbers will move to VILLERS BRETONNEUX on March 1st passing Q4c54 BERNES at 12 NOON, proceeding under command of T.O. 1st ROYAL FUSILIERS to reach FRAMERVILLE on night of 1st March & VILLERS BRETONNEUX on 2nd March.

7. Both convoys will proceed by Route - HANCOURT-VRAIGNES- BRIE-VILLERS-CARBONNEL- ESTREÉ- LA-MOTTE- VILLERS-BRETONNEUX.

8. Cookers will be ready to move from Montigny at 7 am 28th Feb

9. Medical Stores & Officers surplus ~~personal~~ Mess kit will be dumped outside Battn. H.Q. at 7 a.m. 28th Feb.

Issued at 6.15 p.m.

E. S. Dowell.
Capt & Adjutant
8th Bn Queens Regt

Copies to

No. 1	H.Q. Mess	No 7	T.O
2	O.C. 'A' Coy	8	Q.M
3	" 'B' "	9	Sig Off
4	" C "	10	M.O.
5	" D "	11	R.S.M
6	" H.Q "	12	File

No 13 War Diary.

Appendix IX

SECRET. COPY No 12

8th Bn The Queen's R.W.S Regt.

OPERATION ORDER. No. 15.

Map. Ref 62c & Amiens. 28th Feby 1918

1. The Battn will be relieved by the 4th EAST LANCS REGT. at MONTIGNY on the 1st MARCH.

2. On completion of relief the Battn will move by Coys to ROISEL and entrain for VILLERS BRETONNEUX.

3. Coys will move off as follows:-

H.Q. Coy	at	9.35 A.M.
"A"	"	9.40 "
"B"	"	9.45 "
"C"	"	9.50 "
"D"	"	9.55 "

4. DRESS:- Full Marching Order with Steel Helmets fitted on the packs.

5. BAGGAGE:- Blankets in bundles of ten will be ready for loading at 7 a.m. They will be brought direct to the Lorries for Loading. Special care will be taken to ensure that bundles are rolled tightly.
   Officers Valises and all other stores excepting 1 Mess basket per Coy and Camp Kettles will be stacked on the piece of waste ground opposite "A" Coys Hut at 7.30. A.M.
   1 Mess basket per Coy & the Camp Kettle will be ready for Loading at 9.a.m.

6. O.C. Companies will ensure that their billets and surroundings are left clean & tidy and will render a certificate to the Adjutant to this effect by 9 a.m.

7. A marching out state will be handed in to the Orderly Room by 9. a.m.

8. There will be 1 Limber per Coy for Lewis Guns &c. All Lewis Guns &c must be ready for loading by 9 a.m.

9. Completion of relief to be reported by runner.

10. Acknowledge:- O.O 15.

Issued at 1 p.m.

E. D. Dowell
Captain & Adjutant
8th Bn Queens Regt

Copies to.

No 1.	H.Q. Mess.	No 7.	Q.M.
2.	O.C. A Coy	8.	M.O.
3.	" B "	9.	Sig. Off.
4.	" C "	10.	R.S.M.
5.	" D "	11.	File.
6.	" H.Q. "	12.	War Diary

"C" Form

MESSAGES AND SIGNALS.

Army Form C. 2123.
(In books of 100.)

No. of Message.........

Prefix.........Code.........Words.........

£ s. d.

Charges to collect

Service Instructions.

Received From......... By.........

Sent, or sent out At.........m. To......... By.........

Office Stamp.

Handed in at.........Office.........m. Received.........m.

TO ED.

*Sender's Number	Day of Month	In reply to Number	AAA
BM309	28		

On receipt of this KC will be the Battn in Reserve and will be prepared to move on ALARM ACTION to positions as detailed in my G2/138 dated 24th inst for Battn in MONTIGNY FM aaa QE will remain MONTIGNY pending further instructions aaa addsd KC and QE reptd ED IV and HORSE

FROM JA

PLACE & TIME 5.0 am.

* This line should be erased if not required.

(B 8070) Wt. w. 7435—M857 250,000 Pads. 10/16 H & S (E436.) Forms/C.2123/3.

"C" Form.

MESSAGES AND SIGNALS.

Army Form C. 2123.
(In books of 100.)

No. of Message

Prefix SM Code CSDM Words 37	Received.	Sent, or sent out.	Office Stamp.
£ s. d.	From 10	At m.	ED
Charges to Collect	By [illegible]	To	28
Service Instructions NK10		By	

Handed in at 10 Sq Office 3·3 Pm. Received 5·27 P m.

TO ED VIA NK42

*Sender's Number	Day of Month.	In reply to Number	AAA
SC 342	28		

All surplus kit of all units is to be got together now and tomorrow will be stored in a div[l] store probably at VRAIGNES aaa Get it ready

FROM NK10
PLACE & TIME 4·50 PM

* This line should be erased if not required.

9310—W.528—100,000—10/5/17—E.P.Co.—(E1213).

"C" Form.

MESSAGES AND SIGNALS.

Army Form C. 2123,
(In books of 100.)

No. of Message

Prefix SO Code EBWPH Words 21	Received.	Sent, or sent out.	Office Stamp.
£ s. d. Charges to Collect	From NK10 By WH	At m. To	ED 28/2/18
Service Instructions NK10 urgent operation priority		By	

Handed in at 10 Sig Office 3.14P m. Received 3.45P m.

TO ED

*Sender's Number	Day of Month.	In reply to Number	AAA
BM306	28		

Alarm action aaa No moves as detailed in G2/138 of 24 inst will take place until further orders aaa Reliefs will continue as previously arranged aaa Ack ED

FROM
PLACE & TIME NK10

* This line should be erased if not required.

9310—W.528—100,000—10/5/17—E.P.Co.—(E1213).

"C" Form.

Army Form C. 2123.
(In books of 100.)

MESSAGES AND SIGNALS.

No. of Message ________

Prefix PO Code CFRRY Words 81

£ s. d.

Charges to Collect

Service Instructions priority NK10 urgent [illegible]

Received. From 10 By [illegible]

Sent, or sent out. At ____ m. To ____ By ____

Office Stamp. ED 28/2/18

Handed in at 10 [illegible] Office 3.31 p.m. Received 4.30 p.m.

TO ED

*Sender's Number	Day of Month.	In reply to Number	AAA
BM 307	28		

continuation of BM 306 of this date aaa Moves as under will take place preparatory moving MONTECOURT first march aaa Ref map 1/20000 Sheet 62c SE7 central aaa ED to move to HANCOURT forthwith aaa further details will be forwarded later aaa QE to move to MONTIGNY on relief aaa HN and RZ on relief to move to BERNES aaa KC will remain BERNES aaa Report completion of all moves aaa Ack Addsd all concerned

FROM

PLACE & TIME

JH

* This line should be erased if not required.

9310—W.528—100,000—10/5/17—E.P.Co.—(E1213).

Appendix IX.

CORRIGENDA TO 17th I.Bde O. No 227

1. Reference Table "B" - Serials No 8 and 9 "Route"

delete " -do-"

Substitute "As in Serial 1."

2. Table "C" Route.

for " As in Table "A" substitute

"As in Table "B"

27/2/18

W. Mackenzie

Major.

Brigade Major 17th Infantry Brigade.

S E C R E T   Copy No ....

17th INFANTRY BRIGADE ORDER No 227

Ref 1/10,000 HARGICOURT special sheet.
& 1/100,000 AMIENS

1. The 24th Division is being relieved by the 66th Division between 26th Feby and 3rd March and on relief is being transferred from Cavalry Corps to XIX Corps BOVES Area.

2. The 17th Infantry Bde will be relieved by 198th Infantry Bde on the 28th Feby and 1st March, in accordance with Table "A" attached.

3. On 1st March 17th Infantry Bde, less 1st Line Transport, will entrain at ROISEL for VILLERS BRETONNEUX.
Entrainment Orders and necessary Administrative instructions will be issued by the Dtaff Captain.

4. 1st Line Transport will move to VILLERS BRETONNEUX Area by Road on 28th Feby and 1st March in accordance with Tables "B" and "C" attached.
Attention of Units is directed to D.R.O.2930 dated 26/9/17 -Steel Helmets if not worn, should be fastened to the man's shoulder and not hung on the Saddle".

5. Instructions re Advanced Parties of 66th Division have already been issued to all concerned.

6. One Officer per M.G.Coy and One O.R. per Machine Gun(in 6 forward positions) will remain in the Line for 24 hours after relief.

7. All Defence Schemes, Maps, Sun-prints, Aeroplane Photographs, Trench Stores, Details of work in hand and proposed will be carefully handed over.
Receipts for above will be forwarded to these H.Qrs within 36 Hours of relief.

8. Completion of relief will be wired to Bde H.Qrs stating time of relief.

9. All other details will be arranged between O's.C concerned.

10. The Command of the 17th I.Bde front will pass to B.G.C. 198th I.Bde 10 a.m. on 1st March at which hour Bde H.Qrs will close at HERVILLY and open at VILLERS BRETONNEUX on arrival.

11. ACKNOWLEDGE.

Issued to Sigs at
7-30 p.m.
26/2/18

Wa Mackenzie
Major.
Brigade Major 17th Infantry Brigade.

Copy No		Copy No	
1	8th Queens	2	1st Royal Fus.
3	3rd Rifle Bde	4	17th M.G.Coy
5	17th L.T.M.Battery	6	Sigs 17th I.Bde
7	"G" 24th Div.	8	"Q" 24th Div.
9	B.T.O.	10	Right Group R.F.A.
11	104th F.Coy R.E.	12	74th Field Amb.
13	24th Div. Train.	14	195 Coy A.S.C.
15	72nd I.Bde	16	73rd I.Bde
17	198th I.Bde	18	199th I.Bde
19	War Diary	20	File.

Table "C" 17th Inf. Bde Rear Transport.

Date	Unit.	From	To	Starting Point Place	Starting Point Time	Route	Remarks.
Mar 1st	1st Roy.Fus 8th Queens 3rd Rifle Bde 17th M.G.Coy 17th L.T.M.B	BERNES MONTIGNY ROISEL ROISEL ROISEL	FRAMERVILLE	Road junction Q.4.c.5.4 (BERNES)	12 Noon	As in Table "A"	
Mar 2nd	-do-	FRAMERVILLE	Billeting Area.	To be arranged by Officer in charge of Convoy.		As in Tabô "A"	

Note- 1. Above Transport consists of (a) Per Bn... 4 L.G.S.Waggons .... for Lewis Guns.
(b) M.G.C.... 5 " " .... for Vickers Guns.
(c) T.M.B.... 1 G.S.Waggon)
& 1 L.G.S.Waggon) .... for Stokes Mortars.

2. T.O. 1st Royal Fusiliers will be in Command 8th Queens, 3rd Rifle Bde and 17th M.G.Coy will detail 1 Mounted N.C.O. to be in charge of respective detachments.

Table "A" issued with 17th I.Bde Order No 227 dated 28/2/18.

Serial No.	Date	Unit.	From	To	Relieved by.	Rendezvous for guides	Time	Remarks.
1.	28th Feby.	1st Royal Fus.	<u>Brigade Support</u> 2 Coys L.10.a. 2 Coys HESBECOURT Bn H.Q "	BERNES	9th Manchester Rgt	HESBECOURT Fork Roads L.13.c.8.2		Relief to commence after dinners. BERNES will be clear by 3-30pm
2	28th Feb) 1st Mar.)	3rd Rifle Bde	<u>Outpost Zone</u> 3 Coys in Front & Support Lines. 1 Coy in LEICESTER LOUNGE Bn H.Q "	ROISEL	2/5 East Lancs Regt	CRUCIFIX L.3.c.85.65	2-30pm	1 Guide per platoon & 1 per Bn H.Qrs.
3		17th M.G.C	Line	ROISEL	203rd M.G.C.	Under arrangements by O's C concerned.		
4		17th T.M.Btty	Line	ROISEL	198th L.T.M.B.	L.10.a.		Under arrangements by O's C concerned.
5	1st Mar.	8th Queens	MONTIGNY Fme	ROISEL	4th E.Lancs Rgt.			To be clear of MONTIGNY by 10 a.m.
6		1st Royal Fus.	BERNES	ROISEL				To be clear of BERNES by 12-30 p.m.
7		17th I.Bde H.Q	HERVILLY	ROISEL	198th I.Bde			To be clear of HERVILLY by 1 p.m.

<u>NOTE</u> - 3rd Rifle Brigade, 17th M.G.Coy and 17th L.T.M.Battery will be accommodated on relief in Tent Camp K.10.c.9x6.

Table "B"

Serial No.	Date.	Unit.	From.	To.	Starting Point Place	Starting Point Time	Route	Remarks.
1.	Feby 28th	Bde H.Qrs	BERNES	VAUVILLERS & FRAMERVILLE		10 a.m.	HANCOURT-VRAIGNES BRIE-VILLERS CARBONNEL-ESTREES.	
2	"	1st Roy.Fus.	"	"	HANCOURT CROSS ROADS Q.8.d.2.9	10-04 a.m	-do-	
3	"	17th M.G.C.	"	"		10-11 a.m	-do-	
4	"	8th Queens	"	"		10-17 a.m	-do-	
5	"	3rd R.Bde	"	"		10-24 a.m.	-do-	
6	"	10th Dublins	HERVILLY	"		10-31 a.m	[illegible] thence as above.	To follow in rear of [illegible]
7	"	104th F.Coy R.E	MILIEU COPSE Q.1-a.8.8	"		10-38 a.m.	-do-	Not to pass Q.8.d.2.9 till 10th Dublins are clear.
8	"	195 Coy A.S.C	ROISEL	"		10-45 a.m	-do-	
9	"	74th Field Ambulance	HANCOURT	"		11-03 a.m	-do-	
	Mar 1st		FRAMERVILLE VAUVILLERS	Final Billeting Area.	To be arranged by B.T.O. 17th I.B		LA MOTTE-VILLERS BRETONNEUX	Guides will be at X Roads 1200 yds E. of VILLERS BRETONNEUX at 10- a.m

Note- (1) 200 yards interval between Units Transports will be maintained.
(2). Billots in VAUVILLERS will be allotted by Lieut. HAVERS 8th Queens. The B.T.O. 17th I.Bde will send 1 Off. and 2 N.C O's in advance to report to him and act as guides.
(3) The B.T.O. 17th I.Bde will be in Command of the Convoy.
(4) The B.T.O. 17th I.Bde will arrange to send on all Train Supply Waggons on the second day of the march one hour in front of the remainder of the column to proceed to the refilling point O.36.c.central to draw supplies and issue to Units the same day.

17th Brigade.

24th Division.

8th BATTALION

ROYAL WEST SURREY REGIMENT

M A R C H   1 9 1 8

Appendices attached:-

Brigade Orders
Intelligence Reports
Situation Reports
Congratulatory Message.
MAP.

17/24

8th Bn "The Queens" R W S Regt

War Diary

Volume 31 (C)

March 1918

R W Pike

April 20th 1918

2nd Lt & Asst/Adjt
For Officer Comdg
8th Bn The Queens Regt

1917/31

Instructions regarding War Diaries and Intelligence Summaries are contained in F. S. Regs., Part II. and the Staff Manual respectively. Title Pages will be prepared in manuscript.

WAR DIARY
or
INTELLIGENCE SUMMARY
(Erase heading not required.)

March 1918

Army Form C. 2118

Place	Date	Hour	Summary of Events and Information	Remarks and references to Appendices
HANCOURT - MONTECOURT.	1.		The Battn left HANCOURT at 10 A.M. and proceeded to MONTECOURT where it was rejoined by the Transport. The Division passed into Corps reserve.	
MONTECOURT	2.		Musketry and Training under Coy arrangements.	
"	3.		Voluntary Church parade. Lt Col. Amr. Tringham D.S.O. (temp Commanding 17th Bde) left the Battn to take command of the 5th Army Group of Entrenching Battns. Major H.J.C. Peirs D.S.O. took command of the Battn.	
"	4.		Musketry and Training under Bn arrangements.	
"	5.		" " " "	
"	6			
"	7		Musketry and Training under Bn arrangements. Lt. H.V. Carter (3/4 Queens) joined the Bn	
"	8		" " " "	
"	9		The Bn. less one Coy carried out a tactical scheme before the Divisional Commander the remaining Coy did musketry training	
"	10.		The Bn attended Bde church parade in the morning. Bde sports and rifle meeting held in the afternoon in which the Bn competed.	

1875 Wt. W593/826 1,000,000 4/15 J.B.C. & A. A.D.S.S./Forms/C. 2118.

Instructions regarding War Diaries and Intelligence Summaries are contained in F. S. Regs., Part II. and the Staff Manual respectively. Title Pages will be prepared in manuscript.

WAR DIARY
or
INTELLIGENCE SUMMARY
(Erase heading not required.)

March 1918

Army Form C. 2118

2

Place	Date	Hour	Summary of Events and Information	Remarks and references to Appendices
MONTECOURT	11		Musketry and Training under Bn arrangements.	
MONTECOURT -VENDELLES	12		The Bn left MONTECOURT and marched to VENDELLES via TERTRY and FLÉCHIN. Here it came into Bde reserve the Bde relieving the Cavalry and taking over the left sub-sector of the Divisional front on a line east of LE VERGUIER.	
VENDELLES ~~MONTECOURT~~	13		Training under Coy arrangements.	
" "	14		" " " " Lt. J. G. Lovelace joined the Bn from the Royal Flying Corps	
" "	15		" "	
" "	16		Bn found Bde working parties. Training as before.	
" "	17		" "	
VENDELLES - LE VERGUIER	18		The Bn relieved the 1st Royal Fusiliers in the left sub-sector of the Bde front (NAUROY. Special sheet. ED 2³ 24a.5.6 to 30b.9.1) The relief was complete by 10 P.M. Two Coys found outposts in the forward zone ie D and A Coys. C Coy headquarters were at SHEPHERDS COPSE (23D.3.8) and A Coy H.Q at GRAHAM POST (29B.9.0). Two remaining Coys D & B held strong points in and around LE VERGUIER. Battn H.Q were situated in the village.	
LE VERGUIER	19		The day extraordinarily quiet as far as the enemy were concerned but our own artillery very active. A Coy H.Q removed to GRAND PRIEL ~~FARM~~ CRATER (29B.2.8).	
" "	20		Conditions as on the previous day.	

1875 Wt. W593/826 1,000,000 4/15 J.B.C. & A. A.D.S.S./Forms/C. 2118.

Instructions regarding War Diaries and Intelligence Summaries are contained in F. S. Regs., Part II. and the Staff Manual respectively. Title Pages will be prepared in manuscript.

WAR DIARY
or
INTELLIGENCE SUMMARY
(Erase heading not required.)

March 1918

Army Form C. 2118

Page 3

Place	Date	Hour	Summary of Events and Information	Remarks and references to Appendices
LE VERGUIER	21	4-30 AM	At about 4.30 AM the enemy began an intense bombardment of LE VERGUIER and the back areas. For eight hours shells of all calibres, including a large proportion of gas shells, fell on the village and Bn headquarters soon became untenable. Advantage was taken of a lull in the bombardment to shift HQ from the village to a deep sap in a sunken road leading in the direction of VENDELLES. The front or outpost line was comparatively free from shelling. At 4 AM 2/Lt Field and two N.C.O's had been out in front of our line working in the direction of ASCENSION WOOD to investigate a report of noises having been heard by sentries and a wire patrol. Nothing suspicious was seen or heard by this party and the cause was put down to a patrol of "C" Coy which had been due to return through the Right Coy posts but which, it was subsequently discovered, had returned on the left. At 4-30 AM as 2/Lt Field came in the shelling started and he immediately warned GRAHAM and MOLLY groups, proceeding to Right Coy HQ at PRIEL CRATER. Telephonic communication between Bn HQ and the forward Companies was severed before 7 AM, but a message was forwarded from DING POST which	Appendix I Bde Wire 3426 Map LE VERGUIER
		9 AM-9-50 AM	reached A Coy Commander at 9-50 AM. It was sent off at 9 AM but the runners, losing direction in the fog, came via "C" Coy headquarters where everything was in order when they left. The first intimation of the German attack, as far as "A" Coy headquarters were concerned, was the approach of a few men from the right post of "C" Coy at 10-30 AM closely followed by the	
		10-30 AM	enemy. They came from the direction of PRIEL FARM and declared that the Germans had cut off the posts. Fire was opened on the enemy but A Coy H.Q was soon subjected to machine gun fire from a northerly direction on the western side of the PRIEL road. Lt Wand, 2/Lt Field, Sergt Feist and a party of a dozen men suffered from this fire taking up a position in rear of headquarters. They then tried to connect with "C" Coy at SHEPHERDS COPSE. Enemy approaching along the valley from the direction of VILLERETTE, however, prevented this and seeing they were being surrounded, and that the enemy were established between the forward Coys and Bn headquarters, they made for ORCHARD POST which they succeeded in reaching. Lt Mackenzie (Commanding A Coy) had followed Lt Wand's party, with Lt Carter and 15 O.R's but became separated in the fog.	

1875 Wt. W593/826 1,000,000 4/15 J.B.C. & A. A.D.S.S./Forms/C. 2118.

Instructions regarding War Diaries and Intelligence Summaries are contained in F. S. Regs., Part II. and the Staff Manual respectively. Title Pages will be prepared in manuscript.

Army Form C. 2118

Page 4

WAR DIARY
or
INTELLIGENCE SUMMARY
(Erase heading not required.)

March 1918

Place	Date	Hour	Summary of Events and Information	Remarks and references to Appendices
LEVERGUIER	21		He rejoined them at ORCARD POST with the addition of 2/Lt Lovelace who had succeeded in getting away from the left (C) Coy. The fog aided these parties in withdrawing when A Coy HQ were being surrounded. Sergt Feist reported to Bn HQ and also Lt Mackenzie who explained the situation. It appeared that the enemy had succeeded in working round both flanks, cutting the wire under cover of the fog which rendered it difficult to discern a man 10 yds away. By the time the report of the situation reached Bn HQ the front Coys were completely cut off and no further news was obtained concerning them.	

1875 Wt. W593/826 1,000,000 4/15 J.B.C. & A. A.D.S.S./Forms/C. 2118.

Instructions regarding War Diaries and Intelligence Summaries are contained in F. S. Regs., Part II. and the Staff Manual respectively. Title Pages will be prepared in manuscript.

Army Form C. 2118

4/5

WAR DIARY
or
INTELLIGENCE SUMMARY
(Erase heading not required.)

March 1918.

Place	Date	Hour	Summary of Events and Information	Remarks and references to Appendices
LE VERGUIER	21		The Battn soon found that all support to the right and left had given way and the remaining Companies & headquarters, holding the posts in and around LE VERGUIER were subjected to very heavy attacks both flank and frontal. Lewis gun and rifle fire kept the enemy back however; small parties of our men holding up large bodies on the wire.	
		7 P.M.	At 7 PM Lt Col W Peirs came up from the transport lines at BERYES and took over command of the Battn from Major [illegible]. By the evening, the Germans having failed to enter the village, the situation became quieter. The bombardment was then renewed and continued all night. Early in the day it had been considered expedient to burn all papers and books in the Battn Orderly Room in order to avoid the possibility of them falling into the hands of the enemy.	
"	22.	6.30 am	The mist was still heavy and under its cover the enemy again renewed their attacks. They succeeded in surrounding the strong points in and around the village with the exception of two, Fort LEES and Fort GREATHEAD on the western outskirts. Men who were able to retire reinforced these and they held out against repeated attacks. On one occasion the Germans forced an entry into Fort GREATHEAD but were ejected by a counter attack. At about 7 am. an attack was made on Battn headquarters in the sunken road. Servants orderlies cooks and all available men were collected and a spirited fight took place. The enemy got to close quarters but were driven off.	
		9.30 am	At 9.30 Lt Col Peirs went in the direction of Fort LEES to discover what was happening and found this point had been taken. What then remained of the Battn was practically surrounded and the order to retire was given. The men from Fort GREATHEAD and Battn HQ assembled on the sunken road and under cover of the mist marched towards VENDELLES. A Lewis	

1875 Wt. W593/826 1,000,000 4/15 J.B.C. & A. A.D.S.S./Forms/C. 2118.

Instructions regarding War Diaries and Intelligence Summaries are contained in F. S. Regs., Part II. and the Staff Manual respectively. Title Pages will be prepared in manuscript.

WAR DIARY
or
INTELLIGENCE SUMMARY
(Erase heading not required.)

March 1918

Army Form C. 2118

8.6

Place	Date	Hour	Summary of Events and Information	Remarks and references to Appendices
LE VERGUIER – MONTECOURT	22		Gun section covered the rear sweeping the road from side to side. The retirement was carried out in an orderly manner and during it only one casualty was sustained, a man from A Coy being wounded in the hand. The Battn retired to a ridge held by the 1st Royal Fusiliers about 600 yds west of LE VERGUIER and amalgamated with the Fusiliers, helping to get wire out in front of their position. An order to retire was then received from Bde and the remainder of the Battn marched to MONTECOURT via VENDELLES, BERNES and HANCOURT. When passing ~~through~~ by VENDELLES the village was heavily shelled but there were no casualties here. For the excellent defence of LE VERGUIER the 24th Div was the first division mentioned in dispatches and the 8th Battn of The Queens was the Battn first mentioned (for the defence of ~~VENDELLES~~ LE VERGUIER) vide the "Times" of Mar 26. 1918. The strength stood at 11 Officers and 150 other ranks at MONTECOURT where the Battn ~~reog~~ reorganised and went into huts. Rations were issued at MONTECOURT.	
MONTECOURT – LICOURT	23	4 AM.	At 4 AM. orders were received from Bde to proceed to DOUVIEUX to take up an out post line East of this village. The small Coys were disposed in depth, the enemy being reported approaching from a north easterly direction.	Appendix II. BRIGADE WIRES B.M. 312 B.M. 314. B.M. 315 B.M. 316.
		9 A.M.	At 9 AM. the order to fall back on the SOMME line was given and the Battn crossed the river at FALVY and halted at PARGNY where hot meals were served to the men. The whole Bde with first line transport marched across the SOMME, the 3rd Rifle Brigade fighting a rearguard action and the 24th Divisional Depot Battn covering the left or eastern flank. A division of fresh troops passed through (the 8th) and took up a position defending the river on the PARGNY side. The Battn was further ordered to LICOURT and the 17th Bde concentrated there.	
		~~11 P.M~~ 11-30 PM	At 11-30 P.M. the Battn received orders to proceed at once to ST CHRIST	Ref. France Sheet 62c.

1875 Wt. W593/826 1,000,000 4/15 J.B.C. & A. A.D.S.S./Forms/C. 2118.

Instructions regarding War Diaries and Intelligence Summaries are contained in F. S. Regs., Part II. and the Staff Manual respectively. Title Pages will be prepared in manuscript.

WAR DIARY
or
INTELLIGENCE SUMMARY
(Erase heading not required.)

March 1918

Army Form C. 2118

67.

Place	Date	Hour	Summary of Events and Information	Remarks and references to Appendices
ST CHRIST	23	11-30PM	to support the 1st Battn Sherwood Foresters (8th Div), two Companies reinforcing the forward zone and two companies taking up a position in rear. On retiring across the river the Engineers had attempted to blow up all the bridges but in some cases had been only partially successful. These constituted a danger and the 1st Sherwood Foresters had repulsed a party of the enemy attempting a crossing. Sniping and machine gun fire was experienced during the night.	
LICOURT-CHAULNES -OMIÉCOURT	24	7-30AM	As the situation appeared more secure the Battn was ordered back to LICOURT. Here orders were received to march to CHAULNES and the Battn left LICOURT between 7 & 8 AM. On arrival battle positions were taken up between OMIÉCOURT and HYENCOURT. During the night both OMIÉCOURT and CHAULNES were heavily shelled. The R.E. dumps at the latter place were set on fire by the Engineers to prevent them falling into enemy hands.	Sheet 66D. FRANCE Appendix III Bde Memo Z.O.[illegible] — " — Z.O.2.
OMIÉCOURT	25	7am	At 7 am the Battn was ordered to support the French attack at PERTAIN ~~south~~ east of OMIÉCOURT. In the meantime the Germans had heavily attacked the 50th Division and had advanced and got into the outskirts of PERTAIN so the Battn was ordered to take up a position East of OMIÉCOURT. The attack by the French did not take place & the 50th Division were compelled to retire ~~through~~ from PERTAIN through our positions which then became the front line. The enemy debouched from PERTAIN and attempted to force us back by heavy machine gun fire and sniping from the houses, at the same time submitting OMIÉCOURT, now rear, to an intense bombardment. The people on the flanks, especially on the right, were severely tried. The fighting took place in the open and a very stubborn resistance was put up until the order came to ~~retire~~ withdraw through OMIÉCOURT. Very heavy losses were inflicted on the Germans approaching from PERTAIN but the Battn suffered many casualties	Appendix IV Bde Wires B.M 336. B.M 334.

1875 Wt. W593/826 1,000,000 4/15 J.B.C. & A. A.D.S.S./Forms/C. 2118.

Instructions regarding War Diaries and Intelligence Summaries are contained in F. S. Regs., Part II. and the Staff Manual respectively. Title Pages will be prepared in manuscript.

WAR DIARY
or
INTELLIGENCE SUMMARY
(Erase heading not required.)

Army Form C. 2118

4/8.

March 1918

Place	Date	Hour	Summary of Events and Information	Remarks and references to Appendices
OMIECOURT – CHAULNES.	25.		Lt Col Peirs & Lt Sparkes were both wounded. Major Rowland took command and the Battn went back to the positions of the previous day, near CHAULNES. Orders were given that CHAULNES was to be held at any cost so a move was made to trenches on the outskirts East of the town. During the night nothing unusual occurred except that a German patrol encountered on the CHAULNES-OMIECOURT road was driven off. Shelling was very heavy.	
CHAULNES – VRELY.	26	6.0 am 8.30 am	In the morning the enemy resumed attacks with CHAULNES as the objective and the Battn held them up. At 8.30 am orders were received ~~for the Bde to march~~ to proceed to VRELY and the Bde marched over the old SOMME battlefields via LIHONS and MEHARICOURT. Positions were chosen East of the village and as soon as these were arranged the men were allowed to go into the village and were billetted in farms. From this point the troops found themselves in long un inhabited regions with civilians in some instances still in the villages they entered. Advantage was taken of this to live on the land and remove material which if left would only fall into the hands of the enemy.	
VRELY	27		Early in the morning battle stations were taken up. The Germans approached through MEHARICOURT and made a frontal attack in mass. They were well received with very heavy rifle & Lewis Gun fire ~~and~~ which, considering the exceptional target offered, inflicted great ~~casual~~ losses on them. The Lewis Gun fire from D Coy, on the right of the Battn. was especially damaging. The line was well held & after this repulse the enemy did not resume the attack. The night was quiet the men waited in their battle positions.	Appendices V Wires & Memos.
VRELY – CASTEL	28.	6 am	Early in the morning the enemy renewed the attack in extended order. The Battn found itself exposed on both flanks and was obliged to fall back. It now	

1875 Wt. W593/826 1,000,000 4/15 J.B.C. & A. A.D.S.S./Forms/C. 2118.

Instructions regarding War Diaries and Intelligence Summaries are contained in F. S. Regs., Part II. and the Staff Manual respectively. Title Pages will be prepared in manuscript.

WAR DIARY
or
INTELLIGENCE SUMMARY
(Erase heading not required.)

Army Form C. 2118

8/9

March 1918

Place	Date	Hour	Summary of Events and Information	Remarks and references to Appendices
VRELY-CASTEL	28		Composed 200 men of various units. Officers stopped and rallied all available men incorporating them in the Battn. It was at this juncture that all troops became very much disorganised and started falling back coming under heavy machine gun fire. The main feature of the attack was the intensity of the machine gun fire, especially from VRELY village. Many casualties were sustained. Lt B.M.S. Mackenzie, whose services from the outset had been of the highest possible value, was killed here and Lt F.A.S. Hill and 2/Lt Lewin wounded. The retirement was checked at CAIX where the Battn formed up and fought a rearguard action ~~checking~~ holding back the enemy. Eventually the orders to withdraw and reorganise at BEAUCOURT was received. From there the Battn proceeded by night to VILLERS-AUX-ERABLES and CASTEL where it billetted. At BEAUCOURT two Companies were formed, Nos 1 & 2, each composed of about 100 ranks of the Queens and various units.	
HAILLES	29	2 PM	At 2 PM orders came to proceed to HAILLES to defend the river crossing. With the exception of a picket posted on the bridge, the men were all put in good billets and had a quiet night.	Appendix VI Bde Wire BM384
"	30	2 PM	The Battn acting on orders took up a position in a wood (Sheet 66E B.15) on high ground west of HAILLES where it remained till 2 PM. The weather had broken slightly on the 28th, but had been fairly fine up till now when it rained heavily and made things very uncomfortable. The ~~enemy~~ Germans were pressing on & the cavalry attacked & drove them out of a large wood (Sheet 66E D.21) South East of our position into which they had penetrated. At 2 PM the Battn was ordered back & went into billets. All was quiet but the enemy was reported working round from the South.	Appendix VII Wires & Memos.

1875 Wt. W593/826 1,000,000 4/15 J.B.C. & A. A.D.S.S./Forms/C. 2118.

Army Form C. 2118

#10.

Instructions regarding War Diaries and Intelligence Summaries are contained in F. S. Regs., Part II. and the Staff Manual respectively. Title Pages will be prepared in manuscript.

WAR DIARY
or
INTELLIGENCE SUMMARY

(Erase heading not required.)

March 1918

Place	Date	Hour	Summary of Events and Information	Remarks and references to Appendices
THEZY – FOUENCAMPS.	31.		The Battn received orders to march to THEZY and thence to FOUENCAMPS. The 72nd Bde (24th Div) were ordered to defend the river there with the 17th Bde in billets in support. Nos 1 and 2 Companies billetted in FOUENCAMPS and reorganised.	Appendix VIII Wire & Memo
				Miscellaneous Appendix IX 24th Divl Letter p.204 d 3/3/18 Letter from Brigadier 17th I.B.
			CASUALTIES FROM 21/31st OFFICERS. 20 ORANKS 380.	

R H Rowland ~~Major~~ Lt. Col.
Comdg.
8th Bn "The Queens" (RWS Regt)

1875 Wt. W593/826 1,000,000 4/15 J.B.C. & A. A.D.S.S./Forms/C. 2118.

Appendix I

"C" Form.

Army Form C. 2123.
(In books of 100.)

MESSAGES AND SIGNALS. No. of Message

Prefix SB Code FLAD Words 21	Received	Sent, or sent out.	Office Stamp
£ s. d.	From	At m.	V.5
Charges to Collect	By	To	21.3.18
Service Instructions NRI		By	

Handed in at NRI Office 6.55 a m Received 7.12 A

TO NL 115

*Sender's Number.	Day of Month.	In reply to Number.	AAA
BM 266	21		

Move	your	Headquarters	forthwith
to	sunken	road	L.34.c.4/8
aaa	report	when	complete
aaa	ACK		

AWR

FROM N.R.1

TIME & PLACE 6.55 AM

*This line should be erased if not required.

(…)00.—John Bisset Ltd.—4/15—3592 Forms C2123

"A" Form.

Army Form C. 2121
(In pads of 100.)

MESSAGES AND SIGNALS.

No. of Message..........

Prefix.......... Code.......... m. | Words. | Charge.

Office of Origin and Service Instructions.

APPENDIX II

Sent
At..........m.
To..........
By..........

This message is on a/c of:
.... Service.
(Signature of "Franking Officer.")

Recd. at..........m.
Date..........
From..........
By..........

TO: 8th Queens, 1st Royal Fusiliers, 3rd Rifle Brigade, 104th Fd Coy RE., 17th L.T.M. Battery., 24th Div G.

Sender's Number.	Day of Month.	In reply to Number.	
* BH 312	23		AAA

17th Infy Bde will move as under AAA
Starting point V 12 a 7/6 AAA 8th Queens
4 am to occupy GREEN LINE high
ground E of DOUVIEUX from V 29 b 8/8
(in touch with 73rd Infy Bde) to V 24 b 4/0
AAA 1st Royal Fusiliers pass S.P. 4.10 am to
occupy GREEN LINE from left of 8th Queens (V 24 b 4/0)
to V 18 b 4/0 (in touch with 72nd Inf Bde)
AAA 3rd Rifle Bde will pass S.P. 4.15 am
and will concentrate in Valley V 17 d 2/2
in Bde Reserve AAA Bde HQrs will close
MONTECOURT 4 am and open at DOUVIEUX
V 26 c 2/8 on arrival AAA All units will
send a representative to Bde Hqrs there
AAA Staff Captain will issue orders for transport
which will not accompany units
AAA Addsd 3rd T.M. Battery 104th Fd Coy RE. G.

From 17th IB.

Place

Time 3.22 am.

The above may be forwarded as now corrected. (Z)

Censor. | Signature of Addressor or person authorised to telegraph in his name. [illegible] Major

* This line should be erased if not required.

(3795.) Wt. W 492/M1647. 650,000 Pads. 5/17. H.W.&V., Ld. (E. 1167)

"A" Form.

Army Form C. 2121
(In pads of 100.)

MESSAGES AND SIGNALS.

No. of Message..............

Prefix.......... Code.......... m	Words.	Charge.	This message is on a/c of:	Recd. at .... m.
Office of Origin and Service Instructions.	Sent		.... Service.	Date..............
	At .... m.			From ....
	To			
	By		(Signature of "Franking Officer.")	By ....

TO [illegible]

Sender's Number.	Day of Month.	In reply to Number.	AAA
* BM 315	23		

[illegible]

From	
Place	
Time	

The above may be forwarded as now corrected. (Z)

Censor. Signature of Addressor or person authorised to telegraph in his name.

* This line should be erased if not required.

(3796.) Wt. W492/M1647. 650,000 Pads. 3/17. H. W. & V., Ld. (E. 1157.)

"A" Form. Army Form C. 2121 (In pads of 100.)

MESSAGES AND SIGNALS.

No. of Message..............

Prefix............Code............m	Words.	Charge.	This message is on a/c of:	Recd. at.........m.
Office of Origin and Service Instructions.	Sent		......................Service.	Date..............
	At..............m.			From..............
	To..................			
	By..................		(Signature of "Franking Officer.")	By..................

TO

Sender's Number.	Day of Month.	In reply to Number.	AAA
*			

From

Place

Time

The above may be forwarded as now corrected. (Z)

Censor. Signature of Addressor or person authorised to telegraph in his name.

* This line should be erased if not required.

(3796.) Wt. W 492/M1647. 650,000 Pads. 5/17. H. W. & V., Ld. (E. 1187.)

"A" Form.

MESSAGES AND SIGNALS.

Army Form C. 2121
(In pads of 100.)

No. of Message..............

Prefix..........Code..........m.	Words. Charge.	*This message is on a/c of:*	Recd. at ....m.
Office of Origin and Service Instructions.	Sent	.........................*Service.*	Date..............
	At............m.		From ....
	To		
	By..............	(Signature of "Franking Officer.")	By..............

TO { 8th Queens
1st Royal Fusiliers

Sender's Number.	Day of Month.	In reply to Number.	AAA
* BM 314	23		

Bde Report Centre now moved to FLEZ V 23 c 3/8 AAA Addsd 8th Queens 1st Royal

From 17th I Bde

Place

Time 6.20 am

The above may be forwarded as now corrected. (Z)

.... Censor. Signature of Addressor or person authorised to telegraph in his name.

* This line should be erased if not required

(3795.) Wt. W 492/M1647. 650,000 Pads. 5/17. H. W. & V., Ld. (E. 1157)

A" Form.
Army Form C. 2121
(In pads of 100.)

MESSAGES AND SIGNALS.

No. of Message............

Prefix........ Code........ m	Words.	Charge.	This message is on a/c of:	Recd. at .... m.
Office of Origin and Service Instructions.	Sent		.... Service.	Date............
	At........ m.			From............
	To........			
	By........		(Signature of "Franking Officer.")	By............

TO ~~8 Queens~~ ~~1 RF~~ ~~3 RB~~ ✓ 8 Queens

Sender's Number.	Day of Month.	In reply to Number.	AAA
* BM 316	23		

8th Queens and 1 Coy 1st RF will withdraw from DOUVIEUX
keeping in touch with 73 IB via FLEZ
and thence due West and cross
SOMME at FALVY AAA 1st Royal ~~via FLEZ~~
Fusiliers less 1 Coy will withdraw gradually through
(~~via~~ positions held by 73 IB N of
GUIZAINCOURT (cover our withdrawal)
and will cross SOMME at FALVY AAA 3RB
will hold present positions at FLEZ until
8 Queens & 1st RF have passed safely through
AAA They will then cross river at FALVY AAA
Definite orders for time of withdrawal of 3RB
will be notified later AAA Addressed 3 Battns

From 17 IB
Place
Time 8.25 am

The above may be forwarded as now corrected. (Z)

Censor. [illegible signature]
Signature of Addressor or person authorised to telegraph in his name.

* This line should be erased if not required.

(3796.) Wt. W 492/M1647. 650,000 Pads. 5/17. H.W.&V., Ld. (E. 1187)

"A" Form.

MESSAGES AND SIGNALS.

Army Form C. 2121
(In pads of 100.)

No. of Message..............

Prefix........ Code........ m	Words.	Charge.	This message is on a/c of:	Recd. at .... m.
Office of Origin and Service Instructions.	Sent		.... Service.	Date..............
	At..........m.			From..............
	To..............			
	By..............		(Signature of "Franking Officer.")	By..............

TO { 8th Queens
24th Inf Bde

Sender's Number.	Day of Month.	In reply to Number.	AAA
* BM 325	23		

You will move forthwith to reinforce left Battn of 24th Inf Bde – 1st Sherwood Foresters – who have been attacked AAA Send representative to Hqrs 24th IB for necessary instructions and report accordingly AAA Addsd 8th Queens repted 24th Inf Bde.

Report on your dispositions

[signature]

From 17 IB.

Place

Time 10.55 am

The above may be forwarded as now corrected. (Z) [signature]
Major

Censor. Signature of Addressor or person authorised to telegraph in his name.

* This line should be erased if not required.

(3796.) Wt. W492/M1647. 650,000 Pads. 5/17. H. W. & V., Ld. (E 1157)

3 Bns   Appendix III   2 Q. 2.

Following from 20 Div aaa

Following from XIX Corps should present line be broken and unable to be restored troops will reform on following line HATTENCOURT – HALLU – CHAULNE – BRESSOIRE ABLAINCOURT ESTREES ASSEVILLERS HERBECOURT aaa No intention to withdraw but to fight out on line now held aaa 11 am parties of Germans reported across canal PARGNY aaa CRA reports right flank position obscure aaa CRE ordered to reconnoitre line HATTENCOURT HALLU CHAULNE aaa Ends

24/3/18   R. Edwards Lieut for Major
Bde Major 17 Inf Bde

1.30

Appendix III

2Q 1

3 Bns

Following from 24th Division:-

"Message from 19th Corps "I" 9.45 am aaa Prisoners captured near PARGNY last night belong to 11th Div. They state expected to be relieved night 23rd/24th by 6th Div (very good Div) and that attack would be continued on high ground N of PARGNY to-day aaa Reported that small parties crossed river at PARGNY aaa Steps are being taken to turn them out aaa Ends.

24/3/18
12.30pm

Capt for
Brigade Major 17th Inf. Bde

MESSAG[...] SIGNALS.

Army Form C. 2121.

Prefix ... Code ... Charge

Office of Origin and Service Instructions.

Sent At ... m. To ... By ...

This message is on a/c of: ... Service. (Signature of "Franking Officer.")

Recd. at ... m. Date ... From ... By ...

TO 3 Battns — Appendix IV

Sender's Number.	Day of Month.	In reply to Number.	AAA
BM 336	25		

French are attacking from line ROUY-LE-GRAND MESNIL-ST-NICALASE today, with a view to establishing position on canal in vicinity of BETHENCOURT. aaa. 8th Div will cooperate on line MORCHAIN – POTTE to assist left flank of attack aaa 17 IB ~~24 Div~~ will be prepared to support this attack, by concentrating on road DRESLINCOURT – PERTAIN, aaa On word "MOVE units will proceed as follows;–

From

Place

Time

The above may be forwarded as now corrected. (Z)

Censor. Signature of Addressor or person authorised to telegraph.

* This line should be erased if not required.

(25062) Wt. W493/M1647. 600,000 Pads. 2/17. H. W. & V. Ld. E. 1187.

"A" Form.

MESSAGES AND SIGNALS. No. of Message............

Prefix ...... Code ...... m	Words.	Charge.	This message is on a/c of:	Recd. at .... m.
Office of Origin and Service Instructions.	Sent		.... Service.	Date ....
	At .... m.			From ....
	To			
	By		(Signature of "Franking Officer.")	By ....

TO 2

Sender's Number.	Day of Month.	In reply to Number.	AAA
Bm 386			

as quickly as possible aaa

1st R.F. Head of column to X roads immediately N of N in DRESSLINCOURT

8th Queens Head of column at E of Em.

3rd R.B. Head of column at ~~BERSINCOURT~~ OMIECOURT. aaa

It is improbable that any move will take place before ~~8th~~ 5.30 AM. aaa addressed 3 Battns.

From 7 I B

Place

Time

The above may be forwarded as now corrected. (Z) [illegible] Major

Censor. Signature of Addressor or person authorized to telegraph in his name.

* This line should be erased if not required.

(3796.) Wt. W49

"A" Form.

Army Form C. (In pads of 100.)

MESSAGES AND SIGNALS.

No. of Message..............

Prefix........ Code........ m. | Words. | Charge.

Office of Origin and Service Instructions.

Sent At........m. To........ By........

This message is on a/c of: ....*Service.*

(Signature of "Franking Officer.")

Recd. at ....m. Date........ From........ By........

TO 3 batteries — Appendix IV

Sender's Number.	Day of Month.	In reply to Number.	AAA
*BM 337	25		

R/o BM ~~337~~ 336

"MOVE"

From JA

Place

Time 6.5 am

The above may be forwarded as now corrected. (Z)

Censor. Signature of Addressor or person authorised to telegraph in his name.

*This line should be erased if not required.

(E. 1189.)

"A" Form.
MESSAGES AND [illegible]

Prefix .... Code .... m	Words.	Charge.	This message is on a/c of: .... Service.	Recd. at
Office of Origin and Service Instructions.	Sent At .... m. To .... By		(Signature of "Franking Officer.")	Date .... From .... By ....

TO { 8th Queens
~~1st Royal Fusiliers~~
~~3rd Rifle Brigade~~

APPENDIX V

Sender's Number.	Day of Month.	In reply to Number.	AAA
* BM 363	27		

In the event of ALARM ACTION Units will move to the following places as quickly as possible AAA 8th Queens to F 19 c 0/5 – F 20 c 0/5 – F 20 a 3/3 (VRELY–MEHARICOURT Road AAA 1st RF from Junction with 8th Queens to VRELY–ROSIERES Road F 13 b 5/0 AAA 3rd RB to supporting position in vicinity of E 18 d AAA COs must use their own discretion as to moving as warning will be very short owing to the close proximity of the front line AAA OC 1st RF will send all [illegible] attached to him to report to OC 12th Sherwood Foresters AAA Bde [illegible] for communication purposes will be with 3rd RB at E 18 d 4/4 [illegible] Wire Co will be [illegible] alarm AAA Ack AAA Addsd 3 [illegible]

From 17 IB
Place
Time 3.55am

The above may be forwarded as now corrected. (Z) [illegible signature]

Censor. Signature of Addressor or person authorised to telegraph in his name.

* This line should be erased if not required.

(3198.) Wt. W 12952/M1294. 375,000 Pads. 1/17. H. W. & V., Ld. (E. 818.)

Prefix.......... Cod[e] ... Charge.

Office of Origin and Service In[structions]

Urgent

Sent	
At.........m.	
To..........	
By..........	

This message is on a/c of:

.... Service.

(Signature of "Franking Officer.")

Recd. at..........m.

Date..........

From..........

By..........

TO { 8th Queens

Sender's Number.	Day of Month.	In reply to Number.	AAA
* B.M.370	27		

One of your runners report that he was directed to CAIX as being at Brigade Hqrs. AAA This is incorrect we are still in our original location in VRELY. AAA You will be duly informed of any change.

From 17th I.B.

Place

Time 1-5 am.

The above may be forwarded as now corrected. (Z) [signature] Major

Censor. Signature of Addressor or person authorised to telegraph in his name.

* This line should be erased if not required.

(5195.) Wt. W 12952/M1294. 375,000 Pads. 1/17. H.W.&V., Ld. (E. 818.)

Prefix..........Code.........Words

£ s d.

Charges to Collect

Service Instructions.

From ....

By....................

At....................

To ....

By.... Priority

In Urgent Ops

Handed in at..........Office........m. Received..........m

TO E.D.V R.E. Q.E

*Sender's Number	Day of Month	In reply to Number	AAA
G99	27		

Prisoner of 243 Div Captured FRAMERVILLE 4 pm 26th states that enemy will renew attack between 6 and seven this morning aaa added Ja on Eg and 24 Div

FROM Ja

TIME & PLACE

*This line should be erased if not required

W. & B. 7300 Wt. W14822/M1523 100,000 3/17 (E930) Forms C/2128

J. A.

The enemy now appears to be retiring from valley in F15 & 21 N of VRELY – MAHARCOURT Road. our 6 Shrapnel appears to be short of them. Have collected remnants of 2 [illegible] Batt. and have put them in position on S.E. edge of VRELY.
Can you give me any other news and please send runners back.

E D Dowell
E.D.

N.B. Approximate casualties 10 OR from shell-fire on village.

EDD

9.50 am 27.3.18

8th Queens.

The situation on the right appears satisfactory so far as my information goes. Will you however keep in touch with 1st [illegible] who have been ordered to support my left flank.

27/3/18

W A Macfayle
B.G.
17 [illegible]

O.C. "C" Coy

Keep me in touch with the situation on your Left Flank.
Are you in touch with the 1st R.F.

[illegible] Capt & Adjt
F. D.

10.15 a.m. 27. 3. '18

Am in touch on the left.

The exact situation I am not certain. We appear to have advanced in places, & seem to me held up through our artillery firing on ~~the~~ our position.

[illegible] "C" Coy

To

J. A

The 20th Entrenching Battn. have retired
on to S.E edge of village
Troops also seen to be retiring on
our right and left.
The 20th Entrenching Battn say they came
back because the D. L. I. retired on their
left.

E. S. Donnell Capt. & Adjt
E. D.

9 a.m. 27. 3. 18.

T H

Received
10-45 am

To The Adjutant
Duration

From O.C. D Coy

I am in touch on my right with a Tank Capt., who has organised a party of stragglers and this officer is in touch with the 73. Bdge.

21/3/18 1-5 PM

A W Wyatt 2Lt
O C D Coy

GM CCPM AG

JA

ED KC

BM 376 27 AAA

Definite orders have been received the Bde will hold the present line aaa There must be no withdrawal despite any turning the flanks aaa Please inform all ranks aaa addressed 3 Bns and 12 Sherwood Foresters

171 B

3.15 PM

To The Adjutant
E D.

From O. C. D Coy

I reported to the battalion on my right quite as recently as half an hour ago and everything was all right then. I have now sent MR. LEWIN along to get further information

C. Wright 2Lt
O.C. D Coy

27/3/18 3.25 P.M.

OC D Coy.

What Battn. is on your right?

E D Donnell Capt & Adjt
E.D.

3.40 p.m. 22. 3. 18

The 13th MIDDLESEX

The Adjutant E.D. AW 10
From O.C. D Coy

The situation on the right brigade is very satisfactory. All ground lost this morning has been retaken. This message was received by an officer of the MIDDLESEX from Bdge H.Q. The above officer is in charge of 2 half coys forming a counter attack party and they are entrenched in the wood F25 a&c. There is nobody on the right of him but they have 2 lines in front

3/4/18 4.40 PM. [illegible]
O.C. D Coy

To the Adjutant

from O.C. C Coy.

Retiring on the

front, both left

flank & right. Enemy appears

to be making a

salient round us.

The retiring people

crossing our f[illegible]

consequently we are

getting [illegible] shelled

Shall hold on as

[illegible] possible [illegible]

"A" Form.

MESSAGES AND SIGNAL[S]

Prefix .... Code ....m	Words.	Charge.	This message is on a/c of:	Recd.
Office of Origin and Service Instructions.	Sent		.... Service.	Date ....
	At ....m.			From ....
	To			
	By		(Signature of "Franking Officer.")	By ....

TO { 8th Queens. E.D.D.
1st Royal Fusiliers
~~3rd Rifle Bde.~~

Appendix VI

Sender's Number.	Day of Month.	In reply to Number.	AAA
* BM 387	29		

1st Royal Fusiliers will provide the local protection of CASTEL in conjunction with units of 72nd + 73rd Inf Bdes AAA They will immediately take up positions to cover the CASTEL crossing from North, their immediate rôle being to harass any enemy movement towards THIENNES from SE AAA 73rd IB will be in the centre, 72nd IB on the right AAA. Dispositions will be forwarded as soon as possible AAA On relief by 1st RF, LGts of 3rd RB will rejoin their unit AAA 8th Queens + 3rd RB will be ready to move at very short notice and will send officers to reconnoitre bridge crossing & ascertain positions of 1st RF AAA Addressed all ~~Bdes~~ Battns.

From 17th Inf Bde.
Place
Time 10-45 a.m.

The above may be forwarded as now corrected. (Z) [signature] Major

Censor. Signature of Addressor or person authorised to telegraph in his name.

* This line should be erased if not required.

(3796.) Wt. W492/M1647. 650,000 Pads. 5/17. H.W. & V., Ld. (E. 1187.)

"A" Form.

Army Fo[rm]
(In pa[ds])

MESSAGES AND SIGNALS.

No. of Message.........

Prefix.......... Code.......... m	Words.	Charge.		Recd. at ....
Office of Origin and Service Instructions.	Sent		This message is on a/c of:	Date........
	At..........m.		..........Service.	From ....
	To..........			
	By..........		(Signature of "Franking Officer.")	By........

TO { 8th Queens. ✓ / 1st Royal Fusiliers / 3rd RIB } 12th Sherwood Foresters / 24th Div Depot Battn / A Coy ~~24th Div~~ MG Battn (attached)

Sender's Number.	Day of Month.	In reply to Number.	
* BM 396	30		AAA

(1) The 24th Division is being relieved today 30th inst by the 8th Division less one Bde.

(2) On relief the Division moves temporarily to BOIS DE GENTELLES and subsequently in accordance with instructions to be issued later

(3) 17th Inf Bde will be prepared to move from present billets by 8 am and will march to above rendezvous as under:-

ROUTE:- HAILLES - H of HALTE - thence NW to main AMIENS road - A of FOUENCAMPS - track to I of GENTELLES

STARTING PT - H of HALTE

Order of March - Bde HQrs - 1st Royal Fusiliers 3rd Rifle Bde - 8th Queens - 12th Sherwood Foresters - 24 DW Depot Battn. A Coy 24th MG Battn -

From

Place

Time

The above may be forwarded as now corrected. (Z)

Censor. Signature of Addressor or person authorised to telegraph in his na[me]

[signature]

* This line should be erased if not required.

(5796.) Wt. W 492/M1647. 650.000 Pads. 5/17. H.W. & V., Ld. (E. 1187.)

Army Form C. 2121.
(In pads of 100.)

MESSAGES AND SIGNALS. No. of Message..............

Prefix.......... Code.......... m | Words. | Charge. | *This message is on a/c of:* .... *Service.* | Recd. at ......m. | Date .... | From .... | By ....

Office of Origin and Service Instructions.

Sent At.........m. To......... By.........

(Signature of "Franking Officer.")

TO { 8th Queens / 1st R F / 3rd Rifle Brigade

Appendix VII

Sender's Number.	Day of Month.	In reply to Number.	AAA
* BM 309	30		

Move to Cottenchy [illegible] postponed AAA 8th Div have been called to assist the French AAA Acknowledge [illegible]

3 Bns

From 17 I.B.
Place
Time 11-52 am.

The above may be forwarded as now corrected. (Z)

Censor. Signature of Addressor or person authorised to telegraph in his name.

* This line should be erased if not required.

(3796.) Wt. W 492/M1647. 650,000 Pads. 5/17. H.W. & V., Ld. (E. 1187.)

"A" Form. Army Form C. 2121. (In pads of 100.)

MESSAGES AND SIGNALS.

No. of Message..........

Prefix..........Code..........m	Words.	Charge.	This message is on a/c of:	Recd. at..........m.
Office of Origin and Service Instructions.	Sent		..........Service.	Date..........
	At..........m.			From..........
	To..........			By..........
	By..........		(Signature of "Franking Officer.")	

TO { 3 Bn
12 [illegible]
[illegible] }

Sender's Number.	Day of Month.	In reply to Number.	AAA
* BM397	30		

Enemy reported in wood in C21 C22 C27 AAA STAND To and be prepared to move at 10 minutes notice AAA Further orders will be issued

From 17 Bde
Place
Time

The above may be forwarded as now corrected. (Z) [illegible] Major

Censor. Signature of Addressor or person authorised to telegraph in his name.

* This line should be erased if not required.

(3796.) Wt. W 492/M1647. 650,000 Pads. 5/17. H.W. & V., Ld. (E. 1187.)

SECRET. Urgent

8th Queens ✓
~~3rd Rifle Brigade~~ ✓
~~12 Sherwoods~~.
~~Def. Bn.~~ ✓

B.M. 405.

Appendix VIII

1. Units on receipt of these orders will move to THEZY. Road immediately North of the CHATEAU. at 10 minutes interval as follows:-

3rd Rifle Bde
8th Queens
Def. Bn.

2. 12 Sherwoods. Less Transport will move to KTOVEN CAMPS.

3. Acknowledge

31/3/18

[illegible] Major B.M.
17th Inf. Bde.

8th Queens
1st ~~Royal Fusiliers~~
3rd ~~Rifle Brigade.~~

Any men of the 15th & 19th Entrenching Battns should be ordered to report to 72nd Inf Bde if now with you.

31/3/18.

W. A. Mackenzie Major
B M 17 I B

"C" Form

MESSAGES AND SIGNALS.

Army Form
(In books of 100.)

No. of Message.

Prefix...... Code........ Words	Received.	Sent, or sent out.	Office Stamp.
£ s. d. Charges to Collect	From	At m.	
Service Instructions Copy of original	By	To. By	

Handed in at Office m. Received m.

TO 3 Battalions 8 Queens

Sender's Number	Day of Month.	In reply to Number	AAA
DM392			

The enemy appear to be held up on the line MARCELCAVE IGNAUCOURT BEAUCOURT FRESNOY AAA 3 Rifle Bde will transfer to DOMMARTIN and will be responsible for covering the withdrawal of the Brigade over the DOMMARTIN Crossings AAA The men should be given as much rest as possible but units will be prepared to move at very short notice aaa addsd 3 Battns

FROM 17 I Bde

PLACE & TIME 4.25p

* This line should be erased if not required.

1970 50m 4/17 W. & C.

8 Queen's

Appendix IX

24th Division No. A. 204.

The following telegram has been received from Major General Sir L.J. BOLS, K.C.M.G., C.B., D.S.O., late Commanding the 24th Division, and the General Officer Commanding wishes it communicated to all ranks :-

" Commanding 24th Division,
B. E. F. France.

CAIRO. 27th March 1918.

W E L L   D O N E   G O O D   S O L D I E R S.

GENERAL BOLS. "

C. H. McMasey[?]
Major.
A.A. & Q.M.G., 24th Division.

April 2nd 1918.

BELLENGLISE.
SPECIAL SHEET.
Scale 1/10,000.
LATER ENEMY ATTACK ON LEFT FLANK
GARRISON OF FORT LEES ACCOMODATED HERE BEFORE ATTACK
POSTS EACH HELD BY A PLATOON OF 'B' COY.
A Coy H.Q FROM WHICH PARTIES SUCCEEDED IN WITHDRAWING
le Verguier
POSTS EACH HELD BY A PLATOON OF 'D' COY
2nd POSITION OF Bn HQ
SUNKEN RD
1st POSITION OF Bn HQ
LATER ENEMY ATTACK ON RIGHT
L
C
R
M
DIRECTION OF ENEMY ATTACK ON RIGHT FLANK
Grand Priel Farm
Ascension Wood
Ascension Valley
Angle Bank
Red Wood
Victoria Cross Roads
Tumulus
Parker Copse
Pontru
Berthaucourt
Maissemy
Bihécourt
Coolier Quarry
Marengi Copse
Heart Copse
Collins Quarry
Fleming Crater
Arbousiers Wood

APPENDIX I

8 QUEENS

MAR/18

(28)

17th Inf.Bde.
24th Div.

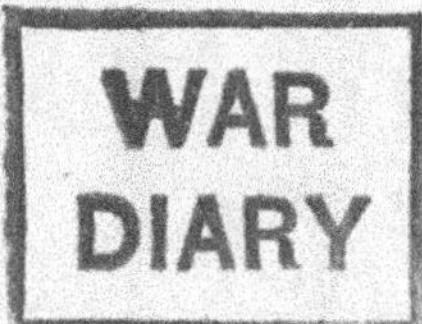

8th BATTN. THE QUEEN'S (ROYAL WEST SURREY REGIMENT).

A P R I L

1 9 1 8

Attached:

Appendices I to IX.

930

8th Bn. THE QUEEN'S R.W.S REGT

WAR DIARY

VOLUME XXXII

4/5/18.

R.H. Cropland
Lieut Colonel
Commanding
8th Bn The Queens RWS Regt

Page I

Instructions regarding War Diaries and Intelligence Summaries are contained in F. S. Regs., Part II. and the Staff Manual respectively. Title Pages will be prepared in manuscript.

WAR DIARY
or
~~INTELLIGENCE~~ SUMMARY

(Erase heading not required.)

Vol No XXXII

Army Form C. 2118

April 1918

Place	Date	Hour	Summary of Events and Information	Remarks and references to Appendices
FOUENCAMPS	1		In billets at FOUENCAMPS, the Bn being in Bde reserve; the 72nd Bde holding the approaches to the river. Message received from Lt. Gen. H. E. Watts, commanding 19th Corps, thanking all ranks of the 24th Division for their efforts during the past 8 ten days.	Appendix I 24th Div No H/16
	2.		Bn still in reserve.	
FOUENCAMPS - BOVES	3.		The Bn marched from FOUENCAMPS to BOVES and received orders to be ready to occupy a reserve position East of GENTELLES.	Appendix II WIRES BM 416 BM 419.
GENTELLES	4.		Further orders received to take up a position by noon extending from the BOIS L'ABBE' to the GENTELLES-CACHY road, with the 8th Royal West Kents on the left and the 1st Royal Fusiliers on the right. The Bn came under the orders of the 72nd Bde. The line occupied was held by a system of posts distributed in depth, No 1 Coy on the left and No 2 Coy on the right. The 18th Division held similar posts immediately in front. There was no enemy action but the village of GENTELLES was heavily shelled. It rained incessantly all the afternoon and night & there was no cover for the troops. Bn HQ situated close to the BOIS DE GENTELLES. Capt HB King (1st Northamptonshire Regt, attached 17th Bde) joined the Bn as temporary second in command.	Appendix III Wires etc
	5		Line held as above. Situation quiet. Information received that the 8th Australian Bde would occupy the BOIS DE GENTELLES & would be used to counter attack if the enemy broke through. Warning order received later that the 58th Division would relieve after dusk and, pending its arrival, the 8th Australian Bde would relieve	Appendix IV Wires.

RR Rose 2/[illegible]

Page 2.

Instructions regarding War Diaries and Intelligence Summaries are contained in F. S. Regs., Part II. and the Staff Manual respectively. Title Pages will be prepared in manuscript.

WAR DIARY
or
INTELLIGENCE SUMMARY
(Erase heading not required.)

April 1918

Volume XXXII

Army Form C. 2118.

Place	Date	Hour	Summary of Events and Information	Remarks and references to Appendices
GENTELLES - LONGEAU	5.		The 1st Royal Fusiliers / 24th Div Depot Battn south of the CACHY - BOVES road. At night the Bn was relieved by the 4th Suffolk Regt (58th Div), relief being	
		10PM.	complete by 10 PM. The Bn then proceeded to an embussing point near LONGEAU on the LONGEAU - DOMART road en route for SALEUX.	
SALEUX - ST VALERY	6.	1.30AM.	Arrived at SALEUX at 1.30 AM. where the men billetted and the officers went into huts. The Bn marched to the station at 2 30 PM where the whole of the 17th Bde entrained for ST VALERY. ~~Gen~~ General Stone B.G.C. 17th Bde was O.C. Train. Left SALEUX at 4 PM and arrived at ST VALERY about 10PM where the Bn went into billets.	Appendix V 17th I.B. Q.4

1875 Wt. W593/826 1,000,000 4/15 J.B.C. & A. A.D.S.S./Forms/C. 2118.

RWB

Army Form C. 2118

Instructions regarding War Diaries and Intelligence Summaries are contained in F. S. Regs., Part II. and the Staff Manual respectively. Title Pages will be prepared in manuscript.

WAR DIARY
or
INTELLIGENCE SUMMARY
(Erase heading not required.)

April 1918 — Volume XXXIII

Place	Date	Hour	Summary of Events and Information	Remarks and references to Appendices
ST VALERY - PENDÉ	7		The Bn spent the night at ST VALERY and marched to PENDÉ in the morning. Headquarters and No 1 Coy billetted at PENDÉ, No 2 Coy at SALENELLES. At 11 PM a draft of 299 OR's arrived a/Capt G. A. R. Slimming (cyclists) taken on the strength of the Battn.	
PENDÉ	8.		Coys placed at the disposal of Os C Coys for an hours steady drill, the rest of the day being spent in refitting and general reorganisation. Four companies formed and billetted as follows:- A B & HQ Coys at PENDE, D Coy at SALENELLES, C Coy at ROUTHIAUVILLE. Five officers and 85 OR's returned from leave. Letter of Congratulation received from Major Gen. Sir E. J. Hamilton K.C.B. Col of the regiment.	Appendix V A
"	9		Bn reorganising and refitting.	
	10		Coys at disposal of Os. C. Coys for drill and completion of reorganisation. 98 OR's joined the Bn. Major. C. R. Elsdaile (3rd Queens) taken on the strength of the Bn as 2nd in Command. D Coy moved from SALENELLES to TILLOY.	Appendix VI Wire H. 4
	11		Inspection by the Commanding officer of N. C. O's and men who had taken part in the recent operations. Training in musketry, drill & Lewis Gun under Coy arrangements. 2/Lt W. E. Kaye (1st H.A.C), 2/Lt H. J. Stallard (3rd [illegible]) 2/Lt E. Plowman (8th Hussars) & 2/Lt N. Parkhill (7th Royal Fusiliers) joined the Bn. Three officers reported from 18th Corps school to assist the Bn in Infantry Bombing and Lewis Gun instruction.	
	12.		Training under Coy arrangements with provision for assistance of specialist officers. Lt J. B. Sturgis joined the Bn.	[initials]

Page 4..

Army Form C. 2118

WAR DIARY
or
INTELLIGENCE SUMMARY
(Erase heading not required.)

Instructions regarding War Diaries and Intelligence Summaries are contained in F. S. Regs., Part II. and the Staff Manual respectively. Title Pages will be prepared in manuscript.

April 1918. Volume XXXIII

Place	Date	Hour	Summary of Events and Information	Remarks and references to Appendices
PENDE'	13		Commanding Officer inspected B C & D Coys. Classes for Bombing & Lewis Gun officers etc., Training under Coy arrangements in Box Respirator drill, musketry etc.	
	14		Church parade at 10 AM. The B. G. C. 17 I Bde inspected the new drafts after church parade and Brig-Gen C. S. Hoare-Nairne, commanding 24th Div., visited the Bn.	
	15		Coys trained under Bn arrangements, one Coy under Infantry instructor, one under musketry instructor; classes for Bombing and Lewis Gunners. Warning order received that the Division would entrain on the 16th for the 1st Army area but that 17 Bde group would not move till after midday. All Corps instructors ordered to report at Bde HQ the following morning. Transport arrangements made for move.	
	16		Instructions received that the Bn would move on the 17th. Major R. C. Rowland appointed A/Lt Col vice Lt Col Piers D.S.O. wounded 25/3/18.	
PENDE' - WOINCOURT	17		The Battn, less D Coy, marched from PENDE' at 5 PM to WOINCOURT and entrained there at midnight for PERNES. D Coy left TILLOY at 2 PM to proceed in advance as Bde unloading party.	Appendix VII Bde OO 231 Bn OO H.1. 17th B Instructions [illegible]
PERNES - MAGNICOURT	18		Detrained at PERNES 1-30 PM. Marched to MAGNICOURT at 4 PM. where, on arrival at 7 PM the Battn went into billets, D Company arriving later.	RWR

1875 Wt. W593/826 1,000,000 4/15 J.B.C. & A. A.D.S.S./Forms/C. 2118.

Page 4.5

Instructions regarding War Diaries and Intelligence Summaries are contained in F. S. Regs., Part II. and the Staff Manual respectively. Title Pages will be prepared in manuscript.

WAR DIARY
or
INTELLIGENCE SUMMARY
(Erase heading not required.)

Army Form C. 2118

April 1918 VOLUME XXXII

Place	Date	Hour	Summary of Events and Information	Remarks and references to Appendices
MAGNICOURT	19		Bn went into training. Lewis gunners of one Coy paraded under Lewis Gun Officer from 13th Corps, remainder of Bn carried out steady drill etc. under Coy arrangements. Three Coys fired group application and rapid practice on range at MONCHY BRETON in the afternoon.	
	20		Training as before. Infantry and Bombing instructors ~~rejoined Bn~~ from 18th Corps rejoined Bn to assist with intensive training. Capt N R Riley (ASC) Lt H. G. Veasey (5th Queens), 2/Lts. C.H. Wingrove and F. J. Posel (3rd Queens) taken on the strength of the Bn. Message received from Div. Commander congratulating units on the entraining & detraining on the 17th & 18th.	Appendix VIII 24th DIV A199/843
	21		Inspection of Box respirators of new draft by Bde Gas NCO. Bn church parade 11.30 a.m. Rapid firing practice on range for 3 Coys with and without gas masks. One Infantry Officer (18th Corps School) & one Musketry Sergt-Instructor attached to Bn to assist with intensive training. 17th Bde Concert party gave an entertainment in the evening.	
	22		Bn route march via FREVILLERS, LE P^T RIETZ, LACOMTE, BAJUS, HOUVELIN – MAGNICOURT. Two platoons detailed for instruction under Infantry ~~& musketry~~ Officers, Lewis Gunners of two companies under Lewis Gun Officer. Capt E.H. Fellowes rejoined the Bn from 72nd Bde and took over command of A Coy. PT and BF instructor attached to Bn to assist with training. Message of appreciation from the town Council of Guildford received respecting defence of LE VERGUIER.	Appendix IX Letter.
	23		Two companies practised tactical schemes on range and whole Bn fired rapid practice. Training under specialist Officers and NCOs as before, remainder of Coys training under Coy arrangements. Lecture to Bn by Divisional Gas Officer.	RWR

1875 Wt W593/826 1,000,000 4/15 J.B.C. & A. A.D.S.S./Forms/C. 2118.

Page 116. Army Form C. 2118

Instructions regarding War Diaries and Intelligence Summaries are contained in F. S. Regs., Part II. and the Staff Manual respectively. Title Pages will be prepared in manuscript.

WAR DIARY
or
INTELLIGENCE SUMMARY
(Erase heading not required.)

April 1918 — VOLUME XXXII

Place	Date	Hour	Summary of Events and Information	Remarks and references to Appendices
MAGNICOURT	24		Coys under Coy Commanders for training, including tactical schemes with [illegible] for special instruction by Infantry Officers of 18th Corps School, Lewis Gun Officer, bombing officer, PT & BF instructor & musketry instructor. At 3.15 PM the Battn was inspected near ROCOURT by General Sir H. S. Horne KCB KCMG commanding the First Army. After the inspection all Coys proceeded to the range for field firing & application practices.	
"	25.		On route march via MONCHY-BRETON, LATHIEULOYE, BAJUS, HOUVELIN back to MAGNICOURT. One Coy Lewis gunners under Lt Reynolds and bombing class as before. Physical training, bayonet fighting and musketry for all Coys in the afternoon. Three officers taken on the strength 2/Lt [illegible] Hall (5th Middx) 2/Lt [illegible] Mitton (5th Middx) and 2/Lt R. P. B. Caking (Rejoined from England).	
"	26.		Tactical training and specialist training as before. Commanding Officer inspected Drums, Pioneers & Stretcher Bearers. C & D Coy carried out night operations.	
"	27		Two Coys on range for field firing and application practices & remainder for tactical training. Training under specialists as before. Commanding Officer inspected runners.	
"	28		Bn Church parade 11.30 AM. In the afternoon the Bn marched to HOUDAIN to attend 1st Army Concert Party. Two Officers taken on the strength, 2/Lt W. R. Hallows & 2/Lt H. Dale (12th E. Surreys).	
"	29		Two Coys carried out tactical training & two Coys fired on range. Order received to send all instructors from Corps schools to Bde & XVIII Corps reinforcement camps cancelled later, only Lt Reynolds lewis gun instructor XVIII Corps school leaving the Bn & CSM Hall, PT & BF instructor, 1st Army school. 2/Lt A. W. White (5th Middx) taken on the strength of the Bn. A & B Coys & signallers carried out night operations.	

1875 Wt. W593/826 1,000,000 4/15 J.B.C. & A. A.D.S.S./Forms/C/2118.

Instructions regarding War Diaries and Intelligence Summaries are contained in F. S. Regs., Part II. and the Staff Manual respectively. Title Pages will be prepared in manuscript.

Page 67/RWR Army Form C. 2118

WAR DIARY
or
INTELLIGENCE SUMMARY

(Erase heading not required.)

April 1918

VOL XXXII

Place	Date	Hour	Summary of Events and Information	Remarks and references to Appendices
MAGNICOURT	30.		Orders received that the Bn would march on the following day to HOUDAIN en-route for the area LES BREBIS – BULLY GRENAY where the Bde would come into Divisional Reserve. All specialist instructors left the Bn.	
			R H Rowland Lt. Col Commanding 8th Bn The Queens (RWS Regt). 6/5/18.	RWR

1875 Wt. W593/826 1,000,000 4/15 J.B.C. & A. A.D.S.S./Forms/C. 2118.

A P P E N D I C E S

I to IX .

Appendix I

24th Division No. A/166.

COPY OF TELEGRAM.

From :- G.O.C. XIXth Corps.

To :- G.O.C. 24th Division.

" Please accept and convey to all ranks my warmest congratu- "
" lations and thanks for your splendid efforts during the "
" last 10 days AAA The fighting spirit and powers of endur- "
" ance shown are beyond all praise and have been of vital "
" importance in maintaining the front of the 19th Corps. "

(sgd) H.E. WATTS.
Lieut-General,
Commanding 19th Corpd.

- 2 -

For information and communication to all ranks.

C. H. H. Massy
Major.
D.A.A.G., 24th Division.

April 1st 1918.

Prefix.............. Code.................. m. | Words | Charge.

Office of Origin and Service Instructions.

Sent

At..................m.

To..................

By..................

This message is on a/c of:

APPENDIX II

.... *Service.*

3

(Signature of "Franking Officer.")

Recd. at..................

Date..................

From..................

By..................

TO

Sender's Number.	Day of Month.	In reply to Number.	**AAA**
B.M. 416.	3.		

Warning order aaa 17th
Inf: Bde. will be prepared
to extend its left
(U.13.b.c.5) northwards along the
BERTEAUCOURT – GENTELLES line
to the BOIS L'ABBE
at about U.1.b.a.5 aaa
1st R.F. will extend their
left to the GENTELLES
– CACHY road at about
U.7. central (GENTELLES inclus:) aaa
24th Div: left batt. will occupy
the line from U.7. central to
the brigade left boundary (U.1.b.a.5)
and will come under the orders of
O.C. 1st R.F. who will [illegible]
the [illegible] front aaa [illegible]

From

Place

Time

The above may be forwarded as now corrected. | **(Z)**

Censor. | Signature of Addressor or person authorised to telegraph in his name

Prefix..........Code..........m. | Words. | Charge. | This message is on a/c of: | Recd. at..........m.

Office of Origin and Service Instructions.

SECRET
Lia Urgent

Sent At..........m. To.......... By..........

APPENDIX II

..........Service.

(Signature of "Franking Officer.")

Date.......... From.......... By..........

TO			
	8th Queens		
	1st RF.	24th Div Depot Bn	73rd Inf Bde
	3rd RB	72nd Inf Bde	24th Div G.

Sender's Number.	Day of Month.	In reply to Number.	AAA
* BM 419	3.		

Cancel my BM 416 of this date AAA
17th Inf Bde will take over the BERTEAUCOURT-
GENTELLES Line by noon 4th April from
left of French T 30 b central to BOIS L'ABBE
U 1 b 0/5 as follows AAA 24th Div Depot Bn from
T 30 b central to LONGUEAU - DOMART Road
U 19 a 0/0 (Right of 1st Royal Fusiliers) and
will rendezvous at X roads T 24 b 8/2 5.30 am
tomorrow 4th April AAA They will be met by a
guide to be provided by 72nd Inf Bde who will
explain the necessary dispositions - HQrs will be
at T 30 a 7/5 AAA 24th Div Depot Bn on taking
over line from units of 72nd Inf Bde will come under
orders of 1st Royal Fusiliers AAA 1st Royal Fusiliers
will remain in their present dispositions in
the line to U 13 b 0/5 AAA 8th Queens will
take over from U 13 b 0/5 to BOIS L'ABBE

From
Place
Time

The above may be forwarded as now corrected. (Z)

Censor. Signature of Addressor or person authorised to telegraph in his name.

…Code……m. | Words. | Charge. | *This message is on a/c of:* | Recd. at……m.

Office of Origin and Service Instructions.

SECRET

Sent At……m. To…… By……

……*Service.*

(Signature of "Franking Officer.")

Date……

From……

By……

TO 8th Queens

APPENDIX III

Sender's Number.	Day of Month.	In reply to Number.	AAA
BM 422	4		

Reference my BM 419 dated 3rd inst AAA 1st RF will prolong their left to GENTELLES - CACHY Road in U7 central AAA This will then become the Right Boundary of the 8th Queens and not as stated in above quoted order AAA Addsd all recipients of BM 419.

From 17th IB

Place

Time 8.50 am

The above may be forwarded as now corrected. (Z) [signature] Major

……*Censor.* Signature of Addressor or person authorised to telegraph in his name.

Prefix SM Code FJ Words 54

£ s. d.

Charges to Collect

Service Instructions

3 adds.

Received	Sent, or sent out.	Office Stamp
From	At ......m.	
By	To	
	By	

Handed in at J.G. Office 10.45a.m. Received 11.8a.m.

TO E.D.

*Sender's Number	Day of Month	In reply to Number	AAA
BM423	4		

Mge	from	Divn	timed
10.25	am	states	AAA
Enemy	attack	this	morning
astride	main	WARFUSEE-ABANCOURT	
AMIENS	road	AAA	Our
troops	now	establishing	a
line	through	P21	P27
P33	AAA	1st	R7
and	8th	Queens	will
keep	closely	in	touch
with	the	situation	in
front	AAA	added	3
Bns			

FROM
TIME & PLACE 17 I Bde 10 45 am

To the Adjutant AW2
E D

From O. C. No 2 Coy

Dispositions of No 2 Coy.

Coy front N of road at U 7 central to
U.1.d 1.6

No 5 Platoon
L G section at U 7 b 1.3
Rifle sections at U 7.a.8.7. U 1.c.8.1
and U 1 d.1.5

In support No 6 Platoon
Rifle sections at U 7 a 7.2 U 7.a.6.5
L G at U 7 a. 5.9
Rifle section at U.1.c.6.3

150x in rear of No 5 Platoon is
Coy HQ + 2 Platoons.

4/9/18 7 PM

[illegible]
O.C.
No 2 Coy

MESSAGES AND SIGNALS. No. of Message

Prefix S/B Code 6 P.M. Words 47 Charge.

Office of Origin and Service Instructions. IV priority

Sent At m. To By

This message is on a/c of: Service.

(Sig. of "Franking Officer.")

Recd. at 7 35 m. Date QE 4 4 18 From JA By Hurst

TO QE KC ED

Sender's Number	Day of Month	In reply to Number	AAA
G 261	4		

situation left & centre 18th div 6 25 pm 53rd IB in centre heavily attacked and forced back One batt ordered to counterattack via U10 and U11 and One batt Australian bde proceeding to counterattack east of VILLERS BRETTONEUX

From IV

Place

Time 7 20 pm

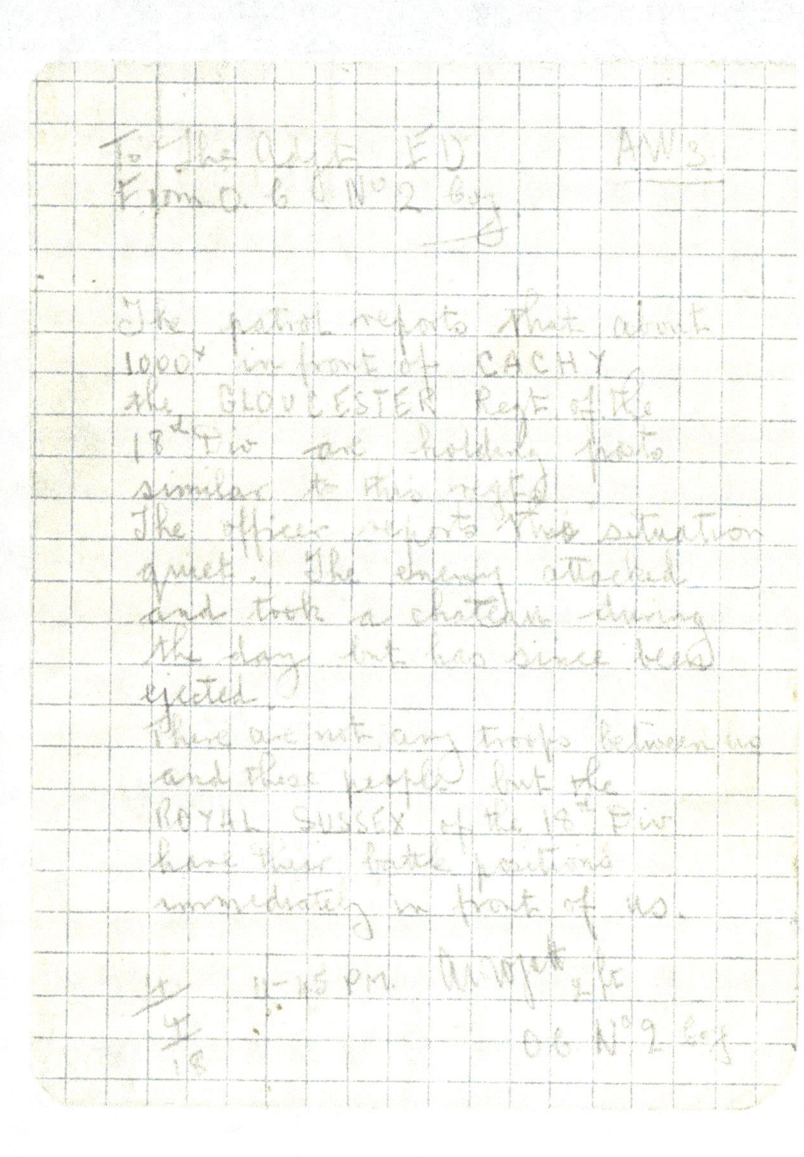

To The O.C. E.D. AW3
From O. C. No 2 Coy

The patrol reports that about
1000x in front of CACHY
the GLOUCESTER Regt of the
18th Div are holding posts
similar to this night
The officer reports the situation
quiet. The enemy attacked
and took a chateau during
the day but has since been
ejected
There are not any troops between us
and these people but the
ROYAL SUSSEX of the 18th Div
have their battle positions
immediately in front of us.

4/4/18 11-45 PM. [illegible] 2/Lt
O.C. No 2 Coy

Prefix..........Code.........Words..........

£ s d

Charges to Collect

Service Instructions. Copy to original

Received From .... By ....

Sent, or sent out. At ....m. To .... By ....

Office Stamp

Handed in at........Office........m. Received........m.

TO 8 Queens

Sender's Number	Day of Month	In reply to Number	AAA
BM 25	4		

For your information AAA 2 Battns 58 Division have been ordered to prolong line 41 to 0/5 north through Bois le abbe AAA added ED Repted OM

FROM BR 12·25pm

MESSAGES AND SIGNALS. No. of Message............

Prefix SM Code M.. Words 42

£ s d

Charges to Collect

Service Instructions. JH 3 adds

Received	Sent, or sent out.	Office Stamp
From........	At..........m.	
By........	To..........	
	By..........	

Handed in at.......................Office........m. Received............m.

TO 8th Queens, 1st RF, 8th RB. [FD KC QE]

*Sender's Number	Day of Month	In reply to Number	AAA
BM. 426	4		

Bureau report line now runs as follows AAA V19 central – V13 central – V7 central – V16 central – P32a central – P26 central – P20 central – Eastern Edge of BOIS de VAIRE – HAMEL inclusive – to River SOMME AAA Addsd 3 Bns

FROM ~~[illegible]~~ JH

TIME & PLACE 12.45 pm.

MESSAGES AND SIGNALS. No. of Message

Prefix SM Code CGB m Words 28 Charge.

Office of Origin and Service Instructions.

JA

Sent At m. To By

This message is on a/c of: Service.

(Sig. of "Franking Officer.")

Recd. at 345 m. Date QE From 4.4.16 JA By Hunt

TO ED

Sender's Number	Day of Month	In reply to Number	AAA
* BM 428	4		

On receipt of this you will come under the order of 72nd Inf Bde aaa Addressed 8th Queens repeated 72nd IB

From
Place 17th Inf Bde
Time

The above may be forwarded as now corrected. (Z)

Censor. Sig. of Addressor or person authorised to telegraph in his name.

To		(Sig. of "Franking Officer.")	By
By			

TO
OC 8 Bn Kents — 10th Essex
OC 15 [illegible] Pos — 7th London
OC 8 Queens — 17 Inf Bde

Sender's Number	Day of Month	In reply to Number	AAA
* BM 166	4		

The BGC has now assumed command of the front from Gentelles – Cachy Rd about U 7 central To O 27 a 7 8
The front is at present held by 8 Queens from U 7 cent to U 1 b 0 5 from thence the line runs O 32 Central – O 27 c 0 0 O 27 a 7 8.
The 10th Essex are holding the line from U 1 b 0 5 To O 32 Central ~~[illegible]~~ HQ O 31 c 7 0
The 7th London are holding the line from O 32 cent To O 27 a 7 8 HQ at O 26 d 0 0
The 8 R W Kents will be responsible for Supporting the line from U 7 central to O 32 c 4 2 (incl) This will include the front held by 8 Queens & half of 10th Essex

From
Place
Time

The above may be forwarded as now corrected. (Z)

Censor. Sig. of Addressor or person authorised to telegraph in his name.

	By	(Sig. of "Franking Officer.")	By

TO

Sender's Number	Day of Month	In reply to Number	AAA
*Bde 166 Cont.	4		

The 15th Entrenching Bn will be responsible for supporting the Northern half of 10th Essex & 7th London. from O. 32 C. 4 2 (excl) – O. 27 a. 7. 8.

Both the 8th R W Kents & 15th Entrenching Bn will get in touch with 10th Essex & 8 RWKents with 8 Queens. HQ T. 11 a. 4. 2 & the 15 Entrenching Bn with 7th Londons.

Both Supporting Bns will send runners to the Batts they are supporting & these Bns will send runners to them.

OC 15th Ent. Bn will move his Batt to position in BOIS de BLANGY about O. 36. b.

OC 8 RWKents will move his Batt to a suitable place further forward to about wood in N. 35 c.

From Positions: once to be reported to BHQ.

Place This front line will be held and counter attack

Time [illegible] necessary.

The above may be forwarded as now corrected (Z) [illegible] Capt

Censor. Sig. of Addressor or person authorized to telegraph in his name.

* This line should be erased if not required.

(7964) Wt. W492/M1647. [E 1187] 130,000 Pads—5/17. M.R.Co.,Ltd. Forms/C.2121.

Prefix .... Code .... m.	Words.	Charge.	This message is on a/c of:	Recd. at .... m.
Office of Origin and Service Instructions.	Sent		.... Service.	Date
	At .... m.			From
	To			
	By		(Sig. of "Franking Officer.")	By

TO ED APPENDIX IV

Sender's Number	Day of Month	In reply to Number	AAA
* G272	5		

The 8th Australian Bde on arrival at AUBIGNY will continue its march to a position in the BOIS DE GENTELLES or in valley in T17 and T22 where it will be in support to the right of their own corps front

From
Place IV
Time

The above may be forwarded as now corrected. (Z)

.... Censor. Sig. of Addressor or person authorised to telegraph in his name.

Prefix............ Code............m	Words. Charge.	This message is on a/c of:	Recd. at..........m.
Office of Origin and Service Instructions.	Sent	...................Service.	Date
Secret	At..........m.		From
	To		
	By	(Signature of "Franking Officer.")	By

TO 8th Queens 3rd R.B. 72nd I.B.
1st R.F. 24th Div Depot Bn 73rd I.B.

Sender's Number.	Day of Month.	In reply to Number.	AAA
*BM 430	5		

Warning order aaa The 17th Inf Bde will be withdrawn from the BERTEAUCOURT—GENTELLES line after dark tonight 5th inst aaa Units will concentrate at LONGUEAU & will embuss from that point aaa Order of march will be as under aaa Starting point cross roads T 9 b 80 1st R.F & Div Depot Bn 9.0 p.m aaa 8th Queens 9.15 p.m aaa 3rd R.B. 9.30 pm aaa Route main DOMART—LONGUEAU road aaa A Bde 58th Div will be occupying line vacated by the Bde but will arrive during the night aaa Units will accordingly leave one officer per Bn & two guides per Coy to assist relieving Units aaa These should be ordered to report to [illegible]

From
Place
Time

The above may be forwarded as now corrected. (Z)
Censor. Signature of Addressor or person authorised to telegraph in his name.

Prefix.........Code......Words...........	Received.	Sent, or sent out.	Office Stamp.
£ s. d. Charges to Collect	From.............. By..................	At..............m.	
Service Instructions Copy		To..................... By.....................	

Handed in at..Office..............m. Received..............m.

TO 8 Queens

* Sender's Number.	Day of Month.	In reply to Number.	AAA
BM 434	5		

Pending arrival of Bns of 58 Div, 8th Australian Bde now at BOIS DE GENTELLES will relieve 1 Roy Fus & Div Depot Bn South of the CACHY - BOVES Road aaa Other arrangement hold good aaa Addd 1RF 8 Queens & Div Depot Bn

FROM 17 Inf Bde
PLACE & TIME

Prefix.........Code.......Words...........	Received.	Sent, or sent out.	Office Stamp.
£ s. d. Charges to Collect	From............. By.............	At..............m.	
Service Instructions		To............. By.............	

Handed in at..Office..............m. Received..............m.

TO 8 Queens

*Sender's Number.	Day of Month.	In reply to Number.	AAA
BM 436	5		

Refce BM430 of this date aaa Units will now await relief by Bns of 58 Divn and 8 Australian Bde respectively aaa 1 Roy Fus Div Depot Bn by 8 Austr Bde SOUTH of CACHY-BOVES Road aaa 8 Queens by Bn of 58 Divn North of this road aaa On relief Units will march to the embussing point along DOMART-LONGUEAU Road concentrating on South side of Road in T2D aaa 3 Rif Bde will march out indefinately passing X roads T9B8/0 at 9-30pm and await arrival of busses at above concentration point aaa acknowledge aaa addd 3 Bns & Div Depot Bn

FROM
PLACE & TIME 17 Inf Bde
5-15pm

Prefix........ Code........ Words........	Received	Sent, or sent out.	Office Stamp
£ s d Charges to Collect	From .... By	At ....m. To .... By	
Service Instructions. SDR.			

Handed in at............ Office ....m. Received ....m.

TO	8th Queens.

*Sender's Number	Day of Month	In reply to Number	AAA
BM 437.	5		

4th Suffolks (58th Division) is now on its way to relieve you AAA Send guides immediately on receipt of this to X roads T9b8/0 where this Bn will rendezvous for tea AAA You can then fix up details of your relief direct with OC. 4th Suffolks AAA On relief you will concentrate in T2d as previously arranged

FROM	17 Inf Bde
TIME & PLACE	5.45 pm

*This line should be erased if not required.

Prefix........Code........m. | Words | Charge.
Office of Origin and Service Instructions.

Sent
At........m.
To........
By........

This message is on a/c of
........Service.
(Signature of "Franking Officer.")

Recd. at........m.
Date........
From........
By........

TO ED, KC

Sender's Number.	Day of Month.	In reply to Number.	AAA
*RB 2	5		

The Brigade Major States that the Brigade will be withdrawn after dusk & will concentrate at LONGEAU from where they will proceed by bus —

From QE
Place
Time

The above may be forwarded as now corrected.
Censor.

(Z)
Signature of Addressor or person authorised to telegraph in his name
[illegible signature] Capt.

Appendix V

3 Bns
B.T.C.

17th I Bde
Q. 7

1. The Divisional Transport will move in the following group on the 6th Inst by road to St Valery.

Group "A": 17th I Bde Group, Div. H Qrs, Train HQrs, CRE, M G Os, 1st Line Tpt Signal Coy, SAA Section DAC.

2. The head of the column Group "A" will pass the starting point at the junction of Saleux - Amiens Road with the Boulevard running round S of Amiens 1 Mile due N of the Lunatic Asylum at 1-45 pm.

3. An interval of at least 1 Mile between each group and 100 yards between each unit will be strictly maintained throughout the march.

The O C Div Train will command the whole column on the march & will be responsible

4. <u>Supplies.</u>

Supplies for consumption on the 6th inst are in possession of all Units. Supplies for consumption on the 7th inst will be issued to all rail parties of Units at the Entraining Station prior to entrainment. For parties proceeding by road supplies will be issued by appropriate Train Coys at the termination of the march on the 6th inst. Supplies for consumption on the 8th inst for rail parties will be delivered direct to Units in the new area. Supplies for consumption on the 8th for road parties will be issued by supplying the Train Coys on the 7th inst. Supplies for consumption on the 9th inst will be delivered to complete Units in the normal way.

5. <u>Train Arrangements</u>

Units will entrain at Saleux and detrain at St Valery as follows:–

<u>1st Train.</u> Depart 3-30pm H.Q. & [illegible] Bde
Pioneer Bn, Camp Comdt, B[illegible].

6. Units will report to R.T.O. Salerno 1 hour prior to departure of trains.

7. Adjt 17 Inf Bde will be O.C. Trains. Units will hand entraining strength to representative.

Acknowledge.

6/3/42

[illegible] Major
Brigade Major 17th Inf Bde

APPENDIX V A

15 Earls Court Gardens
London SW5

~~UNITED SERVICE CLUB.~~

~~PALL MALL, S.W.1.~~

8th April 1918

My dear Tringham
I trust this will find you safe & sound. I wish to send you & the Battn my hearty congratulations on the noble way you have all kept up & added to the record of the Regt. I fear you have had heavy losses, but up to now not very many casualties amongst officers have been reported, but the lists are slowly coming in & increasing in size. Our

Prefix............Code..............m. | Words. | Charge.

Office of Origin and Service Instructions.

Sent

At..............m.

To..............

By..............

This message is on a/c of: ....Service.

(Signature of "Franking Officer.")

Recd. at..........m.

Date..........

From..........

By..........

APPENDIX VI

TO ~~1st Bn.~~ 8 Queen's

Sender's Number.	Day of Month.	In reply to Number.	AAA
* A4.	9		

From tomorrow 10th inst 12 noon the Div. have ordered that SAULINELLE be handed over to 24 MG Bn. aaa You will be given VANDRICOURT ETINCOURT and TILLOY aaa The Bde Interpreter will report to you at 9am 10th to help you in the new arrangement.

From

Place

Time 1.7PM

The above may be forwarded as now corrected. (Z)

Censor.

W.R. [illegible] Captain

Signature of Addressor or person authorised to telegraph in his name.

* This line should be erased if not required.

(3 W.S.) Wt. W12952/M1294. 187,500 Pads. 1/17 McC. & Co., Ltd. (E. 818.)

Appendix VIII

Copy No 1

Amendment to 17th Inf: Bde Order No.231.

Reference Serial No.1, Remarks Column.

For 4.04 p.m. Read 4.04 a.m.

W R G Bye
Captain, for
Brigade Major, 17th Infantry Brigade.

Issued to all recipients
of Brigade Order No.231.

---

3. Entraining Stations..........WOINCOURT - FEUQUIERES.
   Detraining Stations..........PERNES - BRYAS.

4. Detailed instructions re entraining and detraining are being issued.

5. Advanced Billeting Parties of the following numbers will travel by Train No.12, departing from WOINCOURT at 13.04 hours on the 17th instant:,

   X

   Each Battalion..............1 Officer & 4 N.C.Os.
   17th L.T.M.Batty............1 N.C.O
   74th Field Ambce............1 Officer & 1 N.C.O.
   No. 2 Coy Div: Train........1 Officer & 1 N.C.O.

   Billeting Areas will be notified later.

6. There are no restrictions as regards routes to the entraining Stations, but these should be reconnoitred by Units beforehand.

7. Brigade Headquarters will close at CAYEUX at 4 p.m. 17th instant

8. ACKNOWLEDGE.

W R G Bye
Captain, for
Brigade Major, 17th Infantry Brigade.

Issued to Sigs
at 2-45 p.m.
16th April, 18.

Copy No.	To	Copy No.	To
1	8th Queens.	2	1st Royal Fus.
3	3rd Rifle Bde.	4	17th L.T.M.Batty
5	Sigs:17th I.B.	6	B.T.O. 17th I.B.
7	"G" 24th Divn:	8	195 Coy. A.S.C.
9	74th Field Amb:	10	War Diary.
11	File.		

S E C R E T. Copy No 1

17th INFANTRY BRIGADE ORDER No. 231.

Ref: 1/100,000
ABBEVILLE)
LENS) Sheets.

1. The 24th Division (less Artillery) is being transferred to the First Army Area.

2. The 17th Infantry Brigade will move on the 17th & 18th April.

3. Entraining Stations...........WOINCOURT - FEUQUIERES.
Detraining Stations...........PERNES - BRYAS.

4. Detailed instructions re entraining and detraining are being issued.

5. Advanced Billeting Parties of the following numbers will travel by Train No.12, departing from WOINCOURT at 13.04 hours on the 17th instant:,

X

Each Battalion..............1 Officer & 4 N.C.Os.
17th L.T.M.Batty............1 N.C.O
74th Field Ambce............1 Officer & 1 N.C.O.
No. 2 Coy Div: Train........1 Officer & 1 N.C.O.

Billeting Areas will be notified later.

6. There are no restrictions as regards routes to the entraining Stations, but these should be reconnoitred by Units beforehand.

7. Brigade Headquarters will close at CAYEUX at 4 p.m. 17th instant

8. ACKNOWLEDGE.

W.R. J Bye
Captain, for
Brigade Major, 17th Infantry Brigade.

Issued to Sigs
at 2-45 pm
16th April, 18.

Copy No.1 to 8th Queens.
3 3rd Rifle Bde.
5 Sigs:17th I.B.
7 "G" 24th Divn:
9 74th Field Amb:
11 File.

Copy No.2 to 1st Royal Fus.
4 17th L.T.M.Batty
6 B.T.O. 17th I.B.
8 195 Coy. A. .C.
10 War Diary.

Serial No.	Date.	Unit.	From.	To.	To arrive at Entraing Stn.	O.C Train	Remarks.
1.	17th April.	3rd R.Bde (1 Coy)	CAYEUX	WOINCOURT.	3.30 p.m.	O.C.74th F.A	Loading party to travel on train No.22 at 4.04 pm 18th instant.
2.	17th April.	17th Inf: Bde. H.Q & No.2 Signal Sectn	CAYEUX)				
3.	17th April.	17th L.T.M.Battery.	HURT)	WOINCOURT	5.30 p.m.	Major ESDAILE 8th Queens.	
4.	17th April.	1 Coy. 8th Queens.	PENDE Area.)				Unloading Party at detraining Stn for all trains.
5.	17th April.	12th Sherwood Foresters (1 Coy)		FEUQUIERES	5.50 p.m.	O.C.,104 RE.	Loading Party to travel in Train No.23 at 6.19 a.m on 18th instant.
6.	17th April.	1st Roy. Fus. (3 Coys)	LANCHERES.	FEUQUIERES	7.50 p.m.	O.C.,1st R.F.	1 Coy to act as unloading party at detraining stn for all trains.
7.	17th April.	8th Queens. (3 Coys)	PENDE.	WOINCOURT	8.30 p.m.	O.C.,8th Queens.	
8.	17th April.	1st Roy. Fus. (1 Coy)	LANCHERES.	FEUQUIERES	10.30 p.m.	O.C.,24th M.G.Bn.	
9.	17th April.	3rd Rifle Bde. (3 Coys)	CAYEUX.	WOINCOURT	11.30 p.m.	O.C.,3rd R.Bde.	

NOTES.
1. Transport to arrive at entraining station 3 hours before train departure.
2. Officer i/c Entraining at WOINCOURT Station – A Captain 3rd Rifle Brigade.
" " at FEUQUIERES " – A Captain 1st Royal Fusiliers.
" Detraining at PERNES " – Major ESDAILE, 8th Queens.
" " at BRYAS " – Major A.SIMKINS, 1st Royal Fusiliers.
3. O's C Trains will detail Train Guards of 1 N.C.O and 6 men near each end of the trains.

Prefix........ Code........m. | Words. | Charge.

Office of Origin and Service Instructions.

D.R.L.S.

Sent

At........m.

To........

By........

This message is on a/c of:

........*Service.*

(Signature of "Franking Officer.")

Recd. at........m.

Date ....

From ....

By ....

TO ALL UNITS and B.T.O.

Sender's Number.	Day of Month.	In reply to Number.	AAA
*K. 3	16.		

Reference 24th Division No C/425 dated 16th instant forwarded under this office Q.7/16 of date trains now depart as follows - previous times are cancelled :-

Serial No 16 19-04 17 21-19 18 22-04 all 17th instant aaa 19 0-19 20 1-04 21 3-19 22 4-04 23 6-19 all 18th instant aaa Acknowledge.

From 17th I.Bde.

Place

Time

Captain,
for Staff Captain.

The above may be forwarded as now corrected.

(Z)

Censor.

Signature of Addressor or person authorised to telegraph in his name.

Prefix......Code......m.	Words	Charge.	This message is on a/c of:	Recd. at......m.
Office of Origin and Service Instructions.	Sent		......Service	Date ......
	At......m.			From ......
	To			
	By		(Signature of "Franking Officer.")	By ......

TO 8th Queens ~~1st Royal Fusiliers~~, 3rd R.B.

Sender's Number.	Day of Month.	In reply to Number.	AAA
* BM 10	17		

Probable location of units of this Bde in the new area:—

TMB	HOUVELIN
8th Queens	MAGNICOURT + HOUVELIN
1st RF	ORLANCOURT in Tents
3rd RB	DIVION
Fd Coy RE	DIVION.
Coy. Div. Train	DIVION
Field Ambulance	DIVION.

From 17th
Place
Time 10.0 a.m.

The above may be forwarded as now corrected.

(Z) [illegible signature] Capt. for B.M.

Censor.

Signature of Addressor or person authorised to telegraph in his name.

*This line should be erased if not required.

(18965.) Wt. W12952/M1294. 187,500 Pads. 1/17 McC. & Co., Ltd. (E. 818.)

Secret

Appendix VII

Copy No. 12

8th Bn The Queens R.W.S. Regt

Operation Order No. A.1.

Map Ref. ABBERVILLE 1/100.000

16th APRIL 1918.

1. The Battn will entrain at HOINCOURT tomorrow for the 1st Army Area.

2. Route:- Pende - Tilloy - St. Blimont - Friville - Hoincourt.

3. D. Coy will entrain at 7 p.m. and will move off from Tilloy at 2. p.m reporting at Hoincourt Stn. at 5.30 p.m.
[illegible] will accompany them.
This Coy will be responsible for the unloading of all trains of the 17th Bde Group.

4. The remainder of the Battn will move off at 5. p.m.
[illegible] Bn. [illegible] in Pende.
Order of March:- Pioneers & Signallers, Drums, H.Q. Coy, A. B. C. Coys.

5. Transport will move off at 4. p.m.

6. Coys with the exception of D. Coy will render a complete Marching Out State in duplicate to O.R. by 3. p.m.
That of 'D' Coy at 12 noon.

7. Officers Kits less mess Kits will be collected as follows:-
'C' Coy - 10 a.m. D Coy - 11. a.m.
H.Q. A & B. Coys will be dumped at Q.M. Stores at 11. a.m

Con[td]

8. Mess tins will be collected as follows:-
'D' Coy. 12.30 p.m. 'C' Coy. 1.30 p.m.
H.Q. A & B. Coys will be dumped at Transport Lines at 2.15 p.m.

9. Dress: Full Marching Order including Blanket.

Issued at 7.50 p.m.

[illegible]
Capt & Adjutant
8 Queens Regt

Issued to.

No 1. H.Q. Mess	No. 5. O.C. D. Coy	No. 9. Q.M.
2. O.C. A. Coy.	6. — F.S. —	10. R.S.M.
3. O.C. B —	7. T.O.	11. FILE.
4. O.C. C —	8. M.O.	12. WAR DIARY

Appendix VII

24th Division No. Q. 5.425.

SECRET

8th Queens

1/R 9 BDE. Q 7/16

ADMINISTRATIVE INSTRUCTIONS FOR THE ENTRAINMENT OF THE 24th DIVISION, (LESS ARTILLERY).

1. ENTRAINMENT.

The Division will commence entrainment on 16th April in accordance with the attached Table.
Entraining Stations will be :-

(A) WOINCOURT.
(B) FEUQUIERES-FRESSENNEVILLE.

Detraining Stations will be :-

(Y) PERNES.
(Z) BRYAS.

2. TRAFFIC CONTROL.

The A.P.M. will arrange to control traffic on the road approaches to the entraining Stations and no troops or transport should be allowed to enter the yards until the R.T.O. is ready.

3. ENTRAINING OFFICERS.

Each Infantry Brigade will detail two Field Officers (if possible) to be on duty at the entraining station and detraining Station of the Brigade Group. The one detailed for entraining will report to the R.T.O. at the entraining Station half an hour before the arrival of the first unit of the Group, and remain until the last train of the Group is ready to leave. At the Detraining Station he will remain on duty until his Group has detrained.

4. LOADING AND UNLOADING PARTIES.

One of the companies, (with Cookers and teams) shown as entraining on the last train of each Brigade Group from each Station will report to the R.T.O. three and a half hours before the departure of the first train and be responsible for loading all trains of the Brigade Group, and will itself entrain upon the last train.
The Company, Cooker and team shewn as entraining on each Brigade H.Q. train will travel complete to the detraining Station, and be responsible for the unloading of all trains of the Brigade Group.

5. ARRIVAL AT ENTRAINING STATION.

In the case of Infantry, Pioneer and Machine Gun Battalions, the Transport will arrive at the entraining Station 3 hours before the time of departure of the train, and the personnel 1½ hours before. In the case of other units they should arrive complete three hours before the time of departure of the train.

6. STATES.

A complete " Marching Out State" showing the number of men, horses, G.S. Wagons, Limbered G.S., and 2 wheeled wagons, and Cycles will be sent with the Transport of each unit, so that the accommodation on the train can be checked by the R.T.O., the Limbered G.S. wagons being counted as two 2 wheeled vehicles on the state.

(continued).

7. SUPPLY, BAGGAGE WAGONS AND WATER CARTS.

Supply & Baggage Wagons will accompany the units they serve. Supply Wagons should rejoin the Headquarters of their train Companies as soon as possible after the latter have arrived in their new areas. Water Carts should be full on entrainment.

8. BREAST ROPES AND LASHINGS.

B[illegible]opes for horse trucks must be provided by the units[illegible]kes; ropes for lashing vehicles on the flat trucks [illegible]ll be provided by the Railway.

9. CLOSING OF DOORS.

All doors of covered trucks and carriages on the right hand side of the train on the main line will be kept closed.

10. BRAKE VANS.

No personnel or Stores are allowed in the brake Vans at each end of the trains.

11. COMPOSITION OF TRAINS.

(a) All trains consist of 1 Officers Carriage, 17 flat trucks, 30 covered trucks.

(b) Each flat truck will take an average of four axles; each covered truck will take 40 men,or 6 H.D. Horses, or 8 L.D.Horses or mules.

12. SUPPLIES.

Units entraining before 24 hours night 16/17th will have their Supplies for consumption 18th instant issued to them at Entraining Stations. These supplies though really for consumption on 18th instant will be consumed on 17th instant, and the Supplies at present on Supply Wagons for consumption on 17th instant, will be retained for consumption on 18th instant. Preserved Meat and Bread will be issued as far as possible.

Units entraining at and after 24 hours night 16/17th will receive Rations for consumption 18th instant, on the afternoon of 16th instant in the present area.

Instructions as regards Supplies for consumption on 19th instant will be issued later.

13. ACKNOWLEDGE.

R.W. Collins.

Lieut-Colonel,

16th April 1918. A.A.&.Q.M.G., 24th Division.

Issued at 12.45 a.m.

Distribution :-

G.O.C.	"G"	"Q"
17th Inf.Bde.	C.R.A.	D.A.D.V.S.
72nd Inf.Bde.	C.R.E.	A.P.M.
73rd Inf.Bde.	A.D.M.S.	D.A.D.O.S.
224th Emplt.Co.	24th Div.M.T.Co.	12th Sher.Fors.
24th M.G.Bn.	Camp Comdt.	24th Divl.Train.
S.A.A.Sect.	24th D.A.C.	R.T.O. WOINCOURT.

R.T.O.FEUQUIERES-FRESSENNEVILLE. Traffic LONGPRE.

24th Division No. [illegible]

Train Serial No.	Station of Entrainment.	Time of Departure.	Units.
1.	FEUQUIERES.	15.00 16th inst.	72nd Inf. Bde. Hd. Qrs. Brigade Signal Section. Light T.M. Battery. 9th E.Surreys 1 Coy. 1 Cooker 1 Team. One Coy. Machine Gun Battn.
2.	WOINCOURT.	16.00 16th inst.	73rd Inf. Bde. Hd. Qrs. Brigade Signal Section. Light T.M. Battery. 9th Royal Sussex 1 Coy. 1 Cooker 1 Team 1 Coy. Machine Gun Battn.
3.	FEUQUIERES.	18.00 16th inst.	9th E.Surreys less 1 Coy. 1 Cooker and 1 Team.
4.	WOINCOURT.	19.00 16th inst.	9th R.Sussex less 1 Coy. 1 Cooker and 1 Team.
5.	FEUQUIERES.	21.00 16th inst.	8th R.W.Kents less 1 Coy. 1 Cooker and 1 Team.
6.	WOINCOURT.	22.00 16th inst.	7th Northants less 1 Coy. 1 Cooker and 1 Team.
7.	FEUQUIERES.	24.00 night 16/17th.	1st N.Staffs less 1 Coy. 1 Cooker and 1 Team.
8.	WOINCOURT.	1.00 17th inst.	13th Midd'x. less 1 Coy. 1 Cooker and 1 Team.
9.	FEUQUIERES.	3.00 17th inst.	8th R.W.Kents. 1 Coy. 1 Cooker and 1 Team, No. 3 Coy. Div. Train and 103rd Field Coy. R.E.
10.	WOINCOURT.	4.00 17th inst.	Divisional Headquarters. H.Q. & No. 1 Sectn. Divl. Signal Coy. H.Q. Divisional Engineers.
11.	FEUQUIERES.	6.00 17th inst.	1st N.Staffs. 1 Coy. 1 Cooker and 1 Team, 72nd Fie[illegible]

Train Serial No.	Station of Entrainment.	Time of Departure.	Unit.
12.	WOINCOURT.	7.00 17th inst.	7th Northants. 1 Coy. 1 Cooker and 1 Team, 129th Fld.Co. R.E. and No.4 Coy. Divl. Train. ⅓ S.A.A. Sectn. 24th D.A.C.
13.	FEUQUIERES.	9.00 17th inst.	
14.	WOINCOURT.	10.00 17th inst.	13th Midd'x. 1 Coy. 1 Cooker and 1 Team. 73rd Field Ambulance. H.Q. 24th Divl. Train.
15.	FEUQUIERES.	12.00 17th inst.	½ S.A.A. Sectn. 24th D.A.C.
16.	WOINCOURT.	13.00 19.04 D Coy 2 p.m. 17th inst.	17th Inf.Bde. Hd.Qrs. Brigade Signal Section. 1 Coy. Machine Gun Battn. Light T.M.Battery. 8th Queens 1 Coy. 1 Cooker and 1 Team.
17.	FEUQUIERES.	21.19 15.00 17th inst.	1st Royal Fus. less 1 Coy. 1 Cooker and 1 Team.
18.	WOINCOURT.	22.04 16.00 17th inst.	8th Queens less 1 Coy. 1 Cooker and 1 Team.
19.	FEUQUIERES.	18.00 17th inst.	1st Royal Fus. 1 Coy. 1 Cooker and 1 Team. H.Q. and 1 Coy. Mach. Gun Battn. Divisional Employment Coy.
20.	WOINCOURT.	19.00 17th inst.	3rd Rif.Bde. less 1 Coy. 1 Cooker and 1 Team.
21.	FEUQUIERES.	21.00 17th inst.	Pioneer Battn. less 1 Coy. 1 Cooker and 1 Team.
22.	WOINCOURT.	22.00 17th inst.	3rd Rif.Bde. 1 Coy. 1 Cooker and 1 Team. 74th Field Ambulance.

3½ 17

4½

Transport 4 p.m.

P.T.O.

Train Serial No.	Station of Entrainment.	Time of Departure.	Units.
23.	FEUQUIERES.	24.00 night 17/18th.	Pioneer Battn. 1 Coy. 1 Cooker and 1 Team. 104th Field Coy. R.E. No. 2 Coy. 24th Divl.Train.

The Camp Commandant will proceed on Train No.3 and on arrival will arrange billets for Divisional Headquarters.

April 16th 1918.

Issued 12·45 AM.

E. Mason.
Major,
D.A.Q.M.G.,24th. Division.

Flat trucks required 11.

Covered trucks required for	H.D.	3.
" " " "	L.D.	6.
" " " "	Mn	1
		10

T.A.

8th Queens
1st Royal Fusiliers
3rd Rifle Brigade
17th L.T.M.Battery
O.C. No 2 Signal Section.

The following lorries have been ordered to convey blankets to the entraining stations :-

Serial No	No of lorries.	To report to.	At.	Time and date.	To be deposited at.	To convey.
3	1	H.Q. 17th I.Bde.	CAYEUX.	2.p.m. 17th inst.	WOINCOURT.	balnkets of 17th I.Bde H.Q., Bde Signals and L.T.M.Battery.
4.	1	H.Q. 8th Queens.	PENDE.	2.p.m. 17th inst.	WOINCOURT.	blankets.
5.	1.	H.Q. 1st Royal Fusiliers.	LANCHERES.	3.p.m. 17th inst.	FEUQUIERES.	blankets.
6.	1.	H.Q. 3rd Rifle Brigade.	CAYEUX.	7.p.m. 17th inst.	WOINCOURT	blankets.

16/4/18.

A.G.W.

[signature] Captain, for

Staff Captain 17th Infantry Brigade.

Appendix VIII

24th Division No. A.199/14?.

A10/47.

O.C. [illegible]

The Divisional Commander is much pleased with the manner in which the recent entrainment and detrainment were carried out by the units of the Division.

The expeditious and efficient manner in which the working parties loaded and unloaded the trains did much to hasten the completion of the move, the progress of which had been retarded by the lateness of the trains.

R. H. Collins.
Lieut-Colonel,
A.A.& Q.M.G., 24th Division.

20th April 1918.

War Diary

Appendix IX.

Hillcote,
Wodeland Road,
Guildford.

22nd. April 1918.

Sir,

I have pleasure in informing you that it was the unanimous desire of the Town Council at their last Meeting that I should communicate to you the following message:-

" The Town Council and inhabitants of Guildford having read with pride and deep admiration of the magnificent stand made by the Queen's at Le Verguier, while deploring the loss of so many gallant lives and feeling deepest sympathy with the relatives of those fallen townspeople, desire to congratulate all ranks on the noble stand made with our brave troops in defence of freedom and liberty".

I am, Dear Sir,

Yours faithfully,

[signature]

Mayor.

The Officer Commanding,
8th. Batt.
Queen's Royal West Surrey Regiment,

B. E. F.

FRANCE.

G.31

8th Bn THE QUEEN'S R.W.S REGt

WAR DIARY

for

MAY 1918

Volume XXXIII

June 4th 1918 P.C. Esdaile Major
Commanding
8th Bn "The Queens" RWS Regt

Instructions regarding War Diaries and Intelligence Summaries are contained in F. S. Regs., Part II. and the Staff Manual respectively. Title Pages will be prepared in manuscript.

Page 1

Army Form C. 2118

WAR DIARY
or
~~INTELLIGENCE SUMMARY~~
(Erase heading not required.)

May 1918 Vol XXXIII

Place	Date	Hour	Summary of Events and Information	Remarks and references to Appendices
MAGNICOURT - HOUDAIN.	1.	9AM	The Bn marched from MAGNICOURT to HOUDAIN. Arrived at HOUDAIN 11-45 AM and billetted for the night	Appendix I Bde O.O 23 Bn O.O 112 Map ref.
LES BREBIS - MAROC	2		Left HOUDAIN for LES BREBIS; route BARLIN-HERSIN-SAINS EN GOHELLE - PETIT SAINS. On arrival at LES BREBIS (8.15 PM) it was found that billetting accomodation for Bn could not be provided. Transport was accomodated in LES BREBIS with Q.M. Stores & D Coy in GRENAY, the rest of the Bn with Headquarters proceeding to MAROC. The Bde came into Divisional Reserve. Orders received to be prepared to move to positions of assembly in G 33 D and G 33 A in case of attack and to get in touch with 43rd Bde HQ at PREVITE CASTLE, G28 central. (Maps references LENS 36c SW1 and LOOS 36c NW3) Positions reconnoitred	
MAROC	3		Bn carried out Lewis Gun training etc. Warning received to be prepared for all forms of gas attack. Orders to assemble at G 27 D in case of attack and hold village line from G 34 c 4.8 to G 28 D 6.5 inclusive on receipt of orders	
	4		Coy Commanders reconnoitre line as above. Training as before. Coys practice taking up positions by night, marching in box respirators.	
	5		Church service at pumping station, FOSSE 11 DE BETHUNE. Dispositions in case of attack; Bn holding line as above with 12th Sherwood Foresters	

Page 2

Army Form C. 2118

WAR DIARY

or

~~INTELLIGENCE SUMMARY~~

(Erase heading not required.)

Instructions regarding War Diaries and Intelligence Summaries are contained in F. S. Regs., Part II. and the Staff Manual respectively. Title Pages will be prepared in manuscript.

May 1918 Vol XXXIII

Place	Date	Hour	Summary of Events and Information	Remarks and references to Appendices
MAROC	5		on right connecting up with 3rd Rifle Bde holding FOSSE 16 DE LENS and COUGAR POST with one Coy in support at EDGEWARE POST. 1st Royal Fusiliers on left from G 28 c 6.5 to G 23 c 6.0.	
"	6		Range practice and general training.	
"	7		Commanding Officer & Coy Commanders proceeded to 73rd Bde HQ and reconnoitre line which it was proposed to take over.	
"	8		Platoon commanders reconnoitred line and approaches. All arrangements for taking over subsequently cancelled on information received of probable attack by enemy.	
"	9		Orders received to have all transport ready to move and be prepared to take up battle positions at shortest notice.	
"	10		Situation unchanged.	
"	11		Bn notified that relief will proceed as arranged on following day.	
MAROC – TRENCHES.	12		The 17th Bde proceeded to take over part of the Divisional front from N 8 b 45.20 to H.32.D.40.00 held by troops of 72nd & 73rd Bdes. The Bn relieved units of 73rd Inf Bde in sector N 2 d. 35.80 – H 32. d. 40.00 C and D Coys relieving two Coys of the 13th Middlx Regt & A & B Coys taking over from	appendix II Bn OO H 4 Bde OO 233

1875 Wt. W593/826 1,000,000 4/15 J.B.C. & A. A.D.S.S./Forms/C. 2118.

R W Rose 2/Lt

Army Form C. 2118

WAR DIARY
~~or~~
INTELLIGENCE SUMMARY
(Erase heading not required.)

Instructions regarding War Diaries and Intelligence Summaries are contained in F. S. Regs., Part II. and the Staff Manual respectively. Title Pages will be prepared in manuscript.

May 1918

Place	Date	Hour	Summary of Events and Information	Remarks and references to Appendices
TRENCHES	12		C & B Coys. 1st Northamptonshire Regt. On completion of relief at 1 AM Bn came under orders of 73rd Bde. Dispositions were as follows:— Bn H.Q. in THE QUARRY; A Coy in CONDENTRENCH — GORDON ALLEY locality with Coy HQ in O.G.1; B Coy in HARRISON'S QUARRY, HARTS QUARRY and THE QUARRY with Coy HQ in THE QUARRY; C Coy in the front line zone with 3 Pltns and Coy HQ in CATAPULT TRENCH, 2 Pltns in NASH trench, 1 Pltn in MUD trench; D Coy in front line with 3 Pltns and Coy HQ in CATAPULT trench, 1 Pltn holding outposts East of this trench. Between 9 PM and 12 midnight the enemy shelled the back areas and Bn Headquarters intermittently. No damage was done. On the Bn going into the line 4 Officers and 78 ORs were left at the Divisional Wing, MAISNIL BOUCHE. Casualties 2 ORs wounded ~~1 OR wounded at duty~~	Sector LOOS area E of LES BREBIS. Map ref. SHEET ST NAZAIRE RIVER (36B NE. SE. 36C NW. SW.) LENS 36C SW1 & LOOS 36C NW.3
	13		Enemy artillery active especially on our back areas. Our artillery carried out harassing fire at intervals throughout the day and night. Bn HQ shelled by 5-9's between 1 AM and 3 AM. The Bn came under orders of 17th I. Bde.	
	14		Enemy artillery fairly active during the day and night. Between 2 PM and 3 PM several 5-9's fell in the vicinity of the QUARRY. Between 10-30 PM and 12 midnight our artillery carried out a gas shell bombardment on the enemy's support line and back areas just north of	R. Rose 2/Lt

Instructions regarding War Diaries and Intelligence Summaries are contained in F. S. Regs., Part II. and the Staff Manual respectively. Title Pages will be prepared in manuscript.

Page 4 Army Form C. 2118

WAR DIARY
or
~~INTELLIGENCE SUMMARY~~
(*Erase heading not required.*)

May 1918

Place	Date	Hour	Summary of Events and Information	Remarks and references to Appendices
TRENCHES	14		our front. Owing to the direction of the wind some of the gas blew back on our front line, but no damage was done. After dark the following changes in dispositions were made:- 1 Pltn of D Coy took over from the Pltn of C Coy in MUD trench. This pltn of C Coy came into CATAPULT trench & took over the right advanced post of D Coy. Casualties. 1 O.R. wounded. 2/Lt H.V. Shipton (E Surrey Regt) and 2/Lt H.V.D. Kerkhove (~~[illegible]~~) E. Surrey Regt taken on the strength of the Bn.	
	15		Our artillery active throughout the day especially on the enemy back areas. Enemy artillery shelled our front line ~~intermittently~~ with 5·9's, ~~and~~ + 2's and whizz-bangs. Direct hits were obtained on NETLEY and CATAPULT trenches. Casualties 11 O.R. wounded	
	16		Our artillery active with harassing fire day and night. During the day our aircraft exceptionally active. Enemy artillery fairly active during afternoon and evening. CATAPULT and NASH trenches received attention. A few shells fell round Bn HQ's and THE QUARRY.	
	17		Harassing fire by our artillery as before, especially during the night. The enemy guns were active and NETLEY TRENCH and MUD LANE were heavily shelled by 5·9's and 4·2's	R.W. [illegible]

1875 Wt. W593/826 1,000,000 4/15 J.B.C. & A. A.D.S.S./Forms/C. 2118.

Instructions regarding War Diaries and Intelligence Summaries are contained in F. S. Regs., Part II. and the Staff Manual respectively. Title Pages will be prepared in manuscript.

Army Form C. 2118

WAR DIARY
~~or~~
~~INTELLIGENCE SUMMARY~~
(Erase heading not required.)

May 1918

Place	Date	Hour	Summary of Events and Information	Remarks and references to Appendices
TRENCHES – LES BREBIS.	18		Our artillery as before, the heavies being particularly active on back areas. The enemy shelled freely during the day, CATAPULT and METLEY trenches receiving attention. The Bn was relieved ~~on~~ at night by the 3rd Rifle Bde in the northern sub-sector of the 17th Bde front. Relief was complete by 1-50 am on 19th and the Bn went into billets at LES BREBIS coming into Divisional Reserve. Casualties 1 O.R. wounded.	Appendix III Bde OO 234 Bn OO. H.5
LES BREBIS	19.		Training carried out under Bn arrangements. Details rejoined Bn from 24th Divl Reinforcement Camp at MAISNIL BOUCHE.	
"	20		Training as before.	
"	21		" "	
"	22		" " "	
"	23		" " Lt. H.W. Carter left Bn for 21st Div Signal Coy.	
"	24		The Bn relieved the 1st Royal Fusiliers in the right sub-sector of the Bde front. (~~H.22.d.40.00~~ – N.8.b.45.20 – N.2.d.4.8). Owing to the fact that the Battn on our right was carrying out a raid and also that gas projectors were being employed by us the relief was delayed and was not complete until 4.15 am on the 25th. On completion of relief Coys were disposed as follows:– "A" Coy (right front), 2 platoons in front line and 2 pltns in support with Coy H.Q. in DOUGLAS trench; B Coy (left front), one pltn in	Appendix IV Bn O.O. H.6.

1875 Wt. W593/826 1,000,000 4/15 J.B.C. & A. A.D.S.S./Forms/C. 2118.

Instructions regarding War Diaries and Intelligence Summaries are contained in F. S. Regs., Part II. and the Staff Manual respectively. Title Pages will be prepared in manuscript.

WAR DIARY

~~or~~

~~INTELLIGENCE SUMMARY~~

(Erase heading not required.)

Army Form C. 2118

May 1918

Place	Date	Hour	Summary of Events and Information	Remarks and references to Appendices
TRENCHES	24.		front line and 3 in support, Coy HQ in CATAPULT trench. "C" Coy in support manned the RED LINE with H.Q in COWDEN trench. D Coy was in reserve with H.Q in 217 MAIN ST CITE ST PIERRE. Bn HQ were established in HARRISONS CRATER. Previous to relief 6 Officers and 89 O.R's were sent to Divl Reception Camp MAISNIL BOUCHE after H.Q.M.	
	25		The day and night were comparatively quiet. The left hand post of B Coy (1 Pltn) at the junction of NESTOR and NUN trenches was taken over by the 3rd Rifle Bde, the change being complete by 11.30 P.M. The left flank of the Bn then ran by the RAILWAY N.2.d.45.50 - N2C 25.55 - NESTOR TR - N2.C.20.90.	Appendix V Bn O.O. A4.
	26.		At about 1 A.M. the enemy commenced a bombardment of our front line, apparently in retaliation for the Gas Projector ~~attack~~ bombardment. Our casualties were 5 O.R's wounded. Our artillery was not so active as usual	
	27.		Our artillery became again active, especially on back areas and that of the enemy was similarly employed during the day, turning on to the front system at night. Considerable aerial activity was shown on our part in the day time. One enemy aeroplane flew very low over our lines at 7.30 P.M. Casualties four O.R's wounded.	
	28.		Our artillery carried out harassing fire; that of the enemy was more active than usual, the front line being heavily shelled.	[illegible signature]

Instructions regarding War Diaries and Intelligence Summaries are contained in F. S. Regs., Part II. and the Staff Manual respectively. Title Pages will be prepared in manuscript.

WAR DIARY

or

~~INTELLIGENCE SUMMARY~~

(Erase heading not required.)

Page 4

Army Form C. 2118

May 1918.

Place	Date	Hour	Summary of Events and Information	Remarks and references to Appendices
TRENCHES	29		Our Artillery active during the day and night. The enemy fired gas shells round about DOUGLAS TRENCH.	
	30.		Artillery on both sides quieter than usual. Inter-Company reliefs were carried out. "C" Coy relieving A Coy and D Coy relieving "B" Coy. Dispositions as before. Relief was complete at 12 midnight. Two O.R's were wounded.	appendix VI B.2.00 A.8.
	31.		Our Artillery fairly active. The enemy sent over gas projectiles at about 11.45 P.M. Casualties 2 O.R's killed and 7 wounded. Lt. G. A. R. Shimming left for RAF	

P. C. Esdaile Major
Commanding
8th Bn The Queens Regt

Appendix I

SECRET.

Copy No. 1

17th INFANTRY BRIGADE ORDER No. 232.

Ref: Map.
1/40,000
Sheet 36B.

1. 17th Infantry Brigade Group will march tomorrow, 1st Day to HOUDAIN Area in accordance with Table "A" attached.

2. The march will be continued after dinners on the 2nd Day to the area LES BREBIS - PETIT SAINS - BULLY GRENAY when the 17th Infantry Brigade will come into Divisional Reserve.

3. The following intervals will be maintained throughout the march :-

400 Yards between Battalions.
200 " " other Units & Transport.

4. Units will send in advance the usual billeting parties. Billets in HOUDAIN will be allotted by Area Commandant.

5. Lorries will be available for conveyance of blankets. Exact details will be issued later.

6. ACKNOWLEDGE.

L.W. Mackenzie Major,
Brigade Major, 17th Infantry Brigade.

Issued to Sigs
at 9.30 p.m.
30th April, 18.

Copy No. 1.to 8th Bns.
2. 1st Royal Fusiliers.
3. 3rd Rifle Brigade.
4. 17th L.T.M.Battery.
5. 17th I.Bde. Sigs.
6. B.T.O.
7. 195 Coy. A.S.C.
8. 74th Field Ambce.
9. 24th Divn: "G"
10. War Diary.
11. File.
12. 104 Fd Coy R.E.

MARCH TABLE "A" to accompany 17th Infantry Brigade Order No.232.

Serial No.	Date.	Unit.	From.	To.	Starting point Place	Starting point Time.	Route.	Remarks
1.	May 1st.	3rd Rifle Brigade.	OSTREVILLE.	LA COMTE	Road junct: T.4.a.80.30	9.00 am	ORLENCOURT - MONCHY-BRETON - MAGNICOURT - HOUVELIN - LA COMTE - BEUGIN - HOUDAIN.	
2.	May 1st.	17th L.T.M.Battery.	OSTREVILLE.	BEUGIN	-- do --	9.15 am.		To follow rear of 3rd R.Bde
3.	May 1st.	17th I.Bde. H.Qrs.	ORLENCOURT.	HOUDAIN	------	9.25 am.		
4.	May 1st.	1st Royal Fusiliers.	MONCHY-BRETON.	HOUDAIN	Road junct: 0.32.b.20.40	9.30 am.		
5.	May 1st.	8th Queens.	MAGNICOURT.	HOUDAIN	Road junct: 0.29.c.40.20	10.0 am.		
6.	May 1st.	74th Field Ambce.	ORLENCOURT.	BEUGIN	------	10.0 am.		
7.	May 1st.	104th Field Co.R.E.	HOUVELIN.	BEUGIN	Road junct: 0.29.b.0.9	10.0		
8.	May 1st.	195 Coy. A.S.C.	ROCOURT.	BAJUS	--------	---		

MARCH TABLE "B" to accompany 17th Infantry Brigade Order No.232 dated 30/4/18.

Serial No.	Date.	Unit.	From.	To	Starting point. Place.	Time.	Route.	Remarks.
1	May 2nd.	3rd Rifle Brigade	MAGNICOURT.	BULLY-GRENAY.	-	-	FERVILLERS- HERMIN GAUCHIN-LEGAL - FRESNICOURT - VERDREL BOUVIGNY - BOYEFFLES BOYEFFLES.	To clear FREVILLERS by 11.30 am. not to pass Rally Crossing R.8.c.2.3 before 4.30 p.m.
2	May 2nd	104 Field Co. RE.	HOUVELIN	LES BREBIS	Road junc: 0.29.c.8.4	11 am.	As per Serial No. 1 thence Road junct: R,3.d.1.8 - LES-BREBIS.	To follow in rear of 3rd Rifle Bde.
3	May 2nd	17th Inf: Bde H.Q	HOUDAIN	LES BREBIS	Road junc: J.35.d.5.4	2 pm.	BARLIN - Road junc: K.27.c.5.3 - HERSIN - SAINS-en-GOHELLE - PETIT SAINS.	
4	May 2nd	8th Queens.	- do -	- do -	- do -	~~4.5~~ 5.5 pm.	-- do -- do --	
5.	May 2nd	1st Roy. Fus.	- do -	- do -	- do -	5.15 pm	-- do -- do --	
6.	May 2nd	17th L.T.M.B.	DIVION	BULLY-GRENAY	- do -	5.30 pm	HOUDAIN - thence as in Serial No.3	
7.	May 2nd	195 Co. A.S.C.	ROCOURT	BARLIN	--do--	------	----------	

NOTES. 1. Distances of 400 yds between Battalions and 200 yards between other Units.
2. Route from HOUDAIN to Starting Point J.35.d.5.4 Road through junction J.33.a.4.2 thence along Main Road through J.33.d.central - J.34.c. & d.

Issued to Sigs
at 6.15 p.m.
1st May 1918.

To all recipients of 17th Infantry Brigade Order No. 232 dated 30/4/18.

ACKNOWLEDGE.

L.E.M. Mackenzie Major,
Brigade Major, 17th Infantry Brigade.

Acknowledge

Reference MARCH TABLE "B" dated 1st May 1918.

---

1. Add 3 (three) hours to all times stated therein.

2. Units will not arrive in new area before 8 p.m.

3. <u>ACKNOWLEDGE</u>.

L.G. Mackenzie Major,

2nd May, 1918. Brigade Major, 17th Inf: Bde.

Issued to all recipients of MARCH TABLE "B" dated 1/5/18.

SECRET.

Q.7/36.

8th Queens
1st Royal Fusiliers
3rd Rifle Brigade
17th L.T.M.Battery
104th Company R.E.
195th Company A.S.C.
BRigade Transport Officer.

With reference to 17th Infantry Brigade Order 232 dated 30th April (table "B" dated 1/5/18);

(1). Advance parties will proceed to the new area to-morrow 2nd instant by lorry. Two lorries will be at Headquarters 3rd Rifle Brigade MAGNICOURT at 8.a.m. where advance parties of 3rd Rifle Brigade, 195th Company A.S.C. and 104th Company R.E. will meet them. The lorries will then report at this Brigade Headquarter HOUDAIN where remaining advance parties will join. Strengths as follows :-

Each Battalion .... 1 Officer and 6 Other Ranks.
T.M.B., 104 Coy R.E } .... 1 Officer and 2 Other Ranks.
A.S.C.
17th I.Bde H.Q. .... 1 Officer and 3 Other Ranks.

(2). Lorries for packs and blankets will be supplied as follows:-

UNIT.	No of lorries.	To report at.	Time.	Destination.
8th Queens.	5	Church HOUDAIN.	9.a.m.	LES BREBIS.
1st Roy Fus.	5	------ do -----	10.a.m.	LES BREBIS.
3rd Rifle B.	5	Bn H.Q. MAGNICOURT.	10.a.m.	BULLY GRENAY.
17th L.T.M.B.	One	Church DIVION.	10.a.m.	BULLY GRENAY.
17th I.Bde H.Qrs.	2	Bde H.Q. HOUDAIN	2.p.m.	LES BREBIS.
104 Coy R.E.	1	H.Q.HOUVELIN.	10.a.m.	LES BREBIS.

(3). An Officer will be detailed to be in charge of each Battalion lorry-convoy. Officers i/c Advance parties will arrange a guide for lorries at their destination.

(4). Billeting lists will be obtained from the Town Majors of LES BREBIS and BULLY GRENAY.

W Aske Lt
for Captain,
Staff Captain 17th Infantry Brigade.

1/5/18.

A.G.W.

appendix I

SECRET. COPY No ......

8th Bn. THE QUEENS. R.W.S. REGT

OPERATION ORDER. No. A.2

MAP REF. 36B. 30th APRIL. 1918.

1 The Battn will march from MAGNICOURT to HOUDAIN tomorrow 1st May.

2 Starting Point:-
Place O.29.C.40.20. Time.- 10. a.m.

3 Route:- MAGNICOURT - LA COMTE - BEUGIN - HOUDAIN

4 Order of MARCH:- DRUMS, C.D.A.B. H.Q. Coy. Contacts, Transport.
Coy Lewis Gun Limbers will be in rear of each Coy.

5 DRESS:- Full Marching Order.

6 The Battn will follow the 1st ROYAL FUSILIERS, 400x distance.

7 BAGGAGE:
Blankets (tightly rolled in bundles of 10) will be stacked at Q.M. Stores by 8. A.M. . The Blankets of Contacts will be stacked separately outside BILLET No 46, also Rifles & Packs of the Drums, by 8.a.m.
Officers Kits, Coy Boxes, etc., will be stacked at Q.M. Stores 8. a.m.
Mess Kits to be ready for collection by Mess Cart 8.30. A.M.

8 Billeting Party:- A Billeting Party consisting of one N.C.O per Coy & Transport will report to Lieut G.W. Wyatt at Q.M. Stores at 9.AM.
This party will draw bicycles from the Quartermaster.
They will report to the Area Commandant on arrival at HOUDAIN.

9 ACKNOWLEDGE:- O.O. A2.

ISSUED AT. 11.55 p.m

[signature]
Capt & Adjutant
8th Queens Regt.

COPIES TO:- No 1. Commanding Officer.
" 2 2nd in Command

No. 3. O.C. A. Coy	No 7. O.C. H.Q. Coy.	No 11 R.S.M.
" 4. -- B. --	8. M.O.	" 12 FILE.
" 5 -- C --	9. Q.M.	" 13. WAR DIARY.
" 6 -- D --	10. TRANS. Sgt.	

appendix II

SECRET.

Copy No. 1

17th INFANTRY BRIGADE ORDER No.233.

Ref: Maps:
1/10,000, Sheets
LENS & LOOS.
1/40,000, Sheet 36c.

1. The 17th Infantry Brigade will take over part of the Divisional front from N.8.b.45.20 to H.32.d.40.00 (Centre Sector), now held by troops of 72nd & 73rd Infantry Bdes, as under :-

   (a) On the night 12th/13th May, 8th Queens will relieve troops of 73rd Infantry Brigade in the line from N.2.d.35.80 to H.32.d.40.00.
   Relief to be complete by 6 a.m. 13th May.

   (b) On the night 13th/14th May, 1st Royal Fus. will relieve troops of 72nd Infantry Brigade in the line from N.8.b.45.20 to N.2.d.35.80.
   Relief to be complete by ~~6~~ a.m. 14th May.

   (c) 3rd Rifle Brigade will be in Brigade Reserve. They will move to LES BREBIS and will take over billets vacated by 1st Royal Fusiliers. on 13th May.

   (d) 17th L.T.M.Battery will relieve guns of 72nd 73rd Brigades in the sector, on nights corresponding to Infantry reliefs.

2. Move will take place in accordance with attached Table "A".

3. BOUNDARIES :-

   Southern (between 17th & 72nd Infantry Brigades)
   Front Line N.8.b.45.20 - along CANTEEN ALLEY (exc) N.7.a.90.50 - along COUNTER ALLEY inclusive to N.7.a.00.35 - M.12.a.00.85 - M.11.a.8.8 - VILLAGE LINE M.9.b.60.80 - MAROC (inc) to railway M.8.d.35.80 - thence N.W., along railway to BULLY GRENAY (exc)

   Northern (between 17th & 73rd Infantry Brigades)
   Front Line H.32.d.40.00 junction NELSON & NETLEY ALLEY (N.2.a.20.90) OG 1 at N.1.a.25.90 - TOWER BRIDGE G.36.c. (exc) - thence along southern outskirts of LOOS to Cross Roads G.34.d.80.50 - thence due West to MAROC (inc).

   INTER-BATTALION BOUNDARY:-
   NESTOR TRENCH at N.2.d.4.8 - BLUE LINE at N.1.d.8.6 - RED LINE at N.1.c.2.9 - M.6.d.5.7 thence due west - (DOUBLE CRASSIER inclusive to Right Battalion)

4. Trench Stores, Maps, Photographs, Log Books, details of Work in hand and projected will be carefully taken over and receipts forwarded to these H.Qrs within 36 hours of completion of relief.

5. Units will forward Sketch Map showing dispositions by last D.R., 15th May.

6. All other details of relief will be arranged direct between Os.C Units.

7. Command of the Centre Sector will pass to B.G.C., 17th Infantry Brigade at a time to be notified later.

8. Completion of reliefs will be wired to Brigade H.Qrs using the following Code Words :-
   For night 12th/13th May..............BOWLER. 1" for [illegible] "Bowler 2" for [illegible]
   For night 13th/14th May..............HAT.

9. 17th Infantry Brigade Advanced H.Qrs will be established at FOSSE 5 (M.3.b.2.8) 12 noon 13th May.

10. <u>ACKNOWLEDGE!</u>

L.D.A. Mackenzie
Major,
Brigade Major, 17th Inf: Bde.

Issued to Sigs:
at_______p.m.
11th May, 18.

Copy No.		Copy No.	
1	to 8th Queens.	2	to 1st Royal Fus.
3	3rd Rifle Bde.	4	17th L.T.M.Batty.
5	Sigs: 17th I.B.	6	24th Div: "G"
7	24th Div: "Q"	8	C.R.A.
9	72nd Inf: Bde.	10	73rd Inf: Bde.
11	24th Bn. M.G.C.	12	195 Coy. A.S.C.
13	B.T.O.	14	War Diary.
15	File.		

RELIEF TABLE "A" (issued with 17th Inf: Bdo Order 233 dated 1[illegible]th May.)

Serial No.	Date.	Unit.	From	To	Relieving	Rendezvous for Guides.	Remarks.
1.	12th/13th May.	8th Queens 2 Coys.		Northern Subsector.	13th Mid'sx Reg Right front and Support Coys.		1. Times for guides to be arranged by C.Os concerned. 2. 8th Queens will remain under orders of 73rd Inf.Bdo until command of Centre Sector passes to 17th I.B on 14th May. *3. 1 Officer & 4 N.C.Os (1 per platoon) will remain behind until arrival of Coy of 8th Queens to shew Alarm positions. ø4. Accommodation in M.6.b.
		1 Coy.		Quarry M.6.a.	7th Northamptons 1 Coy. *		
		1 Coy. ø	MAROC			HARRISONS CRATER. M.6.c.20.50	
		H.Qrs. Quarry M.6.a.					
2.	13th/14th May.	1st Roy. F. 2 Coys.		Southern Subsector.	(8th R.W.Kents. (In BLUE LINE & forward posts)	Rly crossg M.10.c. 75.25.	1. Times for guides to be arranged by C.Os concerned. *2. 7th Northamptons will leave behind caretakers until arrival of 1st Roy Fus.
		1 Coy.			9th E.Surreys. RED LINE.	- do -	
		½ Coy. ½ Coy.	LES BREBIS	Harrisons Crater. M.12.a.2.8.	----	----	
		H.Qrs. Harrisons Crater M.6.c.20.50					
3.	13th May.	3rd Rifle Bde.	BULLY GRENAY	LES BREBIS	1st Royal Fus.		

Serial No	Date	Unit.	From	To	Relieving	Rendezvous for Guides.	Remarks.
4.	12th/13th May.	17th L.T.M.B 2 Guns.		Line. N.2.a.60.65 N.2.a.45.55	73rd L.T.M.B		Reserve Guns N.7.a.20.90 M.6.b.80.55
	13th/14th May.	2 Guns	LES BREBIS ~~MAROC~~	N.2.d.35.15 N.8.b.30.25	72nd L.T.M.B.		
		H.Qrs. N.12.b.05.65.					

NOTES. 1. There will be no movement E of MAROC + M.8.b.8.0 before 8.45 p.m.

appendix II

SECRET. COPY No. 16.

8th Bn THE QUEEN'S. R.W.S. Regt.

OPERATION ORDER. No. A.4.

MAP REF:- 1/10.000, SHEETS. LENS & LOOS. 1/40.000, SHEET. 36C

12th MAY. 1918.

1. The Battn will relieve 2 Coys and Bn. H.Q., 13th MIDDLESEX REGT and 2 Coys of 7th NORTHAMPTONS in the Centre Sector of the Divl Front on the right of 12th/13th inst.

2. C. Coy. (Queens) will relieve Coy (Middlesex)
   D. --- --- --- --- " --- --- --- --- " ---
   A. --- --- --- --- " --- "C" --- (NORTHANTS)
   B --- --- --- --- " --- B --- --- " ---

3. Coys will move off in the following order:-
   "D" "C", "B". "A". H.Q. Coy will follow the rear platoon of "B" Coy.
   "D" Coy will leave GRENAY at 8. P.M.
   200x interval between platoons.

4. Lewis Gun Limbers will go with the leading platoons of each Coy.

5. TRENCH STORES:- All Trench Stores, Work in hand and proposed, Defence Schemes, etc will be carefully taken over. Certificates of Stores etc taken over to reach O.R. by 12 NOON, 13th inst.

6. Completion of relief will be reported by runner or wire using Code Word "CHAOS".
   "A" & "B" Coy. will report completion of relief to Bn. O.R. Quarry.
   "C" & D --- --- " --- --- " --- --- --- 13th Middx. Hd Qrs

7. ACKNOWLEDGE:- O.O. A.4.

Issued To:- 12.30 p.m.

E. D. Donnell.
Capt & Adjutant
8th Queens Regt.

COPIES TO:-

No. 1. Commanding Officer
2. H.Q. 17. I. B.
3. O.C. A. Coy.
4. --- B ---
5 --- C ---
6 --- D ---
7 --- H.Q. ---
No 8. M.O.
9. T.O.
10. Q.M.
11. Sigs
12. R.S.M.
13. 13th Middx
14. 7th Norths.
No. 15. File. No. 16. War Diary.

SECRET. Appendix III COPY No. 16

8TH BN THE QUEEN'S R.W.S. REGT

OPERATION ORDER No. A.5

MAP REF:- 1/10.000. Sheets. LENS & LOOS 1/40.000 Sheet 36C 17TH MAY 1918.

1. The Battalion will be relieved by the 3rd Bn Rifle Brigade in the northern Sub-Sector of the Brigade front on the night of 18th/19th inst.

2. "A" Coy. (Queens) will be relieved by "B" Coy (3rd RIFLE BRIGADE)
"B" –"– —"— —"— "C" –"– —"—
"C" –"– —"— —"— "A" –"– —"—
"D" –"– —"— —"— "D" –"– —"—

3. On relief the Battalion will be in Divisional Reserve at LES BREBIS.

4. Rear Battn H.Q will make all arrangements for billets and will have 1. Guide per platoon at road junction M.1.d.60.32 to take the men direct to the billets.

5. Company L.G. limbers will be at CROSS ROADS M.5.a.50.85 at 12 M.N. that for H.Q Company at 11 P.M.

6. Guides:- 1 guide per platoon and 1. for each Advance post will be at HARRISON CRATER at 10- P.M.

7. TRENCH STORES:- All Trench Stores, Petrol Tins filled, Work in hand and proposed, Defence Schemes etc will be carefully handed over. Certificates of Stores etc hand over to reach O.R. by 12 NOON 19th inst.

8. Completion of relief will be reported by runner or wire using CODE WORD. "FUN."

9. ACKNOWLEDGE :- O.O. A.5

Issued AT: 8.0c p.m.

E. D. Dowell.
Capt & Adjutant
8 Queens Regt

Copies To:-

No 1 Commanding Officer	No 8 M.O
2. H.Q. 17. I.B	9 T.O
3. O.C "A" COY.	10 Q.M.
4 –"– "B" –"–	11. SIGS
5 –"– "C" –"–	12 R.S.M.
6 –"– "D" –"–	13. 3rd RIFLE BRIGADE
7 –"– H.Q –"–	14 1st ROYAL FUSILIERS
No 15 FILE	No 16 WAR DIARY

To:- O.C. Company
From Adjutant.

Ref O.O.#5 para 6. Guides for "A.B & HQ. Coys" will not be required. There will be a train at "Green Mound Dump" tomorrow night to take back Officers Mess Kits, Trench Bundles, Orderley Room Boxes, Dixies etc. Companies must have all their stuff at dump ready for loading by 9. pm.

E.S. Dowell.
Capt & Adjutant.

appendix III

Secret | Copy No 1

17th INFANTRY BRIGADE ORDER No.234

Ref. Trench Maps
1/10,000

1. The 3rd Rifle Brigade will relieve the 8th Queens in the Northern Subsector of the Brigade front on the night 18/19th MAY 1918.

2. On relief the 8th Queens will be in Divisional Reserve at LES BREBIS and will take over billets vacated by 3rd Rifle Bde.

3. All defence schemes, work in hand and proposed, trench stores, maps etc., will be carefully taken and handed over and receipts forwarded to these Headquarters within 36 hours of completion of relief.

4. All other details of relief will be made direct between O's.C. concerned.

5. Completion of relief will be wired to Brigade Headquarters stating time at which completed.

6. All future reliefs will be carried out in accordance with attached table.

7. ACKNOWLEDGE.

W R ? Bye Captain
for MAJOR.
Brigade Major 17th Infantry Brigade

Issued to
Sigs. at 11 am.
15th MAY 1918.

Copy No	To	Copy No	To
1	8th Queens	2	1st Royal Fus.
3	3rd Rifle Bde	4	17th L.T.M.Btty.
5	Sigs.17th Inf.Bde	6	24th Div.'G'
7	24th Div. 'Q'	8	C.R.A.
9	72nd Inf.Bde	10	73rd Inf.Bde.
11	Centre Group	12	24th Bn M.G.C.
13	195 Coy.A.S.C,.	14	Bde Transport Offr,
15	104 Field Coy R.E.	16	73rd Field Amblnce.
17	War Diary.	18	File

Appendix IV

Secret. Copy No. 14....

8TH BN. THE QUEENS. R.W.S. REGT.

OPERATION ORDER. No. A.6

MAP REF:- 1/10.000 Sheets. LENS & LOOS. 1/40'000 SHEETS 36C MAY. 1918.

1 The Battn will relieve the 1st ROYAL FUSILIERS in the Left Sub Sector of BRIGADE FRONT on the night of the 24th/25th inst.

2 'A' Coy (Queens) will relieve 'A' Coy (R.F.) RIGHT COY.
'B' — — — 'B' — — LEFT —
'C' — — — 'C' — —
'D' — — — 'D' — —

3 ORDER of MARCH: 'A' 'B' 'C' 'D'. 'A' Coy moving off at 8.45 P.M. 200x interval between platoons. H.Q. Coy will fall in with the rear platoon of 'D' Coy proceeding to HARRISON'S CRATER.

4. ROUTE:- Les Brebis - MAROC - FOSSE 11 Rd - X Roads - M 10. C. 5. 4

5 Guides:- 1 Guide per platoon will meet Coys at FOSSE 16. Guides for Forward Posts will be at Forward Platoons H.Q. Guides for A. B & C. Coys. will conduct platoons via Eddy Dump.

6. LEWIS GUNS:- Coy. Lewis Gun Limbers will go with the leading platoon of each Coy. H.Q. Lewis Gun Limber will follow in rear of H.Q. Coy.
Lewis Gun Limbers will proceed as far as possible, but not beyond E. of LENS - BETHUNE Road.

7 BAGGAGE:- Officers Trench Bundles, Mess kits, etc will be dumped at Q.M. Stores ready for collection by 7 p.m.
Officers Valises etc not required for Trenches, will be returned to Q.M. Stores during the day.
Coys will arrange to collect Rations, Baggage, etc at their respective Dumps. i.e. A.B & C Coys, Eddy Dump. D & H.Q. Coy. at M.O.C. 7.2.

8 TRENCH STORES:- All Trench Stores, Petrol Tins filled, Work in hand and proposed, Defence Schemes etc will be carefully taken over. Certificates of Stores etc taken over to reach O.R. by 7.30 A.M. 25th inst.
'D' Coy will detail 1 N.C.O. & 3 men to take over Battn. H.Q. S.A.A. Bombs etc., Dump at Eddy.
This party will go on in advance.

9 Completion of relief will be reported by runner or wire using Code Word "BLUFF".

10 ACKNOWLEDGE O.O. A.6.

Issued at 11.45. p.m.

E. L. Donnell.
Capt & Adjutant
8th Queens Regt

COPIES TO:-

No 1.	COMMANDING OFFICER.	No 8.	T.O.
2	H.Q. 17. I.B.	9.	Q.M.
3.	O.C. A. COY	10.	M.O.
4	— B —	11.	1st R.F.
5	— C —	12.	R.S.M.
6	— D —	13.	A.L.S.
7	— H.Q. —	14.	War Diary

Appendix V

Secret. Copy No. 8.

8th Bn. The Queens R.W.S. Regt.

OPERATION ORDER No A.7.

Map Ref 36c S.W.1. May 25th 1915.

(1) One platoon of "B" Coy (Queens) at present occupying Left Post at junction of Nestor & Nuns Trench will be relieved by a platoon of 3rd Rifle Brigade.
This relief to be completed by 11.30. p.m. this evening.

(2) On completion of this relief the Left Flank of the Queens will be Railway N. 2.d. 45-50 - N. 2 c. 25.55 - Nestor Tr. - N.2.c. 20 70 - thence as before.

3 One platoon "B" Coy (Queens) will relieve Left Platoon of "A" Coy (Queens) (HdQrs in Cosy Tr) and post found there-from. Left Coy (Queens) i.e. "B" Coy will be responsible for Cosy Trench, but "A" Coy (Queens) i.e. Right Coy will have the right of use of Cosy Tr.

4 Trench Stores etc will be carefully handed over and receipt taken. Certificate of Stores etc handed over to reach O.R. by 6.AM 26th inst.

5 Completion of relief will be reported by wire using the Code Word "Wet".

6 Acknowledge. O.O. A.7.

Issued at 7.5.p.m.

[illegible]
Capt & Adjutant
8th Queens Regt.

Copies to.

No 1	Officer Commanding	No 5	O.C. C. Coy
" 2	H.Q. 17 I.B.	" 6	— D. —
" 3	O.C. A Coy	" 7	File
" 4	— B —	" 8	War Diary

No 9 Sig. Off
" 10 Intell Off
" 11 M.O.
" 12. 3rd R.B.

Appendix VI

Secret.

Copy No. 10.

8TH BN. THE QUEENS. R.W.S. REGT.

OPERATION ORDER. No A.8.

Map Ref. Sheet 36c S.W.1 — MAY. 29TH 1918

1 The following inter-Company relief will take place during evening of 30th May. 1918.

(a) "C" Company will relieve "A" Coy in the Right Sector of Bn front.

(b) "D" Company will relieve "B" Coy in the Left Sector of Bn front.

(c) "A" Company will move back to Support position vacated by "C" Company.

(d). "B" Company will move back to Reserve position vacated by "D" Company.

Relief to be completed by 8.p.m.

2 All Trench Stores &c will be handed over and receipts obtained. Certificate of Stores handed over to reach Bn. H.Q. by 8.a.m on 31st inst.

3 Defence Schemes, Maps, Photographs, & "Programmes of Work in hand & proposed" will be handed over by each Company.

4 All details as to any Working & Carrying Parties being supplied by Support & Reserve Coys will be carefully handed over to "A" & "B" Coys by "C" & "D" Coys respectively.

5. Completion of relief will be reported by wire using Code Word "HAPPY".

6 ACKNOWLEDGE:- O.O. A.8

Issued at 5.40 p.m
By RUNNER

A. V. [illegible]
2nd Lieut
for Capt & Adjutant
8th Queens' Regt

Copies to:-

No. 1. COMMANDING OFFICER. — No 7. T.O.
2. H.Q. 17 I.B. — 8. Q.M.
3. O.C. A. Coy — 9. File.
4. — B — — 10. WAR DIARY
5. — C — — 11. [illegible]
6. — D — — 12. S.G.C.

No 13. M.O.
— 14. O.C. [illegible]

932

28031 W3125/M2250 1000m 6/17 M.R.Co.,Ltd. (1367) Forms W3091.

Army Form W. 3091.

VII 34

Cover for Documents.

Natures of Enclosures.

8th Bn The Queen's R W S Regt

WAR DIARY

VOLUME XXXIV

JUNE 1918

H. J. C. Pierse Major

July 2nd 1918

Lieut Col
Commanding
8th Bn The Queens Regt

Notes, or Letters written.

Instructions regarding War Diaries and Intelligence Summaries are contained in F. S. Regs., Part II. and the Staff Manual respectively. Title Pages will be prepared in manuscript.

JUNE 1918

WAR DIARY
or
~~INTELLIGENCE SUMMARY~~
(Erase heading not required.)

Army Form C. 2118
PAGE I

VOLUME XXXIV

Place	Date	Hour	Summary of Events and Information	Remarks and references to Appendices
TRENCHES	1st	-	Battalion holding the Right Sub-sector of 17th Inf: Bde front. N.8.b.45.70 to N.2.d.4.8. (Ref: LENS Map). Artillery on both sides very active on back areas during the night.	
	2nd	-	Situation very quiet during the day. Both Artilleries active during the night. Our Patrols active - nothing seen of enemy patrols	
	3rd	-	Situation unchanged - Hostile artillery more active than usual - bursts of rapid fire opened at intervals throughout the day on both our forward and back areas. Our Patrols again very active. Lieut. P.A. REEVES (Cyclist Corps) Joined the Bn. for duty.	
	4th	-	At 11pm. a Raid was carried out by the 73rd Bde on our left resulting in considerable artillery retaliation on our front. During the	[illegible]

1875 Wt. W593/826 1,000,000 4/15 J.B.C. & A. A.D.S.S./Forms/C. 2118.

Instructions regarding War Diaries and Intelligence Summaries are contained in F. S. Regs., Part II. and the Staff Manual respectively. Title Pages will be prepared in manuscript.

June 1918

WAR DIARY
or
~~INTELLIGENCE SUMMARY~~
(Erase heading not required.)

VOLUME XXXIV

Army Form C. 2118
PAGE II.

Place	Date	Hour	Summary of Events and Information	Remarks and references to Appendices
TRENCHES	4th		night our patrol had to withdraw owing to this enemy retaliation.	
			Captain W.S. MOSSE M.C. to Hospital.	Appendix I.
	5th		The Bn: was relieved in the line by the 3rd Bn: Rifle Brigade and moved into Divisional Reserve at LES BREBIS. During the relief enemy artillery were again active with sharp bursts of fire - Casualties 2 Killed.	O.O. A.9
LES BREBIS.	6th		Battalion in Divisional Reserve and commenced training.	
	7th		Training. Lines of defence to be occupied by the Reserve Bn: in the event of an attack - were reconnoitred by Company and Platoon Commanders. Lieut: L.F. WEIR rejoined the Bn: for duty from 18th Corps Reinforcement Camp. Captain H.C. MORLEY (The Buffs) joined the Bn: for duty.	

1875 Wt. W593/826 1,000,000 4/15 J.B.C. & A. A.D.S.S./Forms/C. 2118.

Instructions regarding War Diaries and Intelligence Summaries are contained in F. S. Regs., Part II. and the Staff Manual respectively. Title Pages will be prepared in manuscript.

June 1918

WAR DIARY
or
~~INTELLIGENCE SUMMARY~~
(Erase heading not required.)

Army Form C. 2118

PAGE III

VOLUME XXXIV

Place	Date	Hour	Summary of Events and Information	Remarks and references to Appendices
LES BREBIS	8th	-	Battalion in Divisional Reserve - Training. &c	
	9th	-	Battalion in Divisional Reserve - Training &c. 400 men supplied for pushing truck of gas cylinders up to left sector for a gas Beam attack. 7 casualties from gas.	
	10th	-	Battalion in Divisional Reserve - Training &c.	
			2/Lieut. E. JENKINS (West Kent) joined the Bn: for duty.	Appendix II
	11th	-	Battalion in Divisional Reserve. During the night the Bn: relieved the 1st Bn: Royal Fusiliers in the left sub-sector of the Brigade front. C Company in Right front line. D Coy in left front line. B Coy in support and A Coy in Reserve. Bn: HQ "THE QUARRIES". 1st Bn: Royal Fusiliers moved back to LES BREBIS in Divisional Reserve. Relief completed at 12.20 a.m. (12th) Following Officers posted to the Bn: for duty:- 2nd Lieuts: W. G. CAMPBELL G.H. NEWMAN and C. BLAND of Sussex Yeomanry.	O.O. 10.

1875 Wt. W593/826 1,000,000 4/15 J.B.C. & A. A.D.S.S./Forms/C. 2118.

Instructions regarding War Diaries and Intelligence Summaries are contained in F. S. Regs., Part II. and the Staff Manual respectively. Title Pages will be prepared in manuscript.

June 1918

WAR DIARY
~~or~~
~~INTELLIGENCE SUMMARY~~

(Erase heading not required.)

Army Form C. 2118

PAGE IV

VOLUME XXXIV

Place	Date	Hour	Summary of Events and Information	Remarks and references to Appendices
TRENCHES	12th	-	During the day large number of our aeroplanes crossed the line flying over to the enemy back area. During the day our artillery were fairly quiet. Between 10 pm and 12 mn Artillery very active on enemy front line. Heavy and field Artillery active during the night on enemy back area. Enemy Artillery was quiet. Slight activity on our front line between 8.30 pm and 10 pm. A few gas shells were fired into our back areas.	
	13th	-	Our aeroplanes again very active. Artillery on both sides very quiet during the day. During the night our Artillery became very active on enemy back area – tracks – dumps &c. Enemy machine guns fairly active on our front and support line. The following honours	

1875 Wt. W593/826 1,000,000 4/15 J.B.C. & A. A.D.S.S./Forms/C. 2118.

Instructions regarding War Diaries and Intelligence Summaries are contained in F. S. Regs., Part II. and the Staff Manual respectively. Title Pages will be prepared in manuscript.

Army Form C. 2118

PAGE V.

WAR DIARY or INTELLIGENCE SUMMARY

(Erase heading not required.)

June 1918 VOLUME XXXIV

Place	Date	Hour	Summary of Events and Information	Remarks and references to Appendices
TRENCHES.	13th	-	and Awards were published in a Special Divisional Routine Order by HQ 24th Division:-	
			T/Major (A/Lt. Col.) A.J.C. PEIRS. D.S.O. = 2nd Bar to D.S.O.	
			Lieut. (A/Captain) E.O. DONNELL = M.C.	
			Lieut. R.D. SPARKES = M.C.	
			2nd Lieut. C.F. OLLEY = M.C.	
			No. 29_5 C.S.M. L. SOLE = D.C.M.	
			No. 3067 C.S.M. W. HAYWARD = D.C.M.	
			No. 24088 Corporal E.L. BLAY = D.C.M.	
	14th	-	Situation unchanged. Our Heavy Artillery shelled the enemy's wire from 2pm to 5pm. Enemy artillery fairly quiet throughout the period. Our Patrols very active during the night - entering the enemy's front line in several places. None of the enemy were seen or	

Instructions regarding War Diaries and Intelligence Summaries are contained in F. S. Regs., Part II. and the Staff Manual respectively. Title Pages will be prepared in manuscript.

June 1918

WAR DIARY
or
INTELLIGENCE SUMMARY
(Erase heading not required.)

Army Form C. 2118
PAGE VI

VOLUME XXXIV

Place	Date	Hour	Summary of Events and Information	Remarks and references to Appendices
TRENCHES			or heard. The enemy apparently very seldom leaves the support line.	
	15th		Artillery quiet on both sides. At 12.30 am a very heavy bombardment took place to the North of our sector. Our aeroplanes were again very active. Patrols also active - again entering the enemy's front line and examining the ground between the front and support line.	
	16th		Situation unchanged. No unusual activity on the part of the artillery. Aeroplanes were active on our side. One or two enemy aeroplanes seen flying high over their own line. Our patrols active.	
	17th		Situation unchanged. Our aircraft extremely active. During the day some 60 machines passed over the enemy's line. During the	[illegible initials]

1875 Wt. W593/826 1,000,000 4/15 J.B.C. & A. A.D.S.S./Forms/C. 2118.

Instructions regarding War Diaries and Intelligence Summaries are contained in F. S. Regs., Part II. and the Staff Manual respectively. Title Pages will be prepared in manuscript.

June 1918

WAR DIARY
or
~~INTELLIGENCE SUMMARY~~

(Erase heading not required.)

VOLUME XXXIV

Army Form C. 2118

PAGE VII

Place	Date	Hour	Summary of Events and Information	Remarks and references to Appendices
			day artillery on both side quiet. The usual firing on back area during the night. During the evening an inter-company relief took place. A Coy relieved C Company in the Right Front Line - and B Company relieved D Company in the left front Line. D Company moved back to support in RED LINE and C Company to Reserve in the QUARRY. Relief was completed by 9pm.	Appendix III O.O. A11.
TRENCHES.	15th		2nd Lieut: W. SKIPTON and H.V. KIRKHOVE cross-posted to 9th Bn. East Surrey Regt. and struck off the strength of the Bn: Lieut: O.K. GRIFFIN (England) struck off the strength of the Bn:	
	18th		Situation unchanged - During the night our artillery shelled CITE St AUGUSTE very heavily. Our patrols very active. Weather very warm.	[initials]

1875 Wt. W593/826 1,000,000 4/15 J.B.C. & A. A.D.S.S./Forms/C. 2118.

Instructions regarding War Diaries and Intelligence Summaries are contained in F. S. Regs., Part II. and the Staff Manual respectively. Title Pages will be prepared in manuscript.

June 1918

WAR DIARY
~~or~~
~~INTELLIGENCE SUMMARY~~
(Erase heading not required.)

Army Form C. 2118

PAGE VIII

VOLUME XXXIV

Place	Date	Hour	Summary of Events and Information	Remarks and references to Appendices
TRENCHES	19th		Situation unchanged. During the night the enemy artillery were very active on our sector – in retaliation for a raid carried out by our troops on our left. Enemy aeroplanes active during the night – some small bombs were dropped near our left front Company H.Q.	
	20th		Fairly quiet day. Our heavy (9.45) T.Ms. carried out a shoot on CITE St. AUGUSTE. Lieut (A/Captain) J. BURRELL and 2nd Lieut C.E. Lyon joined the Bn. for duty.	
	21st		Situation unchanged. Enemy artillery more active than usual. Our patrols active. No enemy patrols encountered.	

1875 Wt. W593/826 1,000,000 4/15 J.B.C. & A. A.D.S.S./Forms/C. 2118.

Army Form C. 2118

PAGE IX

Instructions regarding War Diaries and Intelligence Summaries are contained in F. S. Regs., Part II. and the Staff Manual respectively. Title Pages will be prepared in manuscript.

June 1918

WAR DIARY
or
~~INTELLIGENCE SUMMARY~~
(Erase heading not required.)

VOLUME XXXIV

Place	Date	Hour	Summary of Events and Information	Remarks and references to Appendices
TRENCHES	22nd		No change in situation. Quiet day.	Appendix IV
	23rd		Quiet day - Bn: relieved in the line by 3rd Bn: Rifle Brigade - The Battalion moved back to LES BREBIS in Divisional Reserve.	O.O. A.12.
LES BREBIS	24th		Battalion in Divisional Reserve. Training - Baths and inspections carried out under Company arrangements. Captain F.S. RIDER joined the Bn: for duty from the 11th Bn: The Queens.	
	25th		Divisional Reserve - Training. Company and Platoon Commanders reconnoitred the VILLAGE LINE and lines of approach there to.	
	26th		Divisional Reserve - Training continued. 2nd Lieut A.M. WHITE cross-posted to 2nd Bn: Middlesex Regt and struck off the strength of the Battalion.	
	27th		Divisional Reserve. Training. Company and Platoon Commanders reconnoitred the Right Bn: sector. Major H.J.C. PEIRS D.S.O. joined Bn: and assumed command.	

1875 Wt. W593/826 1,000,000 4/15 J.B.C. & A. A.D.S.S./Forms/C. 2118.

Instructions regarding War Diaries and Intelligence Summaries are contained in F. S. Regs., Part II. and the Staff Manual respectively. Title Pages will be prepared in manuscript.

June 1918

WAR DIARY

or

~~INTELLIGENCE SUMMARY~~

(Erase heading not required.)

Volume XXXIV

Army Form C. 2118

PAGE X

Place	Date	Hour	Summary of Events and Information	Remarks and references to Appendices
LES BREBIS	28th		Divisional Reserve. Training continued. Lieut. L. F. WEIR posted to Base - medically unfit for front line duties. Major P. C. ESDAILE to 2nd in Command of West Kent Regt.	
	29th		Battalion relieved the 1st Bn. Royal Fusiliers in the right-sub-sector of Brigade front. Relief was completed at 1.15 am. D Coy. to Right front sector. C Coy. to left front sector. A Coy. to support. B Coy in Reserve. Bn. HQ HARRISON'S CRATER. 1st Royal Fus[rs] moved back to LES BREBIS in Divisional Reserve.	Appendix V O.O.A.B.
TRENCHES	30th		Quiet day. Slight shelling of back areas.	
			CASUALTIES	
			Total casualties for the period - 17.	
			[signature] Lieut & Act/Adjutant 8th Queens Regt	

1875 Wt. W593/826 1,000,000 4/15 J.B.C. & A. A.D.S.S./Forms/C. 2118.

Appendix I

Secret. COPY No. 17.

8th Bn. Queens. R.W.S. Regt

OPERATION ORDER. No. A. 2

MAP Ref: Sheets 1/10000. Lens & Loos. 1/40.000. Sheet. 36c

4th JUNE. 1918.

1. The Battn will be relieved by the 3rd Rifle Brigade in the Southern Sub-Sector of the Bde front on the night of the 5th/6th inst.

2. "C" Coy (Queens) will be relieved by "D" Coy (Rifle Brigade)
"D" — " — — " — — " — — " — "C" — " — — " —
"A" — " — — " — — " — — " — "A" — " — — " —
"B" — " — — " — — " — — " — "B" — " — — " —

3. Guides. 1 per Platoon as follows:-
"C" & "D" Coys to be at FOSSE 16 by 10.30. p.m.
A.B. H.Q. — " — HARRISONS CRATER at 10.15 — " —

4. On completion of relief, Battn will move into billets at LES BREBIS and come into DIV. RESERVE.
Coys will take over same billets as before.

5. TRENCH STORES:- Trench Stores, Work in hand and proposed, Defence Schemes etc, will be carefully handed over and receipts obtained.
Certificates of Stores handed over to reach O.R by 9. a.m. 6th inst.
Water tins will be handed over full.

6. Officers Trench Bundles, Mess kits, cooking dixies etc, to be ready for loading as follows:-
"A", "C", & "D" Coys at EDDY DUMP at 10. p.m.
H.Q. & "B" — " — — " — M.6.c.6.2 — " — 10.15 p.m.
2 men per Coy to be left in charge and travel back on the trucks.

7. Arrangements for Lewis Gun Limbers as follows:-
"A" Coy at M.11.d.45.60. @ 12.15. a.m.
"B" — " — — " — M.10.c.40.40. @ 12.15. a.m.
"C" — " — — " — M.12.b.45.50. @ 11.45. P.M.
"D" — " — — " — M.12.b.45.50. @ 11.50. P.M.
H.Q. — " — — " — M.5.b.35.80. @ 11. P.M.
This limber will take the Lewis Guns of B. Coy attached to H.Q. Coy.
1 N.C.O. and 2 men will be left i/c of each limber.

8. Completion of relief will be by runner or wire using Code Word "BILLY".

9. ACKNOWLEDGE:- O.O. A.2.

Issued at 7 p.m.

S. A. Dowell.
Capt & Adjutant
8th Queens Regt.

Copies for:-
No 1 Officer Commanding
No 2. 17. I.B.
" 3. O.C. "A" Coy
" 4. — " — "B" — " —
" 5 — " — "C" — " —
" 6 — " — "D" — " —
" 7 — " — M.O.
No 8. T.O.
" 9. Q.M.
" 10. O.C. Details
" 11. Int. Off.
" 12. Sig. — " —
No 13. 1st R. Fusiliers.
" 14. 3rd R. Brigade.
" 15. R.S.M.
" 16. File.
" 17. War Diary.

Appendix II

Secret.

Copy No. ......

8TH Bn. THE QUEEN'S. Regt

OPERATION ORDER. No. A. 10.

Map Ref:- Sheets: 1/10.000 Lens & Loos. 1/40.000. Sheet 36c

10TH JUNE. 1918

1. The Battn will relieve the 1st. Royal Fusiliers in the Northern Sub-Sector of the Brigade front on the night of the 11th/12th inst.

2. "C" Coy (Queens) will relieve "A" Coy (1st R.F.) on the Right.
   "D" --- --- --- "B" --- --- --- Left.
   "B" --- --- --- "D" --- --- in Support.
   "A" --- --- --- "C" --- --- --- Reserve.

3. Order of March. "C.D.B.A." Coy moving off at 8.45. P.M. 200x interval per platoons. H.Q. Coy will fall in with the rear platoon of "A" Coy.

4. Guides:- 1 guide per platoon will meet Coy at The Quarry.

5. Lewis Guns:- Coy Lewis Gun Limbers will follow the leading platoon of each Coy. H.Q. Limber will follow in rear of H.Q. Coy.

6. Baggage:- Officers Trench Bundles, Mess Kits, etc. will be dumped at "Q.M. Stores" ready for collection by 7.30. P.M.
   Officers Valises etc, not required for trenches will be returned to Q.M. Stores during the day.
   Coys will arrange to collect Rations, Baggage etc at Green Mound Dump.

7. Trench Stores:- All Trench Stores, Petrol Tins filled, Work in hand and proposed, Defence Schemes etc., will be carefully taken over. Certificates of Stores etc taken over to reach O.R. by 8. A.M. 12 inst.

8. Completion of relief will be reported by runner or wire, using Code Word "DUFF"

9. Acknowledge:- O.O. A. 10.

Issued at.... 8. P.M.

E. D. Dewell.
Capt & Adjt
8th Queen's Regt

Copies to:-

No.		No.	
1	C. O.	9.	Intell Off.
2.	17. I. B.	10.	T. O.
3.	o/c A. Coy	11.	Q.M.
4.	--- B ---	12.	1st R.F.
5	--- C ---	13.	R.S.M.
6	--- D ---	14	File
7	--- Sigs.	15	War Diary
8	M. O.		

A407 Appendix III

SECRET.

COPY No ....1....

8th BN THE QUEEN'S R.W.S Regt.

OPERATION ORDER No A11.

Map: Ref: Sheets 1/10.000
LENS & LOOS 1/40.000 Sheet 36c

16th June 1918

1 The following inter-coy relief will take place on 17th inst:-

"A" Coy will relieve "C" Coy (RIGHT COY)
"B" " " " "D" COY (LEFT ")

2. On completion of relief "D" Coy will be in support in the RED LINE. Reserve
"C" Coy in ~~support~~ in the "QUARRY".

3. All arrangements for relief will be made between O.C Coys concerned.

4. Relief to be complete by 9 P.M with the exception of the 2 forward posts.

5. TRENCH STORES:- All Trench Stores, Petrol Tins filled, Work in hand and proposed, Defence Schemes etc will be carefully taken over.
Certificates of Stores etc taken over to reach O.R. by 12 NOON 18th inst.

6 Completion of relief will be reported by runner or wire, using CODE WORD:- PIP

7. ACKNOWLEDGE:- O.O. A.11
Issued at 3.P.M. P.M.

Copies to:-

No 1. C.O
2. O/c "A" Coy.
3 -- "B" --
4 -- "C" --
5 -- "D" --
6 -- M.O --
No 7 Q.M.
8 R.S.M.
9 FILE
10 WAR DIARY

E. D. Donnell
Capt & Adjt
8th Queens Regt.

SECRET.

Appendix IV

COPY. No. 2.

8TH BATTN THE QUEEN'S REGT.

OPERATION ORDER No. A. 12.

MAP REF. SHEETS 1/10,000 LENS & LOOS 1/40,000. SHEET 36c

22ND JUNE 1918.

1. The Battalion will be relieved by the 3rd Rifle Brigade in the Northern Sub-sector of the Brigade front on the night of the 23rd/24th inst.

2. 'A' Coy (Queen's) will be relieved by C Coy (3rd R.B.)
   B " " " " D " "
   C " " " " B " "
   D " " " " A " "

3. On relief the Battalion will be in Divisional Reserve. LES BREBIS. Billets will be taken over as before.

4. **Guides.** 1 Guide per Platoon & 1 for Bn. HQ will be at M.5.a.5.9. by 10 p.m.

5. **Lewis Guns.** Company L Gun limbers will be at Cross Roads M.5.b.20.30 by 12 M.N. That for HQ Coy will be at M.5.b.20.30 by 10.45 p.m. for L. Guns, magazines, trench bundles, mess kit etc. 1 N.C.O. & 2 men will be in charge of each limber.

6. Coy. Officers trench bundles, mess kits, dixies, etc to be ready for loading as follows:-
   A & B. Coys at NASH DUMP by 10.30 p.m.
   C & D " " GREENMOUND " " 10.30 p.m.
   2 men per Coy to be left in charge & travel back on the trucks.

7. **Trench Stores.** All trench stores, Petrol Tins filled, work in hand and proposed Defence Schemes etc will be carefully handed over. Certificates of Stores etc handed over to reach Orderly Room by 12 noon 24th inst.

8. Completion of relief will be reported by runner or, wire, using CODEWORD "PIG".

9. Acknowledge O. O. A 12.

Issued at. 11.20 PM.

R.H. Rose. 2nd Lieut.
Asst. Adjt.
8th Queens Regt.

Copies to :-

No. 1 P. O.
2.
3. 17 I. B.
4. o/c. A Coy.
5 — B —
6 — C —
7 — D —
8 — Sigs

No. 9. Intell Off.
10. T. O.
11. Q M.
12. 3rd R. B.s.
13. R. S. M.
14 FILE
15 M. O
16. WAR. DIARY.

Appendix V

Secret. COPY No. 14

8TH BN. THE QUEEN'S REGT.

OPERATION ORDER. No. A. 13.

Map Ref: Lens. St. Nazaire River 28TH JUNE. 1918.

1. The Bn will relieve the 1st ROYAL FUSILIERS in the Right Sub-Sector of the Brigade Front on the night of 29th/30th June.

2. "D" Coy will relieve "A" Coy (Royal Fusiliers) Right Front Line.
"C" --- --- --- "B" --- --- " --- Left ---
"A" --- --- --- "C" --- --- " --- Support.
"B" --- --- --- "D" --- --- " --- Reserve.

3. Order of March:- D.C.A.B & H.Q. Coy. "D" Coy will move off at 9.15 p.m. Intervals of 200x per platoon will be maintained. H.Q. Coy will proceed direct to HARRISON'S CRATER.

4. ROUTE:- Les Brebis - Maroc - Fosse 11 Road - X Roads. M.10.c.4.4.

5. GUIDES:- Platoon Guides will meet Companies at Fosse 16.

6. Lewis Guns:- Lewis Gun limbers will move with the leading platoon of each Coy. H.Q. Coy limber will move off in rear of H.Q. Coy.

7. BAGGAGE:- Officers' Trench Bundles, Mess Kits, etc, will be dumped at Q.M. Stores, ready for collection by 7 p.m. (29th)
Valises &c not required for trenches will be returned to Q.M. Stores during the day (29th)
Rations, Kits &c will be collected by Coys at their respective dumps. A.C. & D Coys at Eddy Dump. "B" Coy & H.Q. Coy at Lens-Bethune DUMP (M.6.C.7.2.)

8. TRENCH STORES:- Trench Stores, Filled Petrol Tins, Programme of work in hand & proposed, Defence schemes &c. will be carefully taken over. Certificates of stores taken over, to reach O.R. by 8 a.m. 30th inst.
"A" Coy will detail 1 N.C.O & 2 men to proceed in advance to take over Bn. H.Q. Dump of Stores, S.A.A., Bombs, etc at Eddy Dump.

9. Completion of Relief will be reported by wire or runner, using Code Word "MERRY".

10. ACKNOWLEDGE:-

Issued at 6 p.m.
By Runner.

A. L. Wright
2nd Lieut
Acting Adjutant
8th Queen's Regt

Copies to:-

No. 1.	C.O.	No. 8.	T.O.
2.	H.Q. 17 I.B.	9.	Q.M.
3.	O.C. A Coy.	10.	M.O.
4.	--- B. ---	11.	1st R.F.
5	--- C ---	12.	R.S.M.
6	--- D ---	13.	File.
7	--- H.Q. ---	14.	War Diary.

(6339) Wt. W160/M3016 1,500,000 10/17 McA & W Ltd (E 1898) Forms W3091. Army Form W.3091.

Cover for Documents.

Nature of Enclosures.

8th BN. THE QUEENS R.W.S REGT

WAR DIARY

VOLUME XXXV
for
JULY 1918

AUGUST 4th 1918 H. J. C. [illegible] LIEUT COLONEL,
COMMANDING
8th QUEENS RWS REGT

Notes, or Letters written.

Instructions regarding War Diaries and Intelligence Summaries are contained in F. S. Regs., Part II. and the Staff Manual respectively. Title Pages will be prepared in manuscript.

WAR DIARY

~~or~~

~~INTELLIGENCE SUMMARY~~

(Erase heading not required.)

July 1918

Vol XXXV

PAGE 1.

Army Form C. 2118

Place	Date	Hour	Summary of Events and Information	Remarks and references to Appendices
Trenches.	1st.		Right sub-sector of Bde front. (N 8.c.45.20 to N 2.d.4.8. Sheet LENS) Quiet day. Our aeroplanes active and slight artillery activity on enemy back areas. Weather exceptionally hot. Between 9.30 PM and 10-30 P.M. enemy shelled Bde front with gas shells.	
"	2nd.		Situation quiet. Our patrols very active. Enemy reported busy in his front line.	
"	3rd		Hostile artillery fairly active on forward areas and our artillery busy during the night on enemy back areas. Our aircraft active. Patrols sent out reached the enemy's wire, but were bombed and fired on. No casualties.	
"	4th.		Artillery and heavy trench mortars active on enemy positions. One E.A. flew low over our trenches. Between 10 PM and 11-15 PM the enemy shelled our forward areas with 4.2's and 77 cm's and dropped heavy minenwerfers and "Darts" on the forward posts. Our artillery retaliated. Casualties one O.R. killed and one wounded. A Coy relieved C Coy. in the left front sector; B Coy relieved D Coy in the right front sector, C Coy in Support. D Coy in Reserve.	Appendix I Bn O.O. A.14
"	5th		A very quiet day.	

R.W.R.

1875 Wt. W593/826 1,000,000 4/15 J.B.C. & A. A.D.S.S./Forms/C. 2118.

2. Army Form C. 2118

Instructions regarding War Diaries and Intelligence Summaries are contained in F. S. Regs., Part II. and the Staff Manual respectively. Title Pages will be prepared in manuscript.

WAR DIARY
or
~~INTELLIGENCE SUMMARY~~
(Erase heading not required.)

July 1918

Place	Date	Hour	Summary of Events and Information	Remarks and references to Appendices
Trenches	6th		Situation quiet during the day. Our artillery carried out the usual harassing fire on back areas. Heavy Minenwerfer again fired on our posts in the neighbourhood of COSY and HAPPY trenches at night.	
	7th		Our artillery very active on the enemy's front and support lines and(?) trench mortar positions. He replied by shelling our forward areas with 77 mm and 4.2's. His minenwerfer were very active on DOUGLAS trench, COSY and HAPPY junction and the forward end of NESTOR trench causing great inconvenience. Our heavy artillery retaliated.	
	8th		Our artillery carried out counter-battery work and our aeroplanes were very active in the evening. The enemy was quiet during the day but his heavy trench mortars were again in action on our forward ~~area~~ posts. Between 9.30 PM and 11 PM about 40 "minnies" containing gas were fired on HAPPY and COSY trenches & CANTEEN ALLEY. Retaliation was called for on all German trench mortar positions.	[initials]

1875 Wt. W593/826 1,000,000 4/15 J.B.C. & A. A.D.S.S./Forms/C. 2118.

Instructions regarding War Diaries and Intelligence Summaries are contained in F. S. Regs., Part II. and the Staff Manual respectively. Title Pages will be prepared in manuscript.

WAR DIARY

~~or~~

~~INTELLIGENCE SUMMARY~~

(Erase heading not required.)

Army Form C. 2118

Place	Date	Hour	Summary of Events and Information	Remarks and references to Appendices
Trenches.	9th.		Our Artillery very active during the night. The heavies fired on back areas and carried out a retaliatory shoot on enemy trench mortars the Cin heavies assisting. Our forward trenches were shelled by salvos of 77 Cms and the enemy trench mortars again became active about midnight. Retaliation was again called for. Hon Lieut. Quartermaster W.H. Burnham was wounded while on his way to Bn H.Qs.	
	10th		Enemy trench mortar fire slackened on retaliation. We registered with 5.9's in the vicinity of our forward posts. On Minnenwerfer again opening at night immediate action was taken by the heavy artillery and they were silenced. Casualties due to early morning trench mortar fire – Killed. Lt B.P.B Calkin and 4 O.R's; wounded 7 O.R's.	
	11th		Heavy artillery shelled enemy back areas. Our aeroplanes active, 16 flying over front lines. Enemy artillery fairly active on HAPPY and NESTOR trenches but his trench mortars quiet. 2/Lt R.C. Brooks (3rd Queens) joined the Bn.	
	12th	3.30 AM	A patrol of B Coy entered the enemy trenches before dawn but were held up by wire and encountered a strong party of the enemy. The party withdrew under a smoke screen and artillery barrage. Casualties 2 O.R's Killed and 1 O.R. wounded. Capt H. C. C Morley left the Bn to join the 1st Bn E. Kent Regt. Major H. J. C. Peirs D.S.O. appointed acting Lieut-Colonel.	

1875 Wt. W593/826 1,900,000 4/15 J.B.C. & A. A.D.S.S./Forms/C. 2118.

Instructions regarding War Diaries and Intelligence Summaries are contained in F. S. Regs., Part II. and the Staff Manual respectively. Title Pages will be prepared in manuscript.

4.

Army Form C. 2118

WAR DIARY
or
~~INTELLIGENCE SUMMARY~~ Vol XXXV
(Erase heading not required.)

July 1918.

Place	Date	Hour	Summary of Events and Information	Remarks and references to Appendices
Trenches - LES BREBIS	13th		The Bn was relieved in the line by the 3rd Rifle Brigade, relief being complete by 1.30 Am. The Bn proceeded to LES BREBIS and passed into Divisional Reserve. An enemy aeroplane dropped bombs in the vicinity of LOOS.	Appendix II Bn O.O. No 16
LES BREBIS	14th		Bn in Divisional Reserve and training commenced.	
" "	15th		" "	
" "	16th		" "	
" "	17th		" "	
Trenches.	18th		The Bn relieved the 1st Royal Fusiliers in the northern sub-sector of the MAROC sector. Relief was complete by 12-45 Am. On completion of relief Coys were disposed as follows:- A Coy. right front Coy; B Coy. left front; D Coy in reserve; C Coy in support. Battn H.Q in THE QUARRY. The following officers were taken on the strength. 2/Lt. A.P. Block, W.B. Heffer, H.P. Coombe, A.P. Pittal (3rd Queens) and L.B. Palmer (West Kent Regt).	Appendix III Bn O.O. No 17
	19th		As well as the usual harrassing fire our artillery was very active	

RWR

1875 Wt. W593/826 1,000,000 4/15 J.B.C. & A. A.D.S.S./Forms/C. 2118.

Instructions regarding War Diaries and Intelligence Summaries are contained in F. S. Regs., Part II. and the Staff Manual respectively. Title Pages will be prepared in manuscript.

5.

Army Form C. 2118

WAR DIARY
~~or~~
~~INTELLIGENCE SUMMARY~~
(Erase heading not required.)

July 1918

Place	Date	Hour	Summary of Events and Information	Remarks and references to Appendices
Trenches	19th		during the night on the enemy back areas. Situation quiet during the day. Our aeroplanes active in the day time and one or two crossed the enemy lines during the night.	
	20th		Our artillery quiet only carrying out the usual harrassing fire at night. Enemy artillery and trench mortars more active than usual especially in the morning and early part of the evening. We patrolled no-man's-land during the night as enemy patrols had been reported active. The weather changed and there was a heavy thunderstorm and rain in the afternoon. The Corps Commander, Lt Gen Sir Aylmer Hunter-Weston, visited the Bn area.	Appendix IV Bde Letter G30/2
	21st		Very quiet on both sides. Patrolled no-man's-land during the night. Weather fair.	
	22nd		Our heavy artillery shelled enemy back areas in the afternoon. Usual harrassing fire carried out. Enemy artillery quiet. At 2 P.M. a raid was undertaken by the Bn on our left	

RWR

1875 Wt W593/826 1,000,000 4/15 J.B.C. & A. A.D.S.S./Forms/C. 2118.

Army Form C. 2118

WAR DIARY

~~or~~

~~INTELLIGENCE SUMMARY~~

(Erase heading not required.)

Instructions regarding War Diaries and Intelligence Summaries are contained in F. S. Regs., Part II. and the Staff Manual respectively. Title Pages will be prepared in manuscript.

July 1918.

Place	Date	Hour	Summary of Events and Information	Remarks and references to Appendices
Trenches	22nd.		but no identification obtained. The enemy artillery retaliated fairly heavily for this but very little fell on our front. Extensive raids were carried out by the Division on our right under cover of a heavy bombardment lasting ¾ hr. The weather was fine. Casualties 1 O.R. wounded.	
	23rd.		Weather fine. Our artillery fairly active. The enemy artillery fired several 3 minute bursts during the day and night indiscriminately on our front. A daylight patrol consisting of 1 Officer and 20 O.Rs entered the enemy trenches and remained there for about five hours. No enemy were seen and it was found that the front line was unoccupied. Casualties 1 O.R. wounded.	Appendix V 17 I B letter C 2/120 23.07.18
	24th.		Weather fine. Both artilleries quiet with the exception of a fair amount of retaliation for a ~~Bn~~ raid ~~on~~ by a Bn on our right which came down on our front line trenches. Heavy trench mortars were also used. Enemy aeroplanes were very active in the early part of the evening and several bombing machines	

1875 Wt. W593/826 1,000,000 4/15 J.B.C. & A. A.D.S.S./Forms/C. 2118.

Instructions regarding War Diaries and Intelligence Summaries are contained in F. S. Regs., Part II. and the Staff Manual respectively. Title Pages will be prepared in manuscript.

WAR DIARY
~~or~~
~~INTELLIGENCE SUMMARY~~
(Erase heading not required.)

7

Army Form C. 2118

July 1918

Place	Date	Hour	Summary of Events and Information	Remarks and references to Appendices
Trenches.	24th		flew over our lines between 10 P.M and 12 M.N. ~~D~~ C and ~~E~~ D Coys relieved A & B Coys in the front line, B Coy coming into Support and A Coy into reserve. The drums played at 8th Corps headquarters.	Appendix VI Bn O.O. H.19.
"	25th		Weather very wet. Both artilleries active, the enemy chiefly devoting his attention to our reserve and support lines. 2/Lt. W. Harding to Machine Gun School, Grantham.	
"	~~27th~~ 26th		Weather wet. Our artillery carried out usual harassing fire and that of the enemy was much more active than usual during the period. A patrol of 1 Officer and 20 O.R's & three double Lewis Gun sections left our lines at N.2.b. 10.30 (Sheet LENS) at 9.45 PM. The Lewis guns were to cover the advance and withdrawal of the patrol which was to penetrate to the enemy support line and secure an identification. Under a brief barrage this party moved up a communication trench at N.2.b. 80.90 and encountered a sentry who tried to escape but was shot and killed in an endeavour to stop him. His shoulder straps were secured and the identity of the opposing	Appendix VII Bde Letter G 2/131. CENTRE GROUP 24th D.A. O.O No 26 Wire W.2 Bn Report on Patrol Enterprise

[initials]

8

Army Form C. 2118

Instructions regarding War Diaries and Intelligence Summaries are contained in F. S. Regs., Part II. and the Staff Manual respectively. Title Pages will be prepared in manuscript.

WAR DIARY

~~or~~

~~INTELLIGENCE SUMMARY~~

(*Erase heading not required.*)

July 1918

Place	Date	Hour	Summary of Events and Information	Remarks and references to Appendices
Trenches	26th		troops established. The party returned after sheltering from the retaliation in the enemy's front line trenches. The conditions on account of the rain were bad. Casualties 6 OR's wounded.	
"	27th		Situation quiet. Casualties incurred in the early morning on account of the raid 1 OR killed; 2 OR's wounded.	
"	28th		Usual harrassing fire by our artillery. Situation quiet.	
"	29th		In the morning at about 9.30 am the enemy shelled Bn Headquarters, five shells falling in the QUARRY, otherwise situation quiet. Major F.C. Esdaile left to take command of the 1st Battn The Queens Regt.	
"	30th		The Bn was relieved by the 3rd Rifle Bde, relief being complete by 2 am on the morning of the 31st. The right front Coy was somewhat held up on account of hostile shelling but no casualties were incurred	Appendix VI Bn OO H20
LES BREBIS.	31st.		The Bn on relief came into Divisional Reserve at in LES BREBIS. The	

1875 Wt. W593/826 1,000,000 4/15 J.B.C. & A. A.D.S.S./Forms/C. 2118.

9

Army Form C. 2118

Instructions regarding War Diaries and Intelligence Summaries are contained in F. S. Regs., Part II. and the Staff Manual respectively. Title Pages will be prepared in manuscript.

WAR DIARY

~~or~~

~~INTELLIGENCE SUMMARY~~

(*Erase heading not required.*)

July 1918

Place	Date	Hour	Summary of Events and Information	Remarks and references to Appendices
LES BREBIS	31st		Corps Commander, Lt Gen Sir Aylmer Hunter-Weston, K.C.B. D.S.O., presented decorations to the following officer, NCOs & men of the Bn at Divisional Headquarters. SAINS-EN-GOHELLE:— Military Cross, 2/Lt C.F. Olley; D.C.M. — C.S.M. W. Hayward, Sergt E.L. Blay; Military Medal — Sergt C. Fear, Sergt J. Heist, Sergt G.W. Jeffries; Ptes (938) F. Wheeler, (24326) C.B. Williams and (8999) H. West.	
			[signature] Lt for. Lt Col Commanding 8th Bn The Queens Regt	

1875 Wt. W593/826 1,000,000 4/15 J.B.C. & A. A.D.S.S./Forms/C. 2118.

W640

Appendix I

SECRET. COPY No. 13.

OPERATION ORDER. No A14
— BY —
LIEUT. COL. H.J.C. PEIRS, D.S.O.
THURSDAY JULY 4th 1918.

1. The following inter-company relief will take place during evening of the 5th inst.
2. (a). A Company will relieve C Company in Left Front Sector.
   (b). B Company will relieve D Company in Right Front Sector.
   (c). C Company will move back to Support positions vacated by A Coy.
   (d). D Company will move back to Reserve position vacated by B Coy.
3. Relief will be completed as far as possible by daylight, arrangements being made between the Company Commanders concerned.
4. The following will be given careful attention when handing over:— Trench Stores - Defence Schemes - Maps and Photos - Details of all Working and Carrying parties - Work on hand and proposed - &c.
5. List of Trench Stores handed over to reach Bn: H.Q. by 9 a.m. 6th inst.
6. Completion of relief will be reported to Bn: H.Q. by wire or runner using code word "SMILE".
7. ACKNOWLEDGE O.O. A14.

[illegible]
[illegible] and Acting Adjt.
8th Queens. R.W.S. Regt.

Issued by Runner at 4 pm.

Copy No 1. to C.O.
2. O.C. A Coy.
3. " B.
4. " C.
5. " D.
6. " H.Q.
7. M.O.
8. 8th Rifle Bde.
9. 1st N. Staffs.
10. 1st [illegible] J.O.
11. Q.M.
12. Office.
13. War Diary.

Appendix II

SECRET

Copy No. 15

8TH BN THE QUEENS RGT.

OPERATION-ORDER No. A.16.

By.

MAP REF. 1/20,000 [illegible] MAJOR. H.J.C. PEIRS. D.S.O. 11th July. 1918

1. The Battalion will be relieved in the Right sub-sector of the Brigade front by the 3rd Rifle Bde on the night of 12th/13th July.

2. Relief of Coys as follows:—

'A' Coy (Queens)	by	[illegible]	Coy (Rifle Bde)
'B' "	"	by	[illegible] " " "
'C' "	"	by	[illegible] " " "
'D' "	"	by	[illegible] " " "

3. On relief Coys will move to LES-BREBIS where Battn will come into Divisional Reserve.

4. Coy. Q.M.Sgt. will be at [illegible] to conduct Coys to their Billets.

5. Coy L.G. limbers will be at M.12.b.0.4. by 11.30.P.M. H.Q. limber will be at Bn H.Q. by 10.45 P.M. and will take H.Q. Officers trench bundles, Spare kit, L.G. [illegible] etc. 1 N.C.O & 2 men will accompany each limber.

6. All Trench Stores, Defence Schemes, [illegible] Patrol [illegible], Sketches, Work [illegible] tables, Aeroplane [illegible], work [illegible] and proposed will be carefully handed over. Trench Store Cards to reach Orderly Room by 12 Noon 13th inst.

7. Coy Officers Kits, Mess Kits, Cooking utensils, etc, will be at respective Ration Dumps by 10 P.M. (D & A Coys. [illegible] [illegible], H.Q. & C. EDDY DUMP.) 2 men will be detailed per Coy to load and accompany these.

8. 1 Guide per platoon will [illegible] unit at Road junction. M.12.b.0.4. [illegible] to be there at 10.15 P.M.

9. Completion of relief will be reported by Code word RAKE

10. ACKNOWLEDGE:- O.O.A.16.

R.M. Pre[illegible] 2nd Lt. A/Adjt
8th Queen's Rgt

Copies to 1 3rd Bn Rifle Bde
2 1st Royal Fusiliers
3 H.Q. 17th Bde
4 C.O
5 A Coy
6 B "
7 C "
8 D "
9 H.Q. Coy
10 H.Q. (mess)
11 Quartermaster
12 Transport Officer
13 O.C. 9th East Surrey Rgt
14 File
15 Diary

Appendix III

14

To Lt Rose for War Diary

Appendix IV

SECRET

17th Infantry Brigade.
G.20/2.

8th Queens.
3rd Rifle Brigade.
17th L.T.M.B. (for information.)

The Corps Commander will visit the Divisional area tomorrow, the 20th inst.

2. He will proceed via the BLACK LINE and will be met by Battalion Commanders concerned at the Northern extremity of their respective sub-sections. Company and Platoon Commanders along the BLACK LINE will meet the Corps Commander at the Northern limits of their respective areas.

3. It is considered that the Corps Commander should arrive at the Northern extremity of the Brigade front (junction of O.G.1 with MARGATE TRENCH) at 12 noon.

4. ~~[illegible]~~.

19/7/18.
K.

W. Mackenzie
Major,
Brigade Major, 17th Infantry Brigade.

appendix V

SECRET. **17th Inf: Bde. No. G.2/120.**

8th Queens. **Ref: Log Map No.2b. ST.AUGUSTE.**
Centre Group.
24th Division "G"

---

1. With the object of securing an identification, 8th Queens are sending a fighting patrol of 1 Officer & 20 O.R. to enter the enemy trenches at N.2.b.65.40 during daylight to-day.

2. The patrol will lie in wait for the enemy and will endeavour to capture the post at N.2.b.85.92 which is usually manned by night.

3. Centre Group will be prepared to assist, should the presence of the patrol be detected.
   The signal for the barrage will be a RED Very Light fired from the enemy front line. Fire will then be directed on enemy M.Gs Nos. 4, 5, 13, on enemy support line (HOOP TRENCH) and on houses about N.3.a.60.90.

   This signal may be fired any time after 7.30 pm.

4. O.C., 8th Queens will arrange to wire Code Word....."STIKIT" to Brigade H.Qrs and Group H.Qrs notifying safe return of the patrol.

5. **ACKNOWLEDGE.**

Wallackefer Major,

23rd July, 1918. Brigade Major, 17th Inf: Bde.

Copy to C.R.A.
3rd Rifle Brigade.
73rd Inf: Bde.

Appendix V

Secret. COPY No. 13.

8th The Queens. Regt. OPERATION ORDER. No. A. 18 by Lt. Col H.J.C. Peirs. D.S.O.

Map Ref. GRAND TRUNK.

JULY. 23rd 1918.

1. An offensive patrol, consisting of 1 Officer and 20 O.R.s will leave our lines from N.2.b. 18.39. at 6.30.p.m. to-day and enter enemy line at N.2.b. 65.40.

2. Object:- To secure identification and inflict casualties.

3. The patrol will return to N.2.b 18.39. at 10.30.pm.(approx).

4. Artillery:- The 18 pdrs and 4.5 Hows will be ready at any time after 7.30.p.m. to fire on M.Gs. 4, 5, 6 and 13 in squares N.2.b. and N.3.a. of ST AUGUSTE LOG MAP, No 2a and to put a light barrage on the enemy support line between N.3.a. 18.99 and N.3.a. 05.40. and in the area of the BRICKSTACKS.
The signal for this will be a Red Very Light fired from the enemy line.

5. The Code Word "HELAS" will be wired to all concerned as soon as the patrol has returned to our lines.

6. ACKNOWLEDGE:- O.O. A. 18.

Issued at 12.30 p.m.
by runner.

F. D. Dowell
Capt & Adjutant
8th Bn The Queens Regt.

Copies to.

No 1.	C. O.	No 7.	O.C. Left Battn.
2.	O.C. "A" Coy	8	--- H. T.M. Batty.
3.	--- "B" ---	9	--- L. --- " ---
4	--- "C" ---	10	--- M. G. Coy.
5	--- D ---	11	H.Q. 17. I. B.
6	--- Rt. Battn.	12	FILE.

No 13. WAR DIARY.
No 14. GROUP. H.Qrs.

Appendix A.19

Secret Copy No. 11

8th Bn. The Queens Regt

Operation Order No. A.19.

by

Lieut. Col. H.J.C. Peirs. D.S.O.

Ref. [illegible]

1. The following inter-Coy Relief will take place to-night:
   - C Coy will relieve A Coy (Right)
   - D " " " B " (Left)

2. Arrangements for relief will be made between Coy Commanders concerned.

3. C Coy will start relieving at 8.30 pm and D Coy [illegible]

4. On completion of relief A Coy will be in Reserve and B Coy in Support.

5. Trench Stores, S.A.A., Bombs, Rifle grenades, defence schemes, aeroplane photographs etc. will be carefully handed over. List of Stores taken & handed over to reach Orderly Room by 8 a.m. 25th inst.

6. Completion of relief will be reported by runner or wire using the code word "[illegible]"

7. Acknowledge. O.O. A.19.

Issued at [illegible] by runner

[illegible]
Capt & Adjutant
8th Bn. The Queens Regt.

Copies to [illegible]

Appendix VII

SECRET. Major Rowland Copy No. 2

17th Inf: Bde. No.G.2/131.

Ref: Log Map.
No.2b. ST: AUGUSTE.

PATROL SCHEME.

1. With the object of securing an identification, 8th Queens are sending a fighting patrol of 1 Officer (2nd Lieut: REEVES) and 20 O.R. to enter the enemy trenches tomorrow night 26th July.

2. About 9.40 pm. the patrol will enter the enemy front line at N.2.b.70.40 and will then move northwards to enemy support trench at approx: N.2.b.85.85. On arrival at this point a message will be sent back by telephone or signal to Battalion H.Qrs. one Gold and Silver Rain rockets will then be fired from vicinity of HARRISONS CRATER - this will be the signal for the artillery barrage to open.

3. ARTILLERY CO-OPERATION.

O.C., Centre Group will assist the operation as under immediately on the Gold and Silver rain rocket signal being seen :,

(a) One minute INTENSE bombardment on enemy trench from N.3.a.10.25 (No.13 M.G. inclusive) to N.3.a.15.60 (No.5.M.G.inclusive)

(b) Box barrage from N.2.b.90.05 - NUTMEG TRENCH N.3.a.50.30 - HOOP TRENCH at N.3.a.40.85 - H.33.c.38.35 - HAKIM TRENCH.

(c) Special attention will be paid to trench junction at N.3.a.15.70 and enemy M.Gs. Nos. 4, 5, 13.

(d) The following targets will also be engaged. Enemy T.Ms. Nos. 12, 13, 6 (H.33.c) Nos. 9, 10, 11, 20 (N.3.a.& b.) and No. 8. Enemy M.Gs Nos. 2 & 3.

(e) A demonstration will be made on NORMAN STACKS with the assistance of 6" Newtons.

4. On the opening of the bombardment a double L.G.Section will be posted on either side of C.T. running through N.2.b.82.90 to cover the flanks of the patrol as it advances down the C.T. and to keep down fire in the enemy support line.

Another double L.G.Section will be posted at N.2.b.70.40 to guard the point of entry and keep down any enemy fire to the S.E.

5. WITHDRAWAL.

The patrol will withdraw through the L.Gs. (O.C., patrol may decide in the event of heavy enemy retaliation to remain in the enemy front line till the barrage has died down).

6. The safe return of the patrol will be wired to Brigade H.Qrs using Code Word....."BUNTER".
A RED Very light will also be fired from HARRISONS CRATER. If this is fired within half an hour of the commencement of the artillery barrage, it will be the signal for "CEASE FIRE"

7. ACKNOWLEDGE.

Issued to Sigs.
at 8.40 pm.
25th July, 1918.

[signature] Major,
Brigade Major, 17th Inf: Bde.

Copy No.1 to Major ROWLAND.)
2 " ")
3 Lt-Col. PEIRS.) 8th Queens.
4 " ")
5 " ")
6 3rd Rifle Brigade.
7 1st Royal Fusiliers.
8 Centre Group, RFA.
9 24th Division "G".
10 72nd Inf: Bde.
11 73rd " "
12 C.R.A.
13 Brigade Sigs. Officer.
14 File.
15 File.
16 War Diary.

"C" FORM.
MESSAGES AND SIGNALS.

Army Form C. 2123
(In books of 100.)
No. of Message ....

Prefix SM Code KCom Words 19

Received from MUQA By SB

Service Instructions
MUQA

Sent, or sent out.
At .... m.
To ....
By ....

Office Stamp.
AH3
26-7-18

Handed in at MUQA Sig Office 10.15 a m. Received 10.55 a m.

TO Home

* Sender's Number.	Day of Month.	In reply to Number.	AAA
W2	26	—	
0026	para	5 last	line
should	read		NO
fuzes	number		106
will	be	used	

FROM MUQA
PLACE & TIME

* This line, except AAA, should be erased, if not required.

(3287) Wt. W54/P738. 691,000 Pads. 3/18. A.P.Ltd. (E3013)

SECRET. Copy No.......

OPERATION ORDER No.26
by
LT.COL.J.C.WALCH,D.S.O.,R.F.A.

COMMANDING CENTRE GROUP 24TH D.A.

Reference LOG MAP No.2b ST AUGUSTE.

1. The 8th Battmn.The Queens Regt.are raiding the enemy's trenches about N.3.a.15.70. on 26/7/18.

2. The Raiding Party is entering the enemy's front line at N.2.b.70.40. about 9.40 p.m.,and is moving northwards to about N.2.b.85.85.,where the party will form up for the raid.

3. The raid will be covered by Centre Group,24th D.A.as follows:-

A/106 - 4 guns - Trench N.3.a.15.60.to N.3.a.15.85.(paying particular attention to M.G.5.and T.J.at N.3.a.15.72) from Zero to Zero plus 1 minute) then lift to line N.3.a.45.40. to N.3.a.40.85.

C/106 - 2 guns - Trench N.3.a.05.45.to N.3.a.15.60.(paying particular attention to M.G.13) from Zero to Zero plus 1 minute,then lift to Trench N.3.a.50.35. to N.3.a.38.42.

B/106 - 4 guns - Trench at H.32.d.90.07.to H.33.c.15.03.to N.3.a.15.90.

18-pdr.Bty.52nd Bde.- 6 guns - Trench N.3.a.35.80.to N.3.a.40.85. to H.33.c.38.35.(paying particular attention to M.G.4).

-do- -do- 4 guns - Trench N.2.b.80.05.to N.3.a.02.38. (90)

-do- -do. 2 guns - Line N.2.b.90.05. to N.3.a.5.3.

D/106 - 4 hows.- Houses along Road N.3.a.6.8.to H.33.c.45.15.

D/52 - 2 hows.- T.M.s No.8 at N.2.b.9.1. and No.12 at N.3.a.2.0.

4. Rate of Fire:-

0 to 0 plus 4 minutes	-	INTENSE.
0 plus 4 to 0 plus 15	-	RAPId.
0 plus 15 to "Cease Fire"	-	NORMAL.

5. Ammunition for 18-pdrs. :-
50% Shrapnel. 50% H.E.
The corrector for Shrapnel will be set to give 50% of bursts on graze.
No.106 Fuzes will be used.

6. No more registration than is absolutely necessary will be done, especially within 200 yards of Trench Junction at N.3.a.15.72.

7. The Heavy Artillery and T.M's are co-operating by firing on the following targets:-

<u>H.A.</u> - T.M's 6, 12 and 13 in H.33.c.
9, 10 and 11 in N.3.a.
20 in N.3.b.
M.G's 2 and 3 in N.3.a.
also Counter Battery Work.

<u>T.M's</u>. NORMAN STACKS and houses about H.33.c.15.75.

8. The signal for open fire will be One GOLD & SILVER RAIN Rocket fired from HARRISON's CRATER (M.6.c.1.6.).
Batteries will open fire immediately this signal goes up.
The signal to cease firing will be One RED VERY Light fired from the same place.
All Batteries will cease firing at Zero plus 30 minutes if the"cease fire" signal has not gone up before then.

9. Guns and Howitzers that have been moved forward for the recent

P T O

OPERATION ORDER NO.26 (contd)

9 (contd). raids will be withdrawn to their main positions on completion of this raid. The return of these guns will be reported to these Headquarters by the code word SAFE.

10. ACKNOWLEDGE.

R Wilmot

Captain, R.F.A.,
Adjutant, Centre Group, 24th D.A.

Issued to Signals at ......

/7/18.

Copies to
1 - A/106
2 - B/106
3 - C/106
4 - D/106
5 - 52nd Army Bde., RFA.
6 - 24th D.A.
7 - 17th I.B.
8 - 8th Queen's
9 - Rt.Group) 24th
10- Lt.Group) D.A.
11- D.T.M.O.
12- 91st Bde.R.G.A.
13- File.

(6–12 for information.)

8th S. Battn The Queens.

Report on Patrol Enterprise. 26/7/1918

Ref. No. 26 St. Auguste

a patrol of 1 officer (2nd Lieut Reeves) and 20 O.R. accompanied by 3 outside Lewis Gun Sections left our lines at N.2.b.10.30 at 9.45 p.m on the evening of the 26th. 7. 1918.

Previous patrols having made it clear that the enemy did not hold his front line, the general scheme of the operation provided for the temporary occupation of his front line by the L.G. sections which would be used to cover the advance of the patrol to the support line.

artillery support including a one minute barrage on the Support line was provided.

The whole party 50 strong occupied the enemy front line unobserved & took up their positions & when ready 2nd Lt. Reeves telephoned back by a line which had been laid across No Mans Land for the artillery to open. A signal visible to all batteries was then fired from Battn Hqrs & the artillery opened simultaneously. On its opening a number of shells fell among the party in the enemy front line and wounded three of the patrol. This mishap disorganised the patrol & when ~~he~~ it reached the enemy support line it had lost its formation.

The communication trench down which the party advanced running from N.2.b.80.90 to N.3.a.15.75 had 4 wire blocks in it. It had been patrolled a fortnight previously & found to be clear.

On reaching the support line through our barrage which is reported to have been shot all through.

A sentry was seen. He tried to bolt & in endeavouring to shoot him in the leg, an N.C.O. hit him in the side & killed him. His epaulettes were taken but he had no papers. Owing to the barrage, 2nd Lieut Rosner who was informed that the patrol had a prisoner, ordered the withdrawal & he did not find out till afterwards that the body of the prisoner had not been brought back. On ascertaining however that his epaulettes had been taken he did not think it advisable to go back into the barrage again to fetch the body. The patrol waited for a quarter of an hour in the enemy front line till the enemy retaliation had died down & then came back.

The enemy retaliation was chiefly from T.M.s & [illegible] not heavy. The conditions owing to the rain were bad but they [illegible] [illegible] [illegible] difficulties in getting across No Man's Land.

[illegible]

guns were not as successful
as they would have been
otherwise. They had shifted [illegible]
from [illegible] & the guns being
put out by action of our artillery.
However they kept down the
enemy fire & the general
opinion is that these were very
a success.

The prisoner was identified as
belonging to the 13 Regt. The N.C.O.
states that he was on [illegible] [illegible] [illegible]
& he must not be carried back.

27.7.1918 A J C [illegible] Lt Col
Comdg [illegible]

SECRET. COPY No.

8th Bn. The Queen's R.W.S. Regt.

OPERATION ORDER No. A.20

by

[illegible]

[illegible]

10.

The following letter is published for promulgation to all ranks.

On leaving the 14th Infantry Brigade, I would like to thank all ranks for the magnificent work they have done, and the loyal and able support they have always given me during 1914 – 1918.

The success of the many operations they have carried out during this period has been due to discipline, good leadership, the cheerful spirit of camaraderie, and the personal gallantry of all ranks. The operations in 1914, at NEVIN, MESSINES, BATTLE WOOD, and YPRES, and in 1918 at LE-VERGUIER, CAUBRIERES WOOD, FLEZ, OMIECOURT, CHAULNES and VRELY, form a record of success unequalled by any Brigade, and one which you, and those who come after you, will be for ever proud to remember. There is much yet to be accomplished, and I know you will keep these great traditions, and the memory of our fallen comrades forever in your thoughts and by your further splendid efforts bring the nation to Victory and Peace.

It is with the greatest regret that I leave the Brigade, and take this opportunity of wishing all ranks the best of good luck, and success in the future

(Signed) P.V.P. Stone. Brig Genl
Commanding 14th Inf Bde.

WR 36

C 34

28031 W3125/M2250 1000m 6/17 M.R.Co.,Ltd. (1367) Forms W3091.

Army Form W. 3091.

17/24

Cover for Documents.

Natures of Enclosures.

8th BN THE QUEEN'S R.W.S REGT

WAR DIARY

VOLUME XXXVI

AUGUST 1918.

September 6th
1918

H. J. C. Peirs.

Lieut Colonel
Commanding
8th Bn The Queens
RWS Regt

Notes, or Letters written.

Instructions regarding War Diaries and Intelligence Summaries are contained in F. S. Regs., Part II. and the Staff Manual respectively. Title Pages will be prepared in manuscript.

WAR DIARY
or
INTELLIGENCE SUMMARY
(Erase heading not required.)

AUGUST 1918

Page 1

VOLUME XXXVI

Army Form C. 2118

Place	Date	Hour	Summary of Events and Information	Remarks and references to Appendices
LES BREBIS	1st		Battn in training in Divisional Reserve. At about 8 P.M. the enemy put several shells into the village, notably in the vicinity of B Coy's billets, 4 O.R.s being wounded	
— " —	2nd		Battn in training in Divisional Reserve. The enemy again shelled LES BREBIS during the night and early morning of the 3rd, but no casualties were incurred. 2/Lieut. A.P. PITEL left the Battn to join the R.A.F.	
— " —	3rd		Battn in training in Divisional Reserve. A Brigade Musketry Meeting was held at MARQUEFFLES Rifle Range, in which the Battn competed. 2/Lieut. E.P. DORRELL joined the Battn.	
— " —	4th		Battn in training in Divisional Reserve. A Parade Service to mark the Commencement of the Fifth Year of the War was held at Army H.Q. and was attended by representatives of all units in the Army and of our Allies. 1 Officer and 23 O.R.'s attended to represent the Battn. The Army Commander General Sir H.S. HORNE K.C.B., K.C.M.G., was present and delivered an address.	
LES BREBIS - TRENCHES	5th		Battn in training in Divisional Reserve. Officers and N.C.O.'s of the Battn attended a lecture in the Cinema Hall, LES BREBIS, by Lord DENBIGH on "War Aims", at which the Army Commander General Sir H.S. HORNE KCB, KCMG, was present. The Battn relieved the 1st Royal Fusiliers in the Southern sub-section of the MAROC sector. The relief was complete at 12.40 A.M. on the morning of the 6th. On completion of relief Coys were disposed as follows:- C Coy - Left Front Coy, D Coy - Right Front Coy, A Coy in Support, B Coy in Reserve, Battn H.Q. in HARRISON's CRATER.	Ref Appendix I. Battn O.O. No A 21

1875 Wt. W593/826 1,000,000 4/15 J.B.C. & A. A.D.S.S./Forms/C. 2118.

C.F.T.

Instructions regarding War Diaries and Intelligence Summaries are contained in F. S. Regs., Part II. and the Staff Manual respectively. Title Pages will be prepared in manuscript.

WAR DIARY
or
INTELLIGENCE SUMMARY
(Erase heading not required.)

Army Form C. 2118

AUGUST 1918 — Page 2 — VOL. XXXVI

Place	Date	Hour	Summary of Events and Information	Remarks and references to Appendices
TRENCHES	5th	Contd	Weather very wet.	
— —	6th		Weather showery. Our artillery fairly active during the day especially on back areas. Enemy artillery quiet. 2/Lieut R T BIRD joined the Battn.	
— —	7th		Weather very fine. The day was marked by great aerial activity on our part, our aeroplanes flying in large numbers all over and behind the enemy's lines. Our artillery fairly active during the day, the Heavies shelling enemy front and support lines on one or two occasions. Enemy artillery was also active in the early morning, and about mid day CITÉ ST PIERRE received attention from Heavies.	
— —	8th		Weather fine. Our aeroplanes were again very active. Our artillery fairly active. Enemy artillery & TM's quiet. Very little enemy aircraft activity. Following awards of the Military Medal announced in Corps Routine Orders:- 10493 Sgt WHITNEY P., 18231 Pte FRENCH I.W., 68313 Pte SHAW W.R.	
— —	9th		Weather fine. Our artillery was active during the day, the Heavies carrying out a shoot on NORMAN STACKS. Our aeroplanes fairly active. Enemy artillery and aeroplanes quiet. At about 5.30 A.M. a patrol of 2 Officers & 1 O.R. went out into NO MANS LAND and did not return and no trace of them was found by patrols subsequently sent out. About 7.45 A.M. a sentry on a forward post heard rifle shots and bombs and about 8 A.M. observers of the 3rd Rifle Brigade and 9th Royal Sussex Regt on our left saw a party of a dozen of the enemy taking 3 men back to their lines, one apparently wounded. Casualties - 2 Officers (Capt. H E WHEATLEY and CAPT C P HAWARD) and 1 O.R. Missing	CF.1

1875 Wt. W593/826 1,000,000 4/15 J.B.C. & A. A.D.S.S./Forms/C. 2118.

Army Form C. 2118

Instructions regarding War Diaries and Intelligence Summaries are contained in F. S. Regs., Part II. and the Staff Manual respectively. Title Pages will be prepared in manuscript.

WAR DIARY
or
INTELLIGENCE SUMMARY
(Erase heading not required.)

AUGUST 1918 — Page 3 — VOL. XXXVI

Place	Date	Hour	Summary of Events and Information	Remarks and references to Appendices
TRENCHES	9th	CONTD.	A Divisional Horse Show and Sports, in which the Battn competed, were held on the Corps Horse Show Ground	
— " —	10th		Our artillery very active on enemy back areas. Aeroplanes also active reconnoitring and flying low and firing on enemy lines. Enemy artillery quiet during the day, but slightly more active at night.	
— " —	11th		Our artillery active especially on LENS and enemy back areas, and Trench Mortars on enemy front line and wire. Normal aerial activity. Enemy artillery quiet except for about 100 5.9's searching for our Heavy Trench Mortars, and some 4.2's on junction of COSY ALLEY and NASH TRENCH. There were also some gas shells and Heavy Trench Mortars on our forward posts during the night. A & B Coys relieved C and D Coys in the front line, C Coy coming into Support and D Coy into Reserve.	Ref Appendix II. Battn O.O. No A22
			From the 7th to 11th inst. a Musketry Competition was held at the Army Musketry Camp open to all units in the 1st Army, each unit entering one team of 1 Officer and 9 O.R's all drawn from the same platoon. The team entered by the Battn won the Anti Gas Competition, for which the Battn received the Congratulations of the G.O.C. Division	Ref Appendix III. Telegram from G.O.C.
— " —	12th		Weather still fine and hot. Our artillery shelled CITÉ ST. AUGUSTE and enemy back areas at intervals. Our aeroplanes were active during the evening and our Trench Mortars during the night. Enemy artillery intermittently active on back areas during the day. A few low flying enemy aircraft appeared over our lines.	
			Capt J R SMITH left the Battn for attachment to Divisional H.Q. on appointment as Divisional Works Officer.	

1875 Wt. W593/826 1,000,000 4/15 J.B.C. & A. A.D.S.S./Forms/C. 2118.

C.F.T.

Instructions regarding War Diaries and Intelligence Summaries are contained in F. S. Regs., Part II. and the Staff Manual respectively. Title Pages will be prepared in manuscript.

WAR DIARY
or
INTELLIGENCE SUMMARY
(Erase heading not required.)

Army Form C. 2118

AUGUST 1918

Page 4

VOL. XXXVI

Place	Date	Hour	Summary of Events and Information	Remarks and references to Appendices
TRENCHES	13th		Our artillery active on enemy forward lines and back areas. Normal activity by our aeroplanes. Enemy artillery active at intervals during the day, especially on CITÉ ST PIERRE, COIN and WALKEM TRENCHES. Enemy night bombing machines were heard at frequent intervals during the night and bombs were dropped in the vicinity of CITÉ ST PIERRE.	
—"—	14th		A quiet day. Very little artillery activity on either side and very few aeroplanes observed until the evening when ours were rather more active.	
—"—	15th		Our artillery very active, especially in the afternoon and evening when two or three organized shoots, each of some 5 minutes' duration, were carried out on LENS and the CARVIN ROAD. Normal activity by our aeroplanes. Enemy artillery fairly quiet. No enemy aircraft observed till 7.30 P.M. when 11 high flying machines attempted to cross our lines but were driven back by A.A. fire.	
—"—	16th		Our artillery quieter than usual, especially at night, this being a "Silent night" for the artillery covering the Brigade front. 2 of our aeroplanes brought down a hostile machine over the enemy lines. Enemy artillery fairly quiet. The award of the Military Cross to 2/Lieut E.F. REEVES was published in Army Routine Orders.	
TRENCHES —LES BREBIS	17th		Weather more unsettled, cloudy and windy. Our artillery very active all day on enemy lines and back areas. Less aerial activity than usual. Enemy artillery fairly quiet during the day but increased during the night, fire being directed especially on the LENS-BETHUNE ROAD and CITÉ ST. PIERRE. The Batt^n was	

1875 Wt. W593/826 1,000,000 4/15 J.B.C. & A. A.D.S.S./Forms/C. 2118.

CF1

Army Form C. 2118

Instructions regarding War Diaries and Intelligence Summaries are contained in F. S. Regs., Part II. and the Staff Manual respectively. Title Pages will be prepared in manuscript.

WAR DIARY
or
INTELLIGENCE SUMMARY
(Erase heading not required.)

AUGUST 1918

Page 5

VOL XXXVI

Place	Date	Hour	Summary of Events and Information	Remarks and references to Appendices
TRENCHES - LES BREBIS	17th	CONTD.	relieved in the line by the 3rd. Rifle Brigade, relief being complete by 12.30 A.M. (18th) As a result of the above mentioned shelling of CITE ST. PIERRE 2 Lewis Gun Limbers were damaged, 2 mules killed and 2 wounded, and 3 O.R.'s wounded. The Battn proceeded to LES BREBIS and passed into Divisional Reserve. Casualties for Tour - MISSING. 2 officers & 1 O.R. WOUNDED 5 O.R.'s. 2/LIEUTS. H.V. ELLIOTT and W.T. EVERETT and a draft of 50 O.R.'s taken on the strength of the Battn	Ref Appendix IV. Battn O.O. No. A.23
LES BREBIS	18th		Battn in training in Divisional Reserve	
—"—	19th		—"—	
—"—	20th		—"— Inspection of the Battn by the G.O.C. Division	
—"—	21st		—"— Address delivered by the Corps Commander, Lieut Gen Sir AYLMER HUNTER-WESTON, K.C.B., D.S.O., at 20th Division H.Q. on "The Battle of the 15th July". Two officers of the Battn attended.	
—"—	22nd		Battn in training in Divisional Reserve. LES BREBIS and vicinity were shelled intermittently by a 5.9 gun between 7 A.M. and 1 P.M., especially in the neighbourhood of B Coy's billets, but no casualties were reported.	
LES BREBIS - TRENCHES	23rd		The Battn relieved the 1st Royal Fusiliers in the northern sub section of the MAROC Sector. The relief was complete by 12.30 A.M. on the morning of the 24th. On completion of relief Coys were disposed as follows:- A Coy - Right Front Coy, B Coy - Left Front Coy, D Coy in Support, C Coy in Reserve, Battn H.Q. in THE QUARRY. Weather fine but cooler. 2/LIEUTS. A.H. FIDDLER and E.S. FRY joined the Battn	Ref Appendix V Battn O.O. No. A.24

CF

1875 Wt. W593/826 1,000,000 4/15 J.B.C. & A. A.D.S.S./Forms/C. 2118.

Instructions regarding War Diaries and Intelligence Summaries are contained in F. S. Regs., Part II. and the Staff Manual respectively. Title Pages will be prepared in manuscript.

WAR DIARY
or
~~INTELLIGENCE~~ SUMMARY
(Erase heading not required.)

Army Form C. 2118

PAGE 6

AUGUST 1918

VOL XXXVI

Place	Date	Hour	Summary of Events and Information	Remarks and references to Appendices
TRENCHES	24th		Very quiet day. Our forward posts received some attention from enemy artillery during the night	
— " —	25		Our forward posts again heavily shelled by hostile artillery. Slight shelling of MARGATE, NOTTINGHAM and MAIDSTONE TRENCHES with Gas Shells	
— " —	26th		A quiet day on the whole, as visibility was poor. MAROC, SOUTH STREET and the "Daylight Track" were very heavily shelled in the late afternoon with 4·2's and 5·9's. Our forward posts again received attention during the night. Heavy rain came on during the evening.	
— " —	27th		Weather cool and showery. Harassing fire by hostile artillery (mostly 4·2's) round THE QUARRY and HARRISON'S CRATER at intervals. Our artillery active. Not many aeroplanes about on either side. Corps Routine Orders contained notification of award of Military Medal to 31154 Pte A G FRENCH, the previous award to 68231 Pte I W FRENCH being cancelled.	
— " —	28th		Weather again showery. Enemy artillery quiet during the day, but considerable harassing fire took place at night over the whole forward area as far back as THE QUARRY, including a large number of gas shells. Our artillery fairly active. Patrols were out at night from both forward Coys to keep touch with the enemy who was suspected of intending a retirement, but no signs of this were noticed, his line being held as usual. A low flying enemy aeroplane was reported to have been brought down by rifle or Lewis Gun fire on the Batt" front.	

1875 Wt. W593/826 1,000,000 4/15 J.B.C. & A. A.D.S.S./Forms/C. 2118.

CH

Instructions regarding War Diaries and Intelligence Summaries are contained in F. S. Regs., Part II. and the Staff Manual respectively. Title Pages will be prepared in manuscript.

Army Form C. 2118

WAR DIARY or ~~INTELLIGENCE~~ SUMMARY

(Erase heading not required.)

AUGUST 1918

PAGE 7

VOL XXXVI

Place	Date	Hour	Summary of Events and Information	Remarks and references to Appendices
TRENCHES	28th	CONTD	in the morning, but this was not confirmed. LIEUT. and QUARTERMASTER W.T. BURNHAM rejoined the Battn from Hospital and England. 2/LIEUT F.T. POPE left the Battn to join the R.A.F. Casualties :- 2 O.R.'s Killed by shell fire.	
	29th		Orders received to make preparations for an advance in the event of the enemy retiring, but later in the evening an Artillery O.P. reported that the enemy was massing in his trenches opposite HILL 70. Our men stood to for longer than usual, but no enemy attack resulted. THE QUARRY and HARRISONS CRATER were rather heavily shelled at night, especially with gas. During the afternoon and evening C and D Coys relieved A and B Coys in the front line, B Coy coming into Support and A Coy into Reserve.	Ref. Appendix VI Battn O.O. No A 25
	30th		In the morning it was reported that the Division on our right had gone forward, and preparations for an advance were again made; but it was found by observation from the O.P.s that the enemy still had his normal sentry groups posted and there was a good deal of movement in his rear lines. At night hostile artillery again shelled THE QUARRY, but retaliation was called for and his guns silenced with gas shells. The night on the whole was fairly quiet except for considerable gas shelling of the area forward of the BLACK LINE. 2/LIEUT. D C G DICKINSON joined the Battn.	Ref. Appendix VII. Patrol Orders
	31st		A very quiet day. The enemy was reported to be still in his normal positions at midnight. During the night the vicinity of THE QUARRY was again shelled	

CFT

1875 Wt. W593/826 1,000,000 4/15 J.B.C. & A. A.D.S.S./Forms/C. 2118.

Army Form C. 2118

PAGE 8

WAR DIARY
or
INTELLIGENCE SUMMARY

(Erase heading not required.)

Instructions regarding War Diaries and Intelligence Summaries are contained in F. S. Regs., Part II. and the Staff Manual respectively. Title Pages will be prepared in manuscript.

AUGUST 1918

VOL. XXXVI

Place	Date	Hour	Summary of Events and Information	Remarks and references to Appendices
TRENCHES	31st	CONTD	and a Sap of A Coy's blown in, 1 O.R being Killed. Orders received to take over the front of the Right Battn of the Division on our left next day. Preparations made for accommodation etc in that Sector.	

C.F. Tatham
Lieut & Asst Adjt
8th Battn The Queen's Regt

CFT

Appendix I

Secret. Copy No. 14

8th Bn. The Queens. Regt.

OPERATION ORDER. No. A. 21.

by

Lieut-Colonel. H. J. C. Peirs. D.S.O.

Map Ref. 1/20,000. St [illegible] — 4th August 1918

1. The Battalion will relieve the 1st Royal [illegible] in the Southern Sub-section of the [illegible] Section on the right of the 5th/[illegible] Line.

2. "A" Coy (Queens) will relieve "[illegible]" Coy. (1st R.F.) Left Front.
   "D" — — — — "C" — — Right —
   "C" — — — — "A" — — Support.
   "B" — — — — "B" — — Reserve.

3. Order of March:- C. D. A. B. H.Q. - C Coy to move at 8.45 p.m. 200x interval between platoons.

4. Guides — [illegible] platoon [illegible] C & D Coys will be at the junction of [illegible] & [illegible]-Bethune [illegible]. There will be no guides for A & B Coys.

5. Lewis Guns:- Coy L. G. limbers will follow the leading platoon of each Coy. H.Q. Coy limber will follow in rear of the Coy.

6. Baggage:- Officers trench bundles, mess kits etc will be dumped at Q.M. Stores ready for collection by 4.30 p.m.
   Officers valises etc not required for the trenches will be [illegible] to Q.M. Stores during the day.
   Coys will arrange to collect baggage, rations, etc. from their respective dumps, i.e., C. D. & A from EDDY, B & H.Q. from Lens-Beth.
   Two men per Coy will be detailed to load and accompany them.

7. Trench Stores:- Trench Stores, Patrol, Sniping, [illegible], Work in hand and proposed, Defence Schemes, etc., will be carefully taken over. Lists of Stores, etc taken over to reach O.R. by [illegible] on the [illegible].

8. Completion of relief will be report by runner or wire using the Code Word "[illegible]".

9. Acknowledge:- O.O. A. 21

Issued at 6 p.m.
by runner.

[illegible]
Capt & Adjutant.
8th Bn The Queens Regt.

Copies to:-

No.		No.	
1.	C.O.	8.	T.O.
2.	O.C. H.Q. Coy	9.	Q.M.
3.	— A —	10.	17th [illegible]
4.	— C —	11.	1st R.F.
5.	— D —	12.	R.S.M.
6.	— B —	13.	File.
7.	— [illegible]	14.	[illegible]

Appendix II

SECRET. Copy No. 14

8TH BN THE QUEEN'S REGT

OPERATION ORDER No. [illegible]

by

MAJOR. R. H. ROWLAND

Ref. 1/20.000 ST. NAZAIRE. 10TH AUGUST [illegible]

1 The following reliefs will take place on the 11th inst.
(a). "A" Coy will relieve "C" Coy (Left Front)
(b) "B" — — — "D" — (R[illegible])

2 Coys will relieve by sections.
"A" Coy moving off at 4.30 p.m. and "B" Coy at [illegible] p.m.

3 Arrangements for relief will be made between Company Commanders concerned.

4 Trench Stores, S.A.A. [illegible], work in hand and proposed, working parties, etc., will be carefully taken over.
[illegible] etc. taken and handed over to reach Orderly Room by 12 noon, 12th inst.

5 Completion of relief will be report by wire or runner using the code word "THE BOY".

6 ACKNOWLEDGE.

Issued at 230 [illegible]
by runner.

[illegible]
Capt & Adjutant
8th Bn The Queen's Regt

Copies to:
No 1. C. O. [illegible]
2. O.C. "A" Coy [illegible]
3. — "B" — [illegible]
4. — "C" — [illegible]
5. — "D" — [illegible]
6. [illegible] [illegible]

Appendix III

Army Form C. 2123.
(In books of 100.)

"C" FORM.

MESSAGES AND SIGNALS. No. of Message 100301

Prefix SM Code KBS pm Words 23

Received from BA2 By JPR

Service Instructions JEWU

Sent, or sent out. At ... m. To ... By ...

Office Stamp. AK25 9.8.18

Handed in at 14th Div. SIGNAL Office 10.12 pm. Received 10.24 pm.

TO Lowe

*Sender's Number.	Day of Month.	In reply to Number.	AAA
G566	9th	—	

Have just heard that you won antigas competition at Army rifle meeting today aaa My heartiest congratulations

FROM GEN. DALY

PLACE & TIME

* This line, except AAA, should be erased, if not required.

(3287) Wt. W54/P738. 691,000 Pads. 3/18. A.P.Ltd. (E3013)

Appendix IV

SECRET. COPY No. 15

8th BN THE QUEEN'S REGT

OPERATION ORDER No. [illegible]

by

Lieut-Colonel [illegible]

MAP REF. [illegible] 15th August 19[illegible]

1. [illegible]

2. "A" Coy [illegible]
"B" [illegible]
"C" [illegible]
"D" [illegible]

3. On [illegible] [illegible]

4. [illegible]
HARRISON'S [illegible] at [illegible]
[illegible] at the junction of [illegible]
BETHUNE ROAD and [illegible] M12
"A" [illegible]
[illegible] 11.30 p.m.
[illegible]

5. Officer's kits, Mess kits, Cooking [illegible] of [illegible] Coys [illegible]
EDDY DUMP at 10 [illegible]
[illegible]
[illegible]
on the [illegible]
[illegible]
with them [illegible]

6. [illegible]
[illegible]
[illegible]
by [illegible]

7. [illegible]
the Code Word [illegible] OOK [illegible] AH

8. ACKNOWLEDGE [illegible]

[illegible] 10

Appendix V

Secret. Copy No. 15.

8th Bn. The Queen's Regt.

Operation Order No. A.24.

By

Lieut. Colonel [illegible] J.C. Petre [illegible] D.S.O.

[illegible] 20th AUG. 191[illegible]

1. The Battn. will relieve the [illegible] [illegible] in the [illegible] section of the [illegible] [illegible] of the [illegible].

2. "A" Coy (Queen's) will relieve "A" Coy (to [illegible]) on the Right
"B" — — — "B" — — — Left
"D" — — — "D" — — — in Support
"C" — — — "C" — — — Reserve

3. Order of March:- "A", "B", "C", "D" & H.Q. Coy. First Coy will move off at 8.45 p.m. 200x interval between platoons.

4. Guides: 1 per platoon will be at the junction of the [illegible] [illegible] [illegible] [illegible] at [illegible] p.m.

5. Lewis Guns: Coy L.G. [illegible] will follow the leading platoon of each Coy. H.Q. Coy [illegible] will [illegible] rear of the Coy.

6. Baggage: Officers' [illegible] [illegible] [illegible] etc. will be dumped at [illegible] ready for collection [illegible]
Officers' valises etc. not required for [illegible] will be returned to [illegible] Stores during the day.
Coys will arrange to collect rations [illegible] from their respective Dumps i.e.
"A" & "B" Coys ... [illegible] Dump
"C", "D" & H.Q. [illegible] ... [illegible] Dump.
[illegible] men will be detailed per Coy to [illegible] [illegible] [illegible]

7. [illegible] Stores: All Trench Stores [illegible] [illegible] [illegible] [illegible] [illegible] etc. to be carefully taken over.
[illegible] Stores taken over to [illegible] [illegible] [illegible]

8. Completion of relief will be reported by [illegible] [illegible] Code Word "GOING UP".

9. Acknowledge: O.O. A.24

Issued at 5.35 p.m. by runner

[illegible]

Copies to:- [illegible]

Appendix VI

11

8th Bn. The Queen's Regt.

Operation Order No A 26

Ref. [illegible] [illegible]

1. The following inter-Coy Relief will take place on the 27th inst

"C" Coy will relieve "A" Coy (RIGHT)
"D" " " "B" " (LEFT)

2. Arrangements for relief will be made between Coy Commanders concerned.
3. C Coy will start relieving at 5.30PM and D Coy at 6PM.
4. On completion of relief A Coy will be in Reserve and "B" Coy in Support.
5. Trench Stores, Petrol tins full, Defence Schemes, work in hand and proposed etc will be carefully handed over. List of Stores taken & handed over to reach Orderly Room by 8 AM [illegible].
6. Completion of relief will be reported [illegible] using the code word "[illegible]"
7. Acknowledge. O.C. A.B.C.D.

[illegible]

Issued at 5 pm by Runner

[illegible]

Copies to [illegible]

SECRET. Appendix VII COPY No. 8

Patrol Orders for night 29/30th Aug. 1918

A Fighting Patrol from the Right Front Coy will leave our line from about N.2.b.40.62 at about 12 midnight tonight. It will proceed across NO MANS LAND in an Easterly direction and reconnoitre enemy front line as far as Railway at about N.2.b.7.7.

Patrol will return to our line at 2.30 A.M.

Object:- To get in touch with enemy & obtain an identification if possible.

C.J. Taka
Lieut & Asst. Adjt
LOWU

29-8-18

COPIES No 1. to O/C 'C' Coy
2 " " 'D' "
3 " " Right Battn
4 " " 17" L.T.M.B.
5 " " X/24 T.M.B.
6 " " 24th M.G.B.
7. FILE.
8 WAR DIARY

9.35

35807. W16879/M1879 500,000 3/17 R.T. (1074) Forms/W3091/3 Army Form W.3091.

9R 37

Cover for Documents.

Nature of Enclosures.

5TH BN THE QUEENS RWS REGT

WAR DIARY

VOLUME XXXVII

SEPTEMBER

1916

OCT 5TH 1916

H.P.C. [illegible] LIEUT COL
COMMANDING
5TH BN THE QUEENS RWS REGT

Notes, or Letters written.

9

Army Form C. 2118

Instructions regarding War Diaries and Intelligence Summaries are contained in F. S. Regs., Part II. and the Staff Manual respectively. Title Pages will be prepared in manuscript.

WAR DIARY
or
~~INTELLIGENCE SUMMARY~~
(Erase heading not required.)

SEPTEMBER 1918

Page 1

VOLUME XXXVII

Place	Date	Hour	Summary of Events and Information	Remarks and references to Appendices
TRENCHES	1st		Battalion holding Northern sub-section of MAROC Sector. During the day the Battalion side stepped to the left taking over a new sector from the Right Battn of the Division on our left and handing over our Right Coy front to the Battn on our right. The new boundaries of the Battn front are shewn in attached O.O. No. A26 paras 2 & 3. After relief Coys were disposed as follows:- C Coy - Left Front Coy, B Coy Centre Front Coy, D Coy Right Front Coy, A Coy in Reserve. Battn H.Q. remained in HARTS QUARRY. About midday it was reported that the enemy had retired from LENS, and B and D Coys were ordered to send out strong patrols to occupy the enemy front line and establish posts there. B Coy's patrol found the enemy line strongly occupied and suffered several casualties from M.G. fire (1 O.R killed, 5 O.R's wounded). Patrols were consequently recalled. Later in the evening the Right Battn also reported enemy trenches to be strongly held.	Appendix I BN OO A26.
—"—	2nd		The enemy was reported to be still holding his line in normal strength. Some readjustment of Coy dispositions was carried out during the day in order to obtain better accommodation. A fairly quiet day. NATAL, MARGATE and MAIDSTONE TRENCHES received some attention from hostile artillery	
—"—	3rd		A quiet day and night. At night 4 Bangalore Torpedoes were taken out to blow up enemy wire. Two were successfully exploded with good results, but the other two failed to act. The Division on our left carried out a Gas Projector attack. Two howitzers were moved close up to Battn H.Q.	

CA

1875 Wt. W593/826 1,000,000 4/15 J.B.C. & A. A.D.S.S./Forms/C. 2118.

Army Form C. 2118

WAR DIARY
or
~~INTELLIGENCE SUMMARY~~
(Erase heading not required.)

Instructions regarding War Diaries and Intelligence Summaries are contained in F. S. Regs., Part II. and the Staff Manual respectively. Title Pages will be prepared in manuscript.

SEPTEMBER 1918

Page 2

VOLUME XXXVII

Place	Date	Hour	Summary of Events and Information	Remarks and references to Appendices
TRENCHES	4th		A quiet day, but very heavy shelling at night round NELSON TRENCH and Battn. H.Q. Retaliation was called for – "SMASH AUGUSTE" and "GAS OVENS" – which effectually silenced the enemy artillery	
— " —	5th		Another quiet day and early part of night, with the exception of a few shells round Battn. H.Q. and on the "Daylight Track". The Battn. was relieved in the line at night by the 3rd Rifle Brigade, relief being complete by midnight. On relief the Battn. proceeded to LES BREBIS and passed into Divisional Reserve.	Appendix II BN OO A.27
– LES BREBIS				
LES BREBIS	6th		Battn. in training in Divisional Reserve.	
— " —	7th		— " — — " — Two Coys proceeded to MARQUEFFLES for training and range practices.	
— " —	8th		Battn. in training in Divisional Reserve. Two Coys again went to MARQUEFFLES for training	
— " —	9th		— " — — " — About 20 shells fell in the vicinity of LES BREBIS in the early morning but no casualties or damage were reported.	
— " —	11th		Battn. in training in Divisional Reserve. Tactical exercises were carried out by the whole Battn. between BULLY and BOIS DE NOULETTE. Weather very wet.	
LES BREBIS – TRENCHES	11th		The Battn. relieved the 1st. Royal Fusiliers in the southern sub section of the MAROC Sector. Relief was complete by midnight. On completion of relief Coys were disposed as follows – A Coy. Left Front Coy, D Coy Centre Front Coy, C Coy Right Front Coy, B Coy in Reserve. Battn. H.Q in HARRISON'S CRATER	Appendix III BN OO A 28

1875 Wt. W593/826 1,000,000 4/15 J.B.C. & A. A.D.S.S./Forms/C. 2118.

Army Form C. 2118

WAR DIARY
or
INTELLIGENCE SUMMARY
(Erase heading not required.)

•Instructions regarding War Diaries and Intelligence Summaries are contained in F. S. Regs., Part II. and the Staff Manual respectively. Title Pages will be prepared in manuscript.

SEPTEMBER 1918

PAGE 3

VOLUME XXXVII

Place	Date	Hour	Summary of Events and Information	Remarks and references to Appendices
TRENCHES	12th		Weather very wet and windy. A quiet day on the whole. Normal activity by our artillery. Enemy artillery active at intervals on forward area. Very little aerial activity.	
– " –	13th		Our artillery active on enemy forward and back areas and Trench Mortars on front line and wire. Enemy artillery quiet during the day except for some retaliation for Trench Mortars, but very active at night over whole forward area with Salvoes of 5.9's and 4.2's in places. Aerial activity slight. 2/Lieut L.A. McDERMOTT joined the Battn. Capt. J. REID SMITH struck off the strength of the Battn on transfer to the R.E's.	
– " –	14th		Normal artillery work on both sides during the day. No aerial activity. At night a fighting patrol of 2 Officers and 27 O.R's left our lines with the object of securing identification. They penetrated to enemy support line in N 3 c and lay up there for over an hour, but saw no enemy at all, and the trench showed no signs of recent occupation though it was in good condition.	
– " –	15th		The weather turned fine and warm again. Normal artillery and aerial activity on both sides during the day. 2 enemy aeroplanes were seen over our lines, and at night hostile night bombers were very active, many bombs being heard to drop. The same fighting patrol went out again at night with orders to establish posts in the enemy support line if there were no enemy in the vicinity. But his line was found to be strongly held and the patrol was	CH

1875 Wt. W593/826 1,000,000 4/15 J.B.C. & A. A.D.S.S./Forms/C. 2118.

Army Form C. 2118

WAR DIARY
or
~~INTELLIGENCE SUMMARY~~
(Erase heading not required.)

PAGE 4
VOLUME XXXVII

Instructions regarding War Diaries and Intelligence Summaries are contained in F. S. Regs., Part II. and the Staff Manual respectively. Title Pages will be prepared in manuscript. SEPTEMBER 1918

Place	Date	Hour	Summary of Events and Information	Remarks and references to Appendices
TRENCHES	15th	CONTD	driven back by M G fire, the moon being too bright for concealment. No casualties were incurred. Lieut. G H S WYNDHAM joined the Battn.	
"	16th		Another warm sunny day. Not much activity beyond the normal either by artillery or in the air. During the afternoon and evening certain readjustments of our dispositions were carried out. C Coy was relieved by C Coy 1st NORTH Staffs (72nd Infantry Brigade) and went into support. D Coy took over one platoon area from A Coy, and A Coy one platoon area from the 3rd Rifle Brigade. The new Battn boundaries are shown in attached O O No A 29 para 9. On completion of relief Coys were disposed as follows:- A Coy. Left Front Coy, D Coy. Right Front Coy, C Coy in Support, B Coy in Reserve, Battn H.Q. remaining in HARRISONS CRATER. The relief of C Coy was observed by the enemy and some shelling of COSY TRENCH ~~resulted~~. The 1st North Staffs suffered some casualties, but we had none.	Appendix IV BH OO A29
— " —	17th		During the afternoon and evening the Battn was relieved by the 1st Royal Fusiliers and itself moved to the Northern sub section of the MAROC Sector to relieve the 3rd Rifle Brigade. The double relief was complete by midnight. On completion of relief Coys were disposed as follows:- B Coy - Right Front Coy, C Coy. Left Front Coy, D Coy in Support, A Coy in Reserve, Battn H.Q. in HARTS QUARRY. A raid during the afternoon by the Division on our left brought	Appendix V BH OO 30 CAF

1875 Wt. W593/826 1,000,000 4/15 J.B.C. & A. A.D.S.S./Forms/C. 2118.

Army Form C. 2118

WAR DIARY
or
~~INTELLIGENCE SUMMARY~~
(Erase heading not required.)

*Instructions regarding War Diaries and Intelligence Summaries are contained in F. S. Regs., Part II. and the Staff Manual respectively. Title Pages will be prepared in manuscript.

SEPTEMBER 1918

PAGE 5

VOLUME XXXVII

Place	Date	Hour	Summary of Events and Information	Remarks and references to Appendices
TRENCHES	17th	CONTD	some retaliation mostly in the neighbourhood of HARRISON'S CRATER. Lieut T E SWAIN joined the Battn.	
" "	18th		A quiet day and night except for some shelling of the Left Forward Coy probably in retaliation for activity of our 6 inch Newtons. The Support Coy was withdrawn from the line at night and proceeded to LES BREBIS for training, the Reserve Coy taking over some of the positions vacated by the Support Coy. 2/Lieut W E KAYE left the Battn for the Labour Corps Base Depot	
" "	19th		A quiet day. One enemy aeroplane came over our lines during the afternoon but was driven back by M.G and L.G fire	
" "	20th		Another quiet day, but some gas shelling at night. The Division on our left received a certain amount of attention from hostile artillery during the day	
" "	21st		Fairly quiet day, except that "B" and "Y M C A" Entrances to HYTHE TUNNEL received a great deal of attention and new slits which were being dug as observation posts were destroyed	
" "	22nd		Quiet during the day, but at night enemy artillery was active with 5.9's on CITÉ ST PIERRE and LOOS and on our left forward post. Our artillery retaliated on BOIS DE DIXHULT with the desired effect.	
TRENCHES – LES BREBIS	23rd		A quiet day. The Battn was relieved at night by the 3rd Rifle Brigade and proceeded to LES BREBIS passing into Divisional Reserve. Relief was complete by 10.40 P.M.	Appendix VI

B110QA31
CA

1875 Wt. W593/826 1,000,000 4/15 J.B.C. & A. A.D.S.S./Forms/C. 2118.

Army Form C. 2118

WAR DIARY
or
~~INTELLIGENCE SUMMARY~~
(Erase heading not required.)

Instructions regarding War Diaries and Intelligence Summaries are contained in F. S. Regs., Part II. and the Staff Manual respectively. Title Pages will be prepared in manuscript. SEPTEMBER 1918

PAGE 6

VOLUME XXXVII

Place	Date	Hour	Summary of Events and Information	Remarks and references to Appendices
LES BREBIS	24th		Battn in training in Divisional Reserve	
— " —	25th		— " — — " — 2/Lieut C.F. OLLEY M.C. left the Battn to proceed to England to join the R.A.F.	
— " —	26th		Battn in training in Divisional Reserve.	
— " —	27th		— " — — " —	
— " —	28th		— " — — " — Practice demonstration of cooperation between Infantry and Tanks, rather spoilt by rain. 2/Lt C.E. WINGROVE left the Battn to proceed to England to join the R.A.F	
— " —	29th		Battn in training in Divisional Reserve.	
LES BREBIS – MAISNIL-LES-RUITZ	30th		The Battn was relieved in Divisional Reserve by the 6th Battn London Regt (T.F) on relief of the Division by the 58th (London) Division. Relief was complete by 2 P.M. On completion of relief the Battn proceeded by March Route to MAISNIL-LES-RUITZ prior to entraining for another area on the 1st prox.	Appendix VII B1100A32

C.F. Tatham
Lieut & Asst Adjt
8th Bn The Queen's Regt

1875 Wt. W593/826 1,000,000 4/15 J.B.C. & A. A.D.S.S./Forms/C. 2118.

APPENDIX I

SECRET

Copy No. 15

8th B.N. THE QUEENS REGT
OPERATION ORDER. No. A 26.

Aug. 5th 1918

1. The 8th Bn the Queen's Regt will [illegible] to the left on [illegible]

2. Northern Batt. Boundary will be
Junction of Heaven Trench and [illegible] Heaven Trench [illegible] Scots Alley (inclusive) [illegible]

3. Southern Batt. Boundary will be
[illegible]

4. C Coy 8th Queens will be relieved by [illegible]
[illegible]

5. On relief C Coy 8th Queens will take over from D Coy [illegible]
1 Platoon [illegible]
1 Platoon [illegible]
1 Platoon Greenmound [illegible]
1 Platoon Gordon Alley [illegible]
Coy H.Q. Gordon [illegible]

6. B Coy 8th Queens will take over [illegible]

7. [illegible]

8. [illegible]

9. [illegible]

APPENDIX A 28

Secret. Copy No. 14.

8th Bn. The Queens Regt.

OPERATION ORDER. No. A.27

Ref. 1/20.000. GRENAY. 4th Sept. 1918.

1 8th Bn. The Queens Regt. will be relieved in the Left Sub-Sector of the Brigade Front on night 5th/6th Sept. 1918.

2 On relief Battn will move to LES BREBIS.

3 Companies will be relieved as follows:-

"A" Coy (Queens) will be relieved by "B" Coy (3rd R.B.)
"D" — " — " — " — "A" — " —
"B" — " — " — " — "C" — " —
"C" — " — " — " — "D" — " —

4. One guide from each Platoon will be at junction of MAROC-LOOS & LENS-BETHUNE ROADS at 9 p.m.

5. Limbers will be at the watertanks on road near BATTN. H.Q. in M.6.A. at the following times:-

"A" Coy & H.Q. at 10.30. p.m.
B. C & "D" Coys. — " — 11.30. p.m.

If platoons on their way out pass this point before the above times, the Lewis Guns, magazines, etc., should be dumped i/c of 1 N.C.O. & 2 men per Coy.

6 Officers Trench Bundles, Mess Kits &c., should be at the Dumps at 10. p.m as follows:-

"A" Coy & H.Q. .... MARTYRS DUMP.
"D" " .... GREENMOUND.
"B" & "C" Coys .... PRATTS DUMP

7 All Trench Stores, Petrol Tins filled, Defence Schemes, work in hand and proposed etc will be carefully handed over and receipts obtained. Lists of Trench Stores handed over to reach O. R. by 12 noon. 6th inst.

8 The Bde Guard at MAROC will be relieved at 6. p.m 5th inst. On relief it will proceed to Les Brebis.

9 The TOWN MAJOR and his Staff will go out with "D" Coy. Their relief will arrive 24 hours in advance.

10. Completion of relief will be notified to Bn. H.Q. by runner or wire using CODE WORD "FAIR & WARMER."

11 ACKNOWLEDGE:-

Issued at 8.30 p.m.
by runner.

E. A. Fellows
Capt. & A/Adjutant
8th Bn The Queens Regt.

Copies to:-

No 1.	C.O.	No 8.	T.O.
2.	H.Q. 17. I.B.	9.	M.O.
3.	o/c "A" Coy	10.	Q.M.
4.	" "D" "	11.	o/c Left Bn.
5	" "C" "	12.	" 3rd R.B.
6	" "B" "	13.	FILE.
7	" H.Q.	14.	WAR DIARY

APPENDIX III

SECRET

Copy No. 15

[illegible] Bn. The Queen's Regt

OPERATION ORDER No. [illegible]

[illegible]

1\. [illegible] will relieve the [illegible] Sub-Sector of the Brigade Sector [illegible]

2\. [illegible] Coy (Queens) will relieve [illegible] Coy [illegible]

3\. Order of March - [illegible] 200x interval between platoons.

4\. Guides - 1 per platoon [illegible] of Church St & [illegible] [illegible] Coy.

5\. Lewis Guns - [illegible] limbers [illegible] will follow in rear of [illegible]

6\. Baggage - Officers [illegible] at [illegible] Stores [illegible]
Officers [illegible]
to [illegible] Stores during [illegible]
[illegible] respective [illegible]

[illegible]

[illegible]

New men per Coy will be detailed [illegible]

7\. Trench Stores - [illegible] and [illegible] [illegible]

8\. Completion of relief will be reported [illegible] using the Code Word "[illegible]"

9\. Acknowledge: O.C. [illegible]

Issued at 5 [illegible]

Copies to:

[illegible]

Appendix IV

SECRET. COPY No. 15...

8th BN. THE QUEEN'S REGT.

OPERATION ORDER No. A.29

Ref. St NAZAIRE 1/20,000. 15th SEPT. 1918.

1. The following readjustments of the Battn dispositions will take place tomorrow 16th inst.

2. "C" Coy (8th Queens) will be relieved by "C" Coy (1st N. STAFFS) during the afternoon starting at 2.30. P.M. The 2 Sections now in CONGRESS TR. will occupy positions in WALKEM TR. prior to relief and the dugout in CONGRESS TR. will be thoroughly cleaned and handed over as Coy HQ of the Right Coy. 1st N. STAFFS.

3. "C" Coy. 1st N. STAFFS. will hold the line as follows:-
   1 platoon in COSY ALLEY, forward of DOUGLAS TR.
   1 — " — — " — DOUGLAS TR.,
   1 — " — — " — WALKEM TR. + 1 Platoon in the BLACK LINE.

4. On relief H.Q. + 2 platoons of "C" Coy. will proceed to CITÉ St. EDOUARD 1 platoon to dugout under the railway in CONDEN TR., 1 platoon [illegible] the junction of MAIDSTONE and HENARK TRENCHES.

5. All Trench Stores, patrol lines fitted, work in hand and proposed etc will be carefully handed over. Lists of Stores etc. handed over to reach O.R. by 8 A.M. 17th inst.

6. The platoon of "D" Coy at present in CITÉ St EDOUARD will be withdrawn to HARRISON'S CRATER before dusk. O.C. Coys concerned will arrange details of relief.

7. "D" Coy will move Coy H.Q. to the junction of CONDEN + MAIDENHEAD TRENCHES and 1 platoon from the BLACK LINE to the dugout in MAIDENHEAD TR. at present occupied by "A" Coy. They will take with them all necessary stores and material as far as possible.
The other BLACK LINE platoon will be [illegible] to the [illegible] post at the junction of NESTOR + TRENCH MORTAR TRENCHES. This platoon will find 1 Rifle Post by day at the junction of NOGGIN, NETLEY + TRENCH MORTAR TRENCHES.
The above moves will be completed before 3 p.m.

8. "A" Coy will vacate MAIDENHEAD TR. and relieve the platoon of the 3rd. RIFLE BRIGADE in NELSON TRENCH by 2.30 p.m.

9. On completion of above reliefs and moves the Battn boundaries will be as follows:-
   LEFT:- NETLEY (inclusive) to NELSON, thence to [illegible], thence to junction of NOGGIN + [illegible] TRENCHES.
   RIGHT:- COSY ALLEY (inclusive) E. of BLUE LINE, thence to [illegible], thence DYNAMITE ROAD (inclusive) to [illegible] thence to junction of MOAT TRENCH + COUNTER ALLEY.
   BATTN. H.Q. will remain in HARRISON'S CRATER.

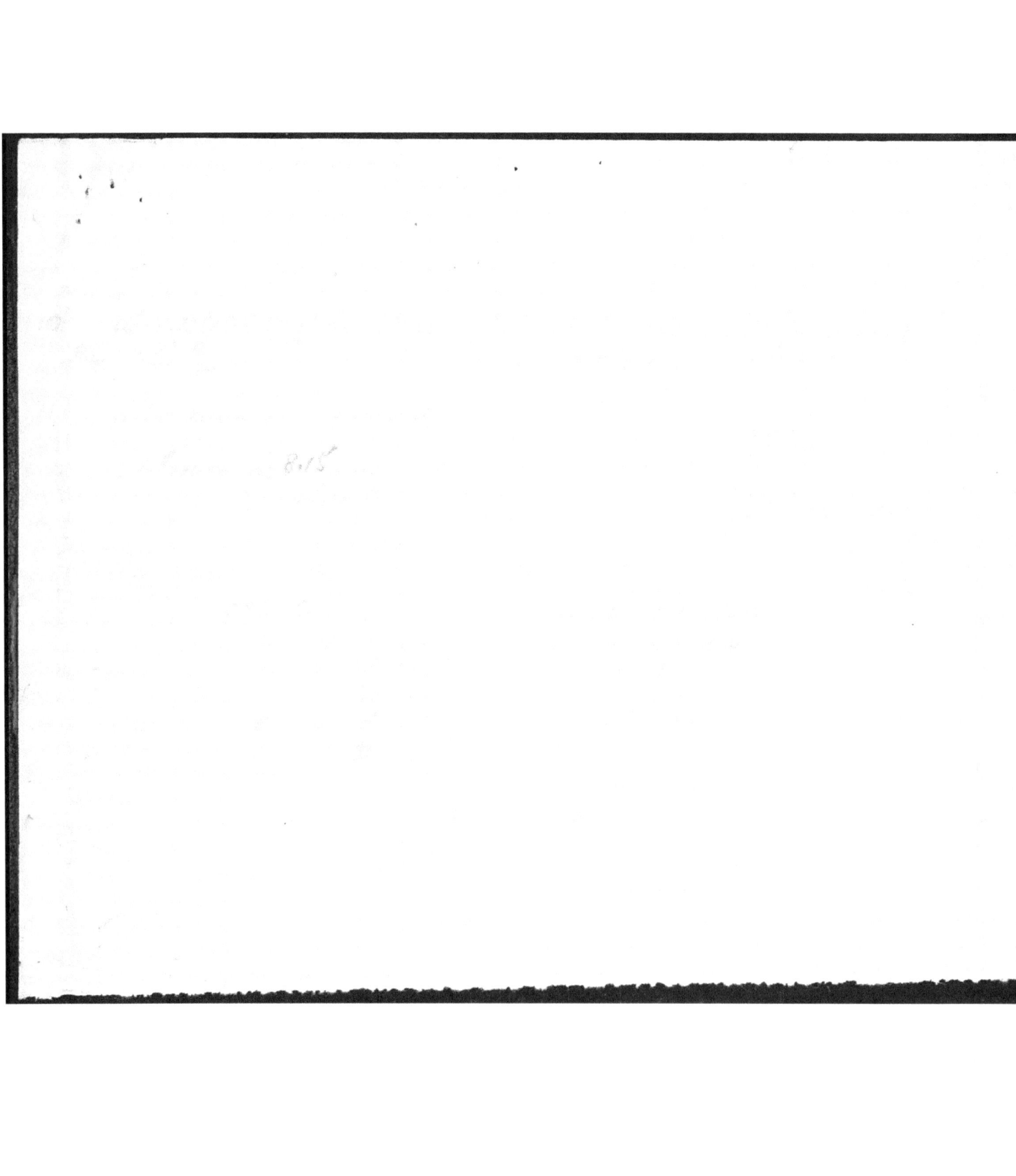

Appendix V

SECRET. COPY No. 16

8th Bn The Queen's Regt
OPERATION ORDER No A30

Ref: [illegible] St [illegible]. 10th Sept. 191[illegible]

1. The Batt[illegible] will be relieved tomorrow night [illegible] by the 1st [illegible] in the Southern Sub-section and on relief will proceed to relieve the 3rd Rifle Brigade in the Northern Sub-section of the [illegible] Sector.

2. "A" Coy (Queens) will be relieved by " " Coy (1st R.F.)
"B" — — — — —
"C" — — — — —
"D" — — — — —

3. "B" Coy (Queens) will relieve "C" Coy (3rd R.B.) Right Front (Right Tunnel)
"C" — — — "D" — — Left —
"D" — — — "A" — — In Support
"A" — — — "B" — — Reserve

4. "A" "C" & "D" Coys will move up to their new positions by platoons as soon as they are relieved, except that the Platoon of "C" Coy in the [illegible] will move independently and will complete relief by 8 p.m.
"B" Coy will also complete their relief in the new [illegible] by 8 p.m.

5. All trench stores etc. will be carefully handed over and taken over on the respective reliefs. Particular care will be taken to ascertain what work is to be carried on in the new sector and the order of its urgency.
List of stores handed and taken over to reach O.R. by 9 a.m. 12th inst.

6. Guides — 1 per platoon of "A", "C" & "D" Companies at M.12.b.05.75. at 8-30 p.m [illegible, struck through]. "B" Coy need not supply guides.

7. [illegible] advance parties will be sent in the early afternoon to take over from 3rd R.B.
Advance parties of 1st R.F. will arrive about 2 p.m. for Support and Reserve Companies.

8. Completion of relief referred to in para [illegible] will be reported by Code Word "METZ" and of that [illegible] in para 3 [illegible] "[illegible]".

9. ACKNOWLEDGE: O.O. A.30.

Issued at 8. pm by runner.

[illegible]
Capt & Adjutant
8th Bn Queen's Regt.

Copies to:
No 1. C.O.
2. H.Q. [illegible]
3. do.

Appendix VI

<u>Secret</u> Copy No. 16

8th Bn. The Queen's Regt
OPERATION ORDER No. 61

22nd Sept. 1918.

[illegible]

1. [illegible]

2. [illegible]

3. Companies will be relieved as under: [illegible]

4. [illegible]

5. [illegible]

6. [illegible]

7. [illegible]

8. [illegible]

9. [illegible]

Appendix VII

Copy No. 13

SECRET.

8th Bn. The Queen's Regt

OPERATION ORDER. No. A.82.

29th Sept. 1918

Map Ref. 36c [illegible]

1. The Battn will be relieved tomorrow by the 6th Bn. [illegible] Relief to be complete by 2 p.m.

2. All Maps, Defence Schemes, [illegible] photographs etc. will be [illegible] handed over on relief and [illegible] will be [illegible] forwarded to Orderly Room by 6 p.m.

3. On completion of relief the Battn will march to [illegible] prior to [illegible] for [illegible] on [illegible]
Route: Fosse 5, Petit Sains, Hersin, Barlin, Maisnil Ruitz.

4. The order of march will be as follows: H.Q., A, B, C, D Coys. 200x interval between Coys. The Drums will [illegible] each [illegible] at the head of H.Q. Coy.
Dress: Full Marching Order, [illegible] Blankets [illegible] to be carried on the Battn transport. The head of H.Q. Coy will pass [illegible]

5. The [illegible] will [illegible] their [illegible] by [illegible] a.m.

6. An advance party of 1 N.C.O. per Coy [illegible] (H.Q. Coy) will parade [illegible] at the [illegible] and proceed to Maisnil Ruitz to [illegible] the [illegible] and to prepare for the arrival of the Battalion. They will report to [illegible]

7. [illegible]

8. [illegible]

9. Officers [illegible]

10. The [illegible] at [illegible] a.m. [illegible]

11. Officers [illegible]

12. [illegible]

13. [illegible]

E

11. [illegible] ways will arrange to evacuate [illegible] the [illegible] by each Platoon [illegible] to enable the [illegible] to [illegible] its dinner under cover.

12. Acknowledge.

Issued at 5.45 pm.

C.F. Talbot [illegible]

[illegible]

[illegible]

Copies to:

No. 1.	C.O.	No. 7.	T.O.
2.	O/c A Coy.	8.	Q.M.
3.	" B "	9.	M.O.
4.	" C "	10.	[illegible]
5.	" D "	11.	R.S.M.
6.	[illegible]	12.	[illegible]

[illegible]

G. 36

(6339) Wt. W160/M3016 1,500,000 10/17 McA & W Ltd (E 1898) Forms W3091.

Army Form W.3091.

W.O. 95/3?

Cover for Documents.

Nature of Enclosures.

8th Bn The Queen's R.W.S Regt

WAR DIARY

VOLUME XXXVIII

OCTOBER 1918

2/11/18

H.J.C. Peirs Lieut Colonel
Commanding
8th Bn The Queens R.W.S Regt

Notes, or Letters written.

14

Army Form C. 2118

WAR DIARY
or
~~INTELLIGENCE SUMMARY~~
(Erase heading not required.)

Page 1

Instructions regarding War Diaries and Intelligence Summaries are contained in F. S. Regs., Part II. and the Staff Manual respectively. Title Pages will be prepared in manuscript. OCTOBER 1918

VOL XXXVIII

Place	Date	Hour	Summary of Events and Information	Remarks and references to Appendices
MAISNIL-LES-RUITZ – LE SOUICH	1st		The Battn left Billets at MAISNIL-LES-RUITZ at 07.00 hours and marched to BARLIN Station where it entrained about 10.30 hours and proceeded by tactical train to BOUQUEMAISON where it detrained and marched to billets in LE SOUICH, the Battn being completely settled in by about 16.30 hours. By this move the Division passed out of the VIIIth Corps into G.H.Q Reserve. A copy of a letter from Lieut General Sir Aylmer Hunter-Weston K.C.B D.S.O. Commanding VIIIth Corps, thanking the Division for its services is attached. Major R.H. ROWLAND left the Battn to proceed to England for the Senior Officers Course at ALDERSHOT.	App. I BN OO A33 App. II 24th DIVL LETTER A 845.
LE SOUICH	2nd		Battn in training in LE SOUICH Area. Lieut. H.P BULLOCK joined the Battn	
"	3rd		" "	
"	4th		" " The Division was now released from G.H.Q. Reserve and passed into the XVIIth Corps	
"	5th		The Brigade carried out a practice attack in the BOUQUEMAISON Area. This was originally intended as a night attack, but subsequently the plans were changed and the attack commenced at 08.30 hrs. The Battn was in support to the 1st Royal Fusiliers and 3rd Rifle Brigade. The objectives were gained by the leading Battns without the Battn being called upon. Operations were completed by 13.00 hrs.	App. III OO A 34
LE SOUICH – GRAINCOURT	6th		The Battn left LE SOUICH at 09.30 and proceeded to BOUQUEMAISON Station where it entrained for the forward area. The train reached HAVRINCOURT about 17.30 where	App. IV BN OO A35

CH

1875 Wt. W593/826 1,000,000 4/15 J.B.C. & A. A.D.S.S./Forms/C. 2118.

Instructions regarding War Diaries and Intelligence Summaries are contained in F. S. Regs., Part II. and the Staff Manual respectively. Title Pages will be prepared in manuscript.

OCTOBER 1918

WAR DIARY
or
~~INTELLIGENCE SUMMARY~~

(Erase heading not required.)

Page 2

VOL XXXVIII

Army Form C. 2118

Place	Date	Hour	Summary of Events and Information	Remarks and references to Appendices
GRAINCOURT	6th	contd	The Battn detrained and marched via HERMIES and DEMICOURT to GRAINCOURT where it was accommodated for the night in bivouacs, tents and dug-outs. Capt E D DONNELL M.C left the Battn for a 6 months tour of duty in England	
GRAINCOURT - ANNEUX	7th		The Battn remained in its bivouacs until the evening when it proceeded by cross-country route to bivouacs in the neighbourhood of ANNEUX, where it arrived about 21.00 hrs relieving the HOOD Battn of the 63rd (R.N) Division. Capt C E S BEADLE joined the Battn	App V BN OO A36 " VI 17 I B OO No 254
ANNEUX - RUMILLY TRENCH	8th		The Battn again remained in its bivouacs all day awaiting orders. The Division was now closed up behind the 63rd (R.N) Division and the 72nd Brigade were ordered to take over the front on the night 8th/9th while the 17 Brigade moved to the RUMILLY Area. The Battn therefore started off from its bivouacs at 18.15 hrs and marched via CANTAING and NOYELLES across the river and Canal de L'ESCAUT to RUMILLY TRENCH about a mile W of RUMILLY, where it bivouaced for the night. All through the night the sky was lit up by the flames of fires in CAMBRAI and in the morning it was learnt that the enemy had finally evacuated the town after setting fire to it in many places. 2/Lieuts A BRINDED and F.S TYLER joined the Battn	App VII BN OO A37
RUMILLY TRENCH - NIERGNIES	9th		The Division now took over the attack, the 72nd Brigade being in the line, the 73rd in Support and the 17 in reserve. The objective of the 72nd Brigade was the railway just east of AWOINGT and this was gained without much trouble by 07.00 hrs. The Battn moved off about 11.00 hrs to resume the advance. The route lay through	App VIII 17 I B OO No 256 " IX BN OO 38.

1875 Wt. W593/826 1,000,000 4/15 J.B.C. & A. A.D.S.S./Forms/C. 2118.

UA

Army Form C. 2118

Instructions regarding War Diaries and Intelligence Summaries are contained in F. S. Regs., Part II. and the Staff Manual respectively. Title Pages will be prepared in manuscript.

OCTOBER 1918

WAR DIARY or ~~INTELLIGENCE SUMMARY~~

(Erase heading not required.)

Page 3

VOL. XXXVIII

Place	Date	Hour	Summary of Events and Information	Remarks and references to Appendices
NIERGNIES	9th	contd	RUMILLY in a N.E. direction, and on the ridge N.E. of RUMILLY there were many signs of a hard fight and a hasty retreat by the enemy. The Battn reached the outskirts of NIERGNIES about 15.30 and halted there to await orders. The 73rd Brigade attacked at 16.30 and after a struggle established the line E. of CAGNONCLES. The Battn received orders to spend the night at NIERGNIES, being partly accommodated in cellars on the edge of the village, but mostly in a trench on the W side of the village. There was considerable shelling of parts of the village, especially the eastern outskirts during the evening and night, but the Battn suffered no casualties, except two men of the Transport Section wounded	
NIERGNIES – CAGNONCLES	10th		Orders had been received for an early start if necessary, but the Battn did not move off till 08.00 hrs. The Brigade was now in Support to the 73rd Brigade who were advancing on AVESNES. The route was past the N edge of AWOINGT, W of CAUROIR to the main CAMBRAI-SOLESMES Road, where a long halt was made. Reports were received of the capture of CAUROIR, CARNIÈRES, BOUSSIÈRES and BÉVILLERS. During the afternoon the Battn moved on a short distance to the Cross Roads S.W of CAGNONCLES where it eventually received orders to stay the night and steps were taken to dig in. A quiet night was spent here	App. X BNOOA39
CAGNONCLES – RIEUX	11th		An early start had to be made in order to get into position by the time fixed for the attack and the Battn moved off soon after 03.00 hrs. and marched to the S.W. edge of RIEUX where it halted to unload the L.G. limbers and wait till it became	App. XI 17 I BOO No 233 " XII LETTER G.T.2 CA

Instructions regarding War Diaries and Intelligence Summaries are contained in F. S. Regs., Part II. and the Staff Manual respectively. Title Pages will be prepared in manuscript.

October 1918

WAR DIARY
or
INTELLIGENCE SUMMARY
(Erase heading not required.)

Page 5

VOL XXXVIII

Army Form C. 2118

Place	Date	Hour	Summary of Events and Information	Remarks and references to Appendices
RIEUX	11th	cont^d	that day, but to continue the attack the following morning, the 8th Queens to pass through the 1st Royal Fusiliers, gain the high ground N of ST AUBERT and turn this village from the north. The Batt^n was withdrawn to the village and made as comfortable as possible for the night in cellars. The casualties during the day had been considerable, comprising 2/Lieut L A M^cDERMOTT Killed, Lieuts T E SWAIN and P A REEVES and 2/Lieut A.B. HEFFER Wounded, and a number of O.R.s Killed and Wounded, A Coy having especially heavy casualties	App XIII " XIV " XV WIRES
	17			
RIEUX – MONTRECOURT	12th		Zero hour had been fixed for 12.00 hrs, but aeroplane patrols at dawn reported that the enemy had withdrawn from the ridge and gone right back, his exact location being uncertain. So by 11.00 hrs. the Brigade was advancing again across country in a N E direction the Batt^n still being in support. About 12.30 hrs. the outskirts of VILLERS EN CAUCHIES were reached and a halt made. A few casualties were suffered as the result of occasional bursts of shell fire over this area. The enemy was now found to be holding the line of the R. SELLE in considerable force and orders were issued for the Batt^n to pass through the leading Batt^ns after dark and try to force the crossings of the river under a barrage. Zero hour for the attack was fixed at 18.30 hrs., but owing to the difficult country to be crossed in the dark and the difficulty of finding its positions the Batt^n was late for the barrage, which however caused the enemy	

1875 Wt. W593/826 1,000,000 4/15 J.B.C. & A. A.D.S.S./Forms/C. 2118.

Instructions regarding War Diaries and Intelligence Summaries are contained in F. S. Regs., Part II. and the Staff Manual respectively. Title Pages will be prepared in manuscript.

October 1918

WAR DIARY
or
INTELLIGENCE SUMMARY
(Erase heading not required.)

Page 4

Vol. XXXVIII

Army Form C. 2118

Place	Date	Hour	Summary of Events and Information	Remarks and references to Appendices
RIEUX	11th	contd	lighter before proceeding. The enemy started shelling the vicinity rather heavily and several casualties were suffered. Soon after 05.00 hrs the Battn moved off again to take up its position in support to the other two Battns. of the Brigade, the 1st Royal Fusiliers being on the left of the attack the 3rd Rifle Brigade on the right. Bn. HQ. were established on the eastern edge of RIEUX village, which was at this time being heavily shelled. A Coy was sent forward with orders to guard the left flank of the 1st Royal Fusiliers, but owing to a misunderstanding it got on the right between that Battn and the 3rd Rifle Brigade. C & D Coys were ordered to dig in on the forward edge of the village and B Coy remained in the village in reserve. Later in the morning C & D Coys were sent forward to stiffen the line which seemed inclined to fall back in confusion owing to the appearance of 2 enemy Tanks, but they were afterwards withdrawn again to the village. The 1st Royal Fusiliers at first made good progress, but then found the crest of the ridge very strongly held and could make no headway against the M.G and rifle fire. A Coy also tried to advance but suffered heavy casualties from shell-fire and M.G's. Much bravery and determination was shown by men of this Coy in the attempt to put enemy M.G's out of action. By mid day it was obvious that the attack was definitely held up on the left, where the 49th Div had at first made good progress under a barrage, and on the right the Guards Divn had orders not to press their attack if strongly opposed. So it was decided to attempt nothing more	C.A.

1875 Wt. W593/826 1,000,000 4/15 J.B.C. & A. A.D.S.S./Forms/C. 2118.

Instructions regarding War Diaries and Intelligence Summaries are contained in F. S. Regs., Part II. and the Staff Manual respectively. Title Pages will be prepared in manuscript.

October 1918

WAR DIARY
or
INTELLIGENCE SUMMARY
(Erase heading not required.)

Page 6

VOL XXXVIII

Army Form C. 2118

Place	Date	Hour	Summary of Events and Information	Remarks and references to Appendices
MONTRECOURT	12th	cont^d	to evacuate MONTRECOURT and the bank of the river. The enemy retaliation for the barrage was particularly heavy on the western edge of MONTRECOURT WOOD where the Batt^n was assembling and some casualties resulted. B & C Coys were ordered to advance to the river bank and attempt to cross the river and establish posts on the further bank, if possible, as far up as the railway embankment. D Coy was in support, with the exception of one platoon sent to clear MONTRECOURT, and A Coy in reserve with Bn. H.Q. at the S.W. edge of MONTRECOURT WOOD. On reaching the river bank B & C Coys found that the river was too deep to wade. Some patrols were pushed across by a broken bridge consisting only of a 6 inch iron rail, and the 103rd Field Coy R.E. built 2 pontoon footbridges further south. The number of men that could be thrown across by the broken bridge was insufficient to deal with the enemy's counter attacks, and it was therefore decided to hold the bridges from the W. side. Throughout the night these bridgeheads were continually under heavy M.G. & rifle fire and some bombing also took place, C Coy suffering a fair number of casualties.	
MONTRECOURT - RIEUX	13th		In the early hours of the morning Bn. H.Q. was subjected to a heavy bombardment with Mustard Gas Shells, and before dawn H.Q. were moved away from the wood into a sunken road about 400 yards west. This place also was subsequently very heavily shelled with gas shells and H.E. mixed with gas, and a large number of casualties, for the most part comparatively slight cases of blindness and blisters, resulted	

1875 Wt. W593/826 1,000,000 4/15 J.B.C. & A. A.D.S.S./Forms/C. 2118.

Instructions regarding War Diaries and Intelligence Summaries are contained in F. S. Regs., Part II. and the Staff Manual respectively. Title Pages will be prepared in manuscript.

October 1918

WAR DIARY
or
INTELLIGENCE SUMMARY
(Erase heading not required.)

Page 7

VOL XXXVIII

Army Form C. 2118

Place	Date	Hour	Summary of Events and Information	Remarks and references to Appendices
MONTRECOURT – RIEUX	13th	contd	on this and the following day. Orders had been received the night before for the relief of the Brigade to-day by the 72nd Brigade, any units at the time E of the R. SELLE to come under the orders of the B.G.C. 72nd Brigade and to be relieved when possible. Most of the Battn accordingly got away in the early afternoon and reached billets in RIEUX by about 19.00 hrs, but C Coy and part of B Coy could not be relieved till dark and did not arrive in billets till nearly midnight. These two Coys continued to have a good deal of spasmodic fighting round the bridgeheads during the day, but they managed to keep the enemy away from the bridges though they were not able themselves to make any progress. The casualties to-day included 2/Lieut. E.P. DORRELL Wounded (Subsequently Died of Wounds) and Capt C.H.T. ILOTT R.A.M.C. (attached) Wounded (Gas). This day also 2/Lieut H.V. ELLIOTT was transferred to England Sick.	
RIEUX	14th		The day was spent in resting and refitting. About 120 Gas casualties reported sick this morning and the large majority of them were sent away, including the C.O., Lieut Col. H.J.C. PEIRS D.S.O., the Adjutant, Capt E.A. FELLOWES M.C., Capt. E.A. MOORE, Lieut. H.G. VERSEY and 2/Lieut. H.P. COMBE. Major H.H. HEBDEN M.C., 1st Royal Fusiliers took over temporary command of the Battn. A Special Order of the Day was issued by the B.G.C. 17th Brigade, copy of which is attached.	App. XVI 17th S. ORDER
— " —	15th		The Battn was engaged in reorganizing and refitting.	
RIEUX – CAGNONCLES	16th		The Battn was relieved by a Battn of the Welsh Regt (58th Inf. Brigade) and proceeded	App XVII

1875 Wt. W593/826 1,000,000 4/15 J.B.C. & A. A.D.S.S./Forms/C. 2118.

Army Form C. 2118

Instructions regarding War Diaries and Intelligence Summaries are contained in F. S. Regs., Part II. and the Staff Manual respectively. Title Pages will be prepared in manuscript.

October 1918

WAR DIARY
or
INTELLIGENCE SUMMARY
(Erase heading not required.)

Page 8
Vol. XXXVIII

Place	Date	Hour	Summary of Events and Information	Remarks and references to Appendices
CAGNONCLES	16th		to billets in CAGNONCLES by cross country march	
— " —	17th		The Batt^n was engaged in training. 2/Lieut L.B. PALMER left the Batt^n to proceed to England to join the R.A.F	
— " —	18th		The Batt^n was engaged in training. Short night operations were carried out, practising the Batt^n in the attack.	
CAGNONCLES – CAMBRAI	19th		The Batt^n was inspected by Brigadier General G. THORPE C.M.G., D.S.O., Commanding 17th Infantry Brigade. In the afternoon the Batt^n moved to billets in FAUBOURG ST. DRUON, CAMBRAI, on relief by a Batt^n of the 61st Div^n. The march was across country via AWOINGT where teas were served, and billets were reached about 20.00 hrs	App XIX " XX 17th I.B. OO 255 BN OO A 40
CAMBRAI	20th		The Batt^n spent the day resting and cleaning up billets and clothing	
— " —	21st		The Batt^n was engaged in training	
— " —	22nd		ditto	
— " —	23rd		ditto	
— " —	24th		The Batt^n carried out a tactical scheme in conjunction with 10th Field Coy R.E. involving the attack over the Canal de L'ESCAUT and the building of footbridges and a pontoon bridge	App XXI OO A 41
— " —	25th		The Batt^n carried out a Route March of about 7 miles	

1875 Wt. W593/826 1,000,000 4/15 J.B.C. & A. A.D.S.S./Forms/C. 2118.

C.B.

Army Form C. 2118

Instructions regarding War Diaries and Intelligence Summaries are contained in F. S. Regs., Part II. and the Staff Manual respectively. Title Pages will be prepared in manuscript.

October 1918

WAR DIARY
or
~~INTELLIGENCE SUMMARY~~
(Erase heading not required.)

Page 9
Vol. XXXVIII

Place	Date	Hour	Summary of Events and Information	Remarks and references to Appendices
CAMBRAI - CAGNONCLES	26th		The Battn was engaged in training in the morning. In the afternoon the Battn proceeded at short notice to billets in CAGNONCLES arriving about 19.00 hrs.	App. XXII 17 IB 00256
CAGNONCLES - ST. AUBERT	27th		The Battn moved on again in the morning and proceeded across country to billets in ST. AUBERT engaging in a Brigade Tactical Scheme on the way.	" XXIII " XXIV
ST. AUBERT	28th		The Battn was engaged in training. Lieuts H.H. RICHARDSON and E.G HOGBIN rejoined the Battn after a 6 months tour of duty in England.	17 IB 00254 BNOO—
— " —	29th		The Battn took part in a Brigade Tactical Scheme involving the capture of MONTRECOURT and the crossing of the RIVER SELLE. Lieut-Col H.J.C PEIRS D.S.O and Capt. E.A. FELLOWES M.C rejoined the Battn from Hospital. Major H.H. HEBDEN M.C relinquished temporary command of the Battn.	" XXV 17 IB LETTER G 4/11
— " —	30th		The Battn was engaged in training. R.S.M L.G TIPPEN awarded the M.M.	
— " —	31st		ditto. Lieut. W.E. WILLSON struck off the strength of the Battn on being ordered a Medical Board in England	

C.F. Tatham
Lieut & Asst Adjt
8 Bn The Queen's Regt

1875 Wt. W593/826 1,000,000 4/15 J.B.C. & A. A.D.S.S./Forms/C. 2118.

Appendix I

SECRET. COPY No. 8

8th BN. The Queens Regt

OPERATION ORDER No. H 33

Map Ref. 36B 1/40000 30th Sept. 1918.

1 The Battn will entrain at BARLIN at 0830 tomorrow and proceed to Bouquemaison.

2 The Battn will march to BARLIN Station [illegible] in the following order D, C, B, A, HQ [illegible] 100x interval. The Drums will march at the head of "C" Coy.
STARTING POINT – [illegible] TIME [illegible]
DRESS – [illegible]

3 Blankets will be [illegible] rolled in bundles of 10 and labelled and stacked at the Q.M. Stores at the entrance to the Camp by 0500. Cooking [illegible], Officers [illegible] kits, Coy [illegible], Drummers [illegible] etc, will be stacked at the same place by 0645.

4 On arrival at BOUQUEMAISON, C.Q.M.S. will proceed at once by cycle to LE SOUICH and report to Lieut [illegible] HYATT M.C. who will allot them the [illegible] allotted to their Coys.
They will draw [illegible] the [illegible].

5 On detraining the Battn will march to LE SOUICH in the same order as laid down in para 2.

6 DISCIPLINE – An N.C.O. will be detailed in charge of each compartment on the train. [illegible] that they are not to [illegible] and at the [illegible] on the foot board.
[illegible] to report to the [illegible] station.

7 REVEILLE – at [illegible].

Lieut C.F. Tasker [illegible]

Copies to –

No 1 [illegible]
2 " B [illegible]
3 " C [illegible]
4 " D [illegible]
5 [illegible]
6 [illegible]
7 [illegible]
8 [illegible]

Appendix II

1st Inf Bde R 25/1

24th Division No. A. 845.

8 Queens

The following letter which has been received by the Divisional Commander from Lieutenant-General Sir Aylmer Hunter-Weston, K.C.B., D.S.O., Commanding VIIIth Corps, is forwarded for information and communication to all ranks :-

" My Dear Daly,

Please express to the Brigades and Battalions concerned my appreciation of the excellent work that has been done by the 24th Division in the vigorous patrolling, and many minor operations, that you have carried out on your front. The success that has attended these operations in tying strong forces of the enemy to our front, and the valuable information that has been obtained as regards the enemy's dispositions by the prisoners that you have taken, has been of very material assistance towards the general scheme of the operations.

2. It is with great regret that I part (I hope only temporarily) with the 24th Division. I am sure that it will give a very fine account of itself wherever it goes, and I shall watch its doings, and the career of each individual in the Division with the greatest personal interest.

May good luck attend each and all of you.

Yours sincerely,

(sd) Aylmer Hunter-Weston. "

R.K. Collins. Lt Col.

A.A.&.Q.M.G., 24th Division.

30th September 1918.
HPM.

Appendix III

SECRET.

Copy No 12

8th Bn. The Queen's Regt

OPERATION ORDER No. [illegible]

Ref Map Sheet 51c [illegible]

1. The 17th Inf Bde will carry out a [illegible] attack at [illegible] on 5th inst.

2. The Battn (less H Coy) will be in Bde Reserve, [illegible] Fusiliers being on the Right of the attack, the 3rd Bn [illegible] Bde on the Left.

3. H Coy will [illegible] the [illegible].

4. The Battn (less H Coy) will march to its [illegible] of assembly in [illegible] squares S.13.c. & [illegible]
Route: via Bougainville and [illegible].
Order of March: B Coy, C Coy, D Coy, [illegible] [illegible] will pass the last house in Le [illegible] village at [illegible].

5. [illegible] Bearing [illegible] from [illegible] to [illegible] is 65° T.B.

6. Zero hour will be 05.30.

7. Coy of [illegible] will [illegible] at the head of the Coys and [illegible] and [illegible]. [illegible] will be [illegible] there without delay. H Coy [illegible] the orders of O.C. H Coy.

8. [illegible] will [illegible] in rear of the Battn [illegible] will be [illegible].

9. Coy Cookers will proceed under the [illegible] to [illegible] by 0710. Breakfast [illegible] on arrival.

10. Reveille 02.45. Tea will be served [illegible].

11. Acknowledge. O.C. [illegible]

Issued at 6.15 p.m.
by runner.

[illegible]
[illegible]
[illegible]

Copies to: No 1. [illegible]
2. [illegible]
3. [illegible]
4. [illegible]

Appendix IV

Copy No. 13

8th Bn. The Queen's Regt.

OPERATION ORDER No. A.35

Map Ref:- Sheet 57c

8th Oct 1915

1. The Battn will entrain [illegible] at Bouquemaison for Hermies (XVIIth Corps Area).

2. The part of the transport which has not already [illegible] entrain in accordance with orders issued to the Transport Officer.

3. The Battn will march to Bouquemaison in the order A, B, C, D, M.G. Sect. The head of A Coy will pass the [illegible] in the Doullens village at [illegible] [illegible] between [illegible].

4. On arrival at the Station [illegible] A Coy will detail a [illegible] party of 2 sections who will report to the Q.M. [illegible].

5. All blankets will be rolled in bundles of 10 [illegible] and dumped at the QM. Stores by [illegible]. Officers [illegible] valises [illegible] will be dumped at the same place [illegible].

6. Dinners will be [illegible] [illegible] on the train.

7. [illegible] will render to O.C. by [illegible] a certificate [illegible] billets have been left in a clean and sanitary condition.

8. [illegible] will be [illegible] [illegible] [illegible].

9. [illegible] will be detailed to be in charge of each [illegible] compartment on the train. [illegible] to get out [illegible] except at [illegible] stopping place [illegible] the permission of [illegible] [illegible] [illegible] [illegible] [illegible] compartment [illegible].

10. [illegible] will [illegible] the [illegible] Brigade [illegible] at Hermies [illegible] immediately on the arrival of the train.

11. Acknowledge [illegible].

Issued at 19.15 [illegible]

By [illegible]

[illegible]

[illegible]

Copy to [illegible]

SECRET Appendix V Copy No. 8.

8th Bn. The Queens Regt

OPERATION ORDER. No. A. 36

Map Ref. 57c N.E. 7th Oct. 1918.

1. The Battn will move today to the neighbourhood of ANNEUX.

2. STARTING POINT:- Road fork K. 4. d. 6. 5.
Order of March. A, B, C, D, H.Q. Coys and Battle Surplus.
The head of A Coy will pass the starting point at 1700. Route - By Cross Country Tracks to the S of GRAINCOURT. Movement will be by Platoons at 100x interval.
Battle Surplus will parade separately under Capt RILEY and march in rear of the Battn.
Transport will move by the road running just N. of K. 5. central and just S of E. 30. central.

3. Guides from advance parties will be at Road Fork E. 30. b. 70. 05. at 1630.

4. Men will carry their blankets on their packs.
Officers Trench Bundles & Mess Kits will be dumped at the Cookers by 1630
Officers Valises will be taken to 1st Line Transport Lines at K. 4. c. 5. 4. by 1600. These will be taken back to 2nd Line Transport Lines MOEUVRES tonight.

5. Transport will return to present area and be parked.

6 ACKNOWLEDGE.

C F Lasher
Lieut & A/Adjt
8th Bn Queens Regt

Copies to:-
No. 1. o/c. A. Coy
2 " B. "
3 " C "
4 " D "
5 " H.Q. "
6 " T.O.
7 - H.Q. 17 I.B.
8. War Diary.

S E C R E T. Appendix VI Copy No 1

17th INFANTRY BRIGADE ORDER No.254.

Ref: Sheet 57c & 57b. 1/40,000

1. (a) The 3rd and 4th Armies continue the attack on October 8th. 63rd Division is attacking on the right of 17th Corps with final objective Road from A.30.b.9.1 to H.1.c.9.9.
6th Corps, with 2nd Division on its left, attacks on the right of 17th Corps.
The objectives of the 6th Corps are WAMBAIX - FONTENVILLE line to Road H.7.b. to H.1.d.
If the 6th Corps meet with a little opposition, the GUARDS DIVISION may be passed through the Right Division of the 6th Corps and be directed to IGNIEL DIT LES FRISETTES.

(b) The 63rd Division attacks on a 2 Brigade front; the 188th Infantry Brigade on the right, 189th Infantry Brigade on the left, and 190th Infantry Brigade in support to 188th Infantry Brigade.

(c) The enemy is retiring on the front of 4th and 5th Corps.

2. The 24th Division will be disposed by 08.00 hours on October 8th and will be prepared to act ;-

(a) 72nd Infantry Brigade H.Q.rs and 2 Companies 24th Bn. M.G.C. in square G.14 West of MASNIERES - CAMBRAI Road. Route via NOYELLES Sur L'ESCAUT - RUMILLY Road and convenient crossings over the Canal, prepared to :-

(1) Support the 63rd Division in case of need with the objectives it may have gained e.g., should 63rd Division be driven out of final objective, to make a deliberate counter attack to regain and hold it under Divisional orders.

(2) ~~To be ready to relieve the 63rd Division if ordered, on~~ night Octr: 8/9th or Octr: 9/10th.

(3) To protect the left flank against possible counter attack from CAMBRAI, made between the MARCOING to CAMBRAI railway line on the canal de L'ESCAUT.

(b) 73rd Infantry Brigade, 1 Coy. 24th Bn. M.G.C and 129th Field Coy. RE in squares L.3.,L.4., or L.9, ready to take the place of 72nd Infantry Brigade should latter be ordered forward.

(c) 17th Infantry Brigade, 'D' Coy. 24th Bn. M.G.C. and 104th Field Coy. RE will be at 2 hours notice from 08.00 hours on 18th instant, ready to take the place of the 73rd Infantry Brigade should latter be moved forward.

3. All concerned will reconnoitre the assembly positions and routes thereto. In the event of a move forward only 5 Lewis gun limbers will accompany Battalions, the remainder of the transport will be prepared to move forward when ordered by Brigade to assembly positions on the W. side of BOIS ~~des Neuf~~ de L'ORIVAL.

4. 'D' Coy. M.G.C. will be prepared to move at 30 minutes notice after 08.00 hours on 8th instant as may be required.

5. On the 8th instant a Contact aeroplane will call for flares from leading troops at ZERO plus 2 hours, ZERO plus 3½ hours, ZERO plus 4½ hours.
A Counter attack aeroplane will be up from ZERO onwards.

6. ZERO hour is 04.30 hours on October 8th.

P.T.O.

7. Advanced Divisional H.Qrs will be at CANTAIN MILL moving, if necessary, to vicinity of MT. Sur L'OEUVRE.

8. ACKNOWLEDGE.

Ronald Hutchison

Issued to Sigs
at 22.30 hours,
7th October 18.

Captain,
Brigade Major, 17th Infantry Brigade.

Copy No. 1 to 8th Queen.
2 1st Royal Fusiliers.
3 3rd Rifle Brigade.
4 17th L.T.M.Battery.
5 Sigs. 17th Inf: Bde.
6 24th Division 'G' (2)
7 104th Field Coy. RE.
8 'D' Coy. 24th Bn. M.G.C.
9 Brigade Major,
10 Staff Captain.
11 I.O., 17th Inf: Bde.
12 War Diary.
13 File.
14)
15)
16) Spare.

8th Oct[illegible]

Appendix VIII

9-10-18

17th Infantry Brigade Ord. No 256

1. 24th Divn. (72nd Inf Bde) is attacking to-morrow 9th inst in conjunction with [illegible] Corps ([illegible] Division) on the right and Canadian Corps on the left.
2. Objectives of 72nd I.B. are railway line from H2 Central to B.20 a.7.2.
3. 73rd Inf Bde will be in support ready to exploit the attack if successful towards CAUROIR, in conjunction with Guards Divn.
4. 17th Inf Bde will be in Divisional Reserve in its present position, ready to move at 15 minutes notice from [illegible]
5. In the [illegible] of a [illegible] will be [illegible] in present [illegible].
6. 1st Line Transport of 17th I. Bde. is moving to BOIS DE L'ORIVAL by dawn to-morrow 9th/10th inst.
7. Zero hour will be 05.20 hours on 9th
8. Acknowledge.

Issued to Battalions & 17th LTM [illegible] 10.15

[illegible]
Major, 17th Inf Bde

To OC — Coy

The 17th Bde will be in reserve in support of an attack by the 42nd I B ready to move at 15 minutes notice from Zero hour onwards.

Zero hour is 0520

One days rations will be issued & water bottles filled before this hour.

Coys will make their own arrangements for cooking & issuing fresh meat as early as possible.

Coys will maintain an officer in the immediate vicinity of BHQ for the purpose of taking orders.

9/10/18
Issued at 0430

Lieut & A/Adjt
8/Queens

SECRET.

Appendix X

Copy No....

8th Bn THE QUEENS REGT.

OPERATION ORDER. No A.39

10th Oct. 1918.

1. The Battn. will move at 0515 or on 10 minutes notice later to proceed to CAUROIR area in Support to the 14th I.B. which is in Support to the 73rd I.B.
Order of March - 'C', H.Q. 'D', 'B'. 'A'.
Starting Point. NIERGNIES Church.
Time - 0515.

2 Cookers will be in rear of the Battn.
L.G. Limbers will be with their Coys.

3. Breakfast will be taken before starting.

Issued at 0030.

C.F. Tatham
Lieut & A/Adjt
8' Queens Regt

Appendix VII

SECRET. Copy No. 9..

8TH BN THE QUEENS REGT

OPERATION ORDER. No A.37.

Oct 8th 1918.

1. The Battn will move tonight to bivouacs in G.13 & 14 (Ref. Map 57c) W of RUMILLY. The Battn will concentrate on W. side of BOIS DE NEUF. (L.10.c. Ref Map. 57c N.E.) where guides will meet them.
2. Coys will move by Platoons at 50x intervals in the following order – H.Q, A, B, C, D Coys. L. G. Limbers to accompany Coys. Dress – Battle Order. Packs will be stacked by Coys at the edge of the road on the W. side of the Camp. Coys will detail 1 man to remain in charge till they are collected by Transport. These men will proceed with the packs to Transport lines and rejoin their Coys at first opportunity.
3. On reaching BOIS DE NEUF, Coy Comdrs will report to Battn. H.Q. at L.10.c.60.70.
4. First Coy to move off at 1815.
5. Officers Valises will be packed on the G. S. Wagon tonight. Officers Mess Baskets will be packed on Coy Limbers.
6. Acknowledge.

C.H. Tatham [?]

Lieut & A/Adjt
8th Queens Regt.

Copies to:-

No 1. O/c A. Coy.
2. " B "
3. " C "
4. " D "
5. " H.Q "
6. T.O.
7. H.Q. 17. I.B.
8. Q.M.
9. War Diary

Appendix XI

Copy No.___

17th Infantry Brigade Order No.253.

1. The 24th Division will continue the advance tomorrow 11th instant on LA SELLE River and establish bridgeheads on east bank. When completed the advance will be continued.

2. VI Corps will advance on a similar line and Canadian Corps has been directed on VALENCIENNES keeping touch with 24th Division just S. of CAMBRAI-SMULZON road and with left flank on Canal de L'ESCAUT.

3. 17th Brigade Group as under will form the advance guard :-

17th Infantry Brigade.
1 Brigade R.F.A.
1 Section 60 pounders.
1 Section 104th Field Coy. RE.
'B' & 'C' Coys. 24th Bn. M.G.C.
XVII Corps Cyclist Battalion
1 Troop cavalry.

4. The Brigade Group will pass through troops of 73rd Brigade on the general line U.30.c. - U.18 as arranged with C.Os at the conference and will continue the advance by bounds as under :-

1st BOUND.
Road junction V.20.c. - ridge through V.13.b. - V.8.c and V.1.d. and b.

2nd BOUND.
Spur through V.13.d. - V.9.b. and V.3.a.

3rd BOUND.
Crossings of LA SELLE river and bridgeheads east of it.

4th BOUND.
High ground W.1.d. and spur running from it through W.1.b. and V.36.

5. 3rd Rifle Brigade will advance on the right, 1st Royal Fusiliers on the left. 8th Queens will be in reserve moving behind the left flank and paying particular attention to maintaining touch with the Brigade on our left.

1 section R.F.A. and 1 section 17th L.T.M.Battery will accompany each leading battalion. 'C' Company 24th Battalion M.G.C. will accompany the right battalion under orders of C.O.3rd Bn. The Rifle Brigade.

Sections R.F.A. will be at U.27.c.0.4 and U.19.d.8.8 respectively at 05.30 hours.

6. The Northern boundary of the Brigade is the CAMBRAI-SMULZOIR Road exclusive -

The Southern boundary - HAUSSY inclusive - Cross roads MAISON BLANCHE W.1.d. inclusive - ESCARMAINE exclusive.

7. Inter-battalion boundary will be L'ERECLIN River - U.18.b.4.5. - Road fork V.7.d.8.4 - road through V.8.central (inclusive to 1st Royal Fus.) also wood in V.3.c. and V.9.a. (inclusive to 1st Royal Fus) - river crossing P.34.c.1.1 (inclusive to 1st Royal Fus)

8. XVII Corps Cyclist battalion will push forward at 05.00 hours on 11th inst. and will establish posts on the E. side of ST. AUBERT.

9. 'B' Coy. 24th Bn. M.G.C. will be at B.6.c.9.4 on the road at 05.00 hours on 11th inst.

10. 6th Dragoon Guards, in case of slight opposition being encountered are pushing forward to line of LA SELLE River to establish bridgeheads on the E. bank. They will also detail Officer patrols to maintain touch with the Divisions on our flanks.

11. 72nd Infantry Brigade with 1 Coy. 24th Bn. M.G.C. are also passing through the 73rd Infantry Brigade to follow 17th Infantry Brigade in close support.

12. Brigade and Battalion H.Q. will be established as under at 05.00 hours :-

Brigade H.Q. .... U.27.central.
1st Bn. Royal Fusiliers .... U.15.d.central.
3rd Rifle Brigade)
'C' Coy. M.G.C.) .... U.28.b.central.
8th Queens .... U.20.d.60.90.

13. Cable head will be established at 05.00 hours at Brigade H.Q. U.27.central. Cable will be extended along the AVESNES-ST.AUBERT-MONTRECOURT Roads.

14. Information obtained from prisoners indicates that there are few of the enemy in front of us.
The pursuit will be pressed on with the utmost vigour.

15. <u>ACKNOWLEDGE</u>.

Issued to Sigs. Captain,
at 1.45 hours.
12th October. 18. Brigade Major, 17th Inf: Bde.

Copy No.1 to	8th Queens.	Copy No.2 to	1st Royal Fusiliers.
3	3rd Rifle Bde.	4	17th L.T.M. Battery.
5	Sigs. 17th I.B.	6	24th Divn. 'G' (2)
7	103rd Field Coy.	8	74th Field Ambce.
9	Att: Artillery Gp (2)	10	72nd Inf; Bde.
11	73rd Inf: Bde.	12	6th Dragoon Gds.
13	XVII Corps Cyclist Bn.	14	24th Bn. M.G.C.
15	'B' Coy. M.G.C.	16	'C' Coy. M.G.C.
17	Major Lagdon (2)	18	Major Hobdon (2)
19	Brigade Major.	20	Staff Captain.
21	I.O., 17th Inf: Bde.	22	War Diary.
23	File.	24	Spare.
25	Spare.	26	Spare.

"A" Form
MESSAGES AND SIGNALS.

App. XII

Army Form C. 2121
(in pads of 100).

No. of Message..............

Prefix..........Code..........m. | Words. | Charge. | This message is on a/c of: | Recd. at..........m.

Office of Origin and Service Instructions.

Sent
At..........m.
To..........
By..........

..........Service.

(Signature of "Franking Officer.")

Date..........
From..........
By..........

TO ~~1st~~ R.F | 17 L.T.M. | ~~24 Div.~~
8th Queens | C. 6 M.G.C. | ~~73 Bde~~
~~3rd~~ R.B | 74 F.A

Sender's Number.	Day of Month.	In reply to Number.	AAA
G.T 2.	10		

73 Bde have captured CAGNONCLES and are advancing to first ~~bo~~ bound C 7 central to U 24 d 0.0 AAA MIDDX will then push through two leading battalions to second bound C 3 d 2.2 to ~~U~~ U 13 d 3.8 AAA 1st R.F ~~and~~ will follow up advance of 73 Bde paying special attention to guarding northern flank. AAA C Co M.G.C and 3rd Bde will be echeloned about 1000 yards behind R.F right flank AAA 8th Queens and 17 L.T.M will follow 3rd R B at about 1000 yards distance AAA Bde H.Q are established at B 20 C 2.3
~~AAA ACKNOWLEDGE~~

From 17 I.B
Place
Time 07.06

The above may be forwarded as now corrected. (Z) G. Thorpe B.G.

..........Censor. Signature of Addressor or person authorised to telegraph in his name.

* This line should be erased if not required.

(18765.) Wt. W12952/M1294. 187,500 Pads. 1/17 McC. & Co., Ltd. (E. 818.)

"A" Form. App. XIII

MESSAGES AND SIGNALS.

Army Form C. 2121. (In pads of 100.)

No. of Message..........

Prefix........Code........m | Words. | Charge. | This message is on a/c of: ....Service. | Recd. at........m. Date........ From........ By........

Office of Origin and Service Instructions.

Sent At........m. To........ By........

(Signature of "Franking Officer.")

TO 3 Battns CRA G
24 M G Bn Flank Bdes
TMB

Sender's Number. *GT 10 | Day of Month. 11th | In reply to Number. | AAA

WARNING ORDER. The attack will be resumed at 0830 12th inst aaa RBs will hold their present front and keep touch with right of left battalions advance aaa 8th Queens will pass through 1st RF and attack under a creeping barrage aaa Objective railway line between ST AUBERT and VILLERS CAUCHIES both exclusive aaa 49th Divn are attacking simultaneously aaa VILLERS CAUCHIES will be bombarded by heavies but will not be entered till the railway line has been reached on either side aaa Queens mop up village South 49th Div N of main road aaa RBs will push into ST AUBERT from N as objective is gained aaa ack

From 17th Inf Bde

Place

Time

The above may be forwarded as now corrected. (Z)

Censor. Signature of Addressor or person authorised to telegraph in his name.

* This line should be erased if not required.

(3198.) Wt. W 12952/M1294. 375,000 Pads. 1/17. H. W. & V., Ld. (E. 818.)

"A" Form.

Army Form C. 2121.
(In pads of 100.)

MESSAGES AND SIGNALS.

No. of Message...............

Prefix .... Code .... m	Words. 75	Charge.	This message is on a/c of:	Recd. at .... m.
Office of Origin and Service Instructions.	Sent		Service.	Date.
	At .... m.			From
	To..			
	By..		(Signature of "Franking Officer.")	By

TO 3 Battns Flank Bde Sigs
TMB G
2nd M. G. C CRA

Sender's Number.	Day of Month	In reply to Number.	AAA
* GT. 10/2	11th		

Reference GT. 10 Zero hour will be 12 noon aaa Details of artillery and MG co-operation have been explained to all concerned aaa 17th L.T.M Battery will be attached to 3rd R Bde aaa 72nd L.T.M Battery will be attached to Queens and will report at Queens HQ at 9 am aaa Correct time will be given at Battalion HQ at 8 am and Brigade HQ at 9 am.

From 17th Inf Bde
Place
Time 2315

The above may be forwarded as now corrected. (Z)

Censor. [signature] Captn for B G C 17th IB

Signature of Addressor or person authorised to telegraph in his name.

* This line should be erased if not required.

(3198.) Wt. W 12952/M1294. 375,000 Pads. 1/17. H. W. & V., Ld. (E. 818.)

"A" Form. App. XIV

Army Form C. 2121.
(In pads of 100.)

MESSAGES AND SIGNALS.

No. of Message..............

Prefix.......... Code.......... m | Words. | Charge. | This message is on a/c of: .... Service. (Signature of "Franking Officer.") | Recd. at ......m. Date.......... From.......... By..........

Office of Origin and Service Instructions.

Sent At..........m. To.......... By..........

TO	3 Battns	CRA
	24th M.G.C.	Flank Bdes
	T.M.B.	G.

Sender's Number.	Day of Month.	In reply to Number.	AAA
* G.T. 10/1	11th		

Reference G.T. 10 Zero has been put off till 12 noon aaa Battalions will patrol ~~in the morning~~ to see whether the enemy still holds his positions during night and ~~afternoon~~ after dawn, aaa If not occupied the line ST AUBERT - VILLERS will be occupied

From 17th Inf Bde
Place
Time 23 hours

The above may be forwarded as now corrected. (Z) [signature] Capt

Censor. Signature of Addressor or person authorised to telegraph in his name.

* This line should be erased if not required.

(3198.) Wt. W 12952/M1294. 375,000 Pads. 1/17. H. W. & V., Ld. (E. 818.)

19

Appendix XVI

SPECIAL ORDER OF THE DAY
** by **
BRIGADIER GENERAL G.THORPE C.M.G. D.S.O.
Commanding 17th Infantry Brigade.

ueens.
oyal Fusiliers.
ifle Brigade
T.M.Battery.

During the last few days the Brigade has been ed in a form of warfare different from that it has encountered during this war, and the way in which all have responded to the new conditions is beyond praise. The attack of the 1st Royal Fusiliersband 3rd Rifle Brigade on the 11th instant, meeting as it did obstinate resistance demonstrated the gallantry of all ranks.

The vigilance and rapid pursuit of the enemy on the 12th instant was all the more creditable in view of the fatigue caused by the fighting of the preceeding day. The night attack of the 8th Queens on the 12/13th was conducted in the face of great difficulties and secured a valuablehtactical success.

I fully realise the strain the recent fighting has imposed and wish to express my admiration for the gallantry and self sacrifice displayed by all Units of the Brigade.

Please bring the above to the notice of all men under your command.

G. Thorpe

14th October 1918. B.G.C., 17th Infantry Bde.

Appendix XVII.

SECRET.

17th Infantry Brigade Order No.254.

1. The 17th Infantry Brigade will be relieved in RIEUX by the 58th Infantry Brigade on the 16th instant and will march to billets in CAGNONCLES on relief.

2. Units of 17th Infantry Brigade will take over billets of Units of 58th Infantry Brigade as under :-

8th Battalion The Queens from a battalion The Welsh Regt.
3rd Battalion The Rifle Brigade from a battalion The Wiltshire Regt.
1st Battalion Royal Fusiliers from a battalion The Welsh Fusiliers.
17th L.T.M.Battery from 58th L.T.M.Battery.

3. Advance parties will proceed to CAGNONCLES to take over billets on the morning of the 16th instant.

4. Units will march out of RIEUX independently as soon as incoming Units have arrived and will proceed by cross country routes.
Full marching order and blankets will be carried.
Transport may proceed by road.

5. First line transport will be accommodated in battalion areas.

6. Location of H.Q. will be reported to Brigade H.Q. as soon as possible.

7. 17th Infantry Brigade Headquarters will close at RIEUX and will open at CAGNONCLES T.28.d.60.45 on relief.

8. ACKNOWLEDGE.

Ronald McScobie
Captain,
Brigade Major, 17th Infantry Brigade.

Issued to Sigs.
at 19.30 hours
15th October 18.

Copies to 8th Queens.
1st Royal Fusiliers.
3rd Rifle Brigade.
17th L.T.M.Battery.
Sigs. 17th Inf: Bde.
24th Division 'G' (2)
Brigade Major,
Staff Captain.
I.O., 17th Inf: Bde.
72nd Inf: Bde.
73rd Inf: Bde.
War Diary.
File.
Spare.

Appendix XVIII

Secret   Copy No [illegible]

8th Bn The Queen's Regt

OPERATION ORDER No [illegible]

Map Ref Sheet 51B   16th Oct [illegible]

1. The Battn will be relieved by a Battn of the WELSH REGT (58th I.B.) today & will march to billets in CAGNONCLES on relief.

2. ORDER OF MARCH: HQ, A, B, C, D Coys. 200x interval between Coys. Time of starting will be announced later.

3. Full marching order & blankets will be carried.

4. Transport will proceed by road.

5. Officers' valises must be dumped at Q.M. Stores [illegible]. [illegible] must be ready to be dumped at the same place at [illegible] hours notice.

6. O.C. Coys will ensure that the billets are left [illegible] & will render a report to Orderly Room [illegible] leaving.

7. Guides will meet Coys on arrival at [illegible] in CAGNONCLES & conduct them to their billets.

8. Completion of relief will be reported [illegible].

Issued at [illegible] by runner.

[illegible] Capt & Adjt

Copies [illegible]

War Diary

Appendix XIX

- Amendment to -

17th INFANTRY BRIGADE ORDER No. 255

To all recipients of 17th Inf.Brigade Order No 255 dated 18th Oct.

Reference above quoted order

1. The 183rd Infantry Brigade is not moving out of FAUBOURG ST DRUON until 19.15 hours to-day.

2. The head of the column will therefore pass starting point at 15.45 hours and Units will carry out night operations on the way in order not to arrive before 19.45 hours.

3. Head of Transport column will pass the starting point at 15.15 hours.

4. Guides from Advanced parties will be at the same rendevouz from 19.00 hours.

5. ACKNOWLEDGE.

For
CAPTAIN.
Brigade Major 17th Infantry Brigade.

19th October 1918.
Issued to Sigs
at 11.15 hours.

SECRET

17th INFANTRY BRIGADE ORDER No 255

Ref.57B. 1/40,000.

1. 17th Infantry Brigade Group will move to Billets in FAUBOURG ST DRUON (CAMBRAI) to-morrow 19th instant.

2. Advance parties,with bicycles, will meet Staff Captain at 17th Infantry Brigade H.Qrsz at 08.00 hours on 19th instant to arrange billets. Accomodation is limited.

3. Order of march :-
   3rd Battalion The Rifle Brigade.
   8th Battalion The Queens.
   1st Battalion The Royal Fusiliers.
   17th L.T.M.Battery.
   74th Field Ambulance.

4. Starting point Road junction B.4.a.80.90. Head of column will pass starting point at 14.00 hours.

5. Personnel will proceed by Cross country route to avoid congestion on the roads.

6. Intervals, 100 yards between companies, 400 yards between Battalions.

7. All transport will proceed by road, in same order as given in para 3, under the Brigade Transport Officer. Head will pass starting point at 13.30 hours.

8. One lorry per Battalion and one for Brigade H.Q. and 17th L.T.M.Battery will report at H.Qrs. of Units at 13.00 hours to carry blankets and stores.

9. Guides from Advance parties will be at Road junction A.23.b. 90.05. at 14.30 hours.

10. Brigade H.Qrs will close at CAGNONCLES at 14.30 hours 19th instant and will open at A.16.c.5.3. at the same hour.

11. ACKNOWLEDGE.

Ronald M Scobie

CAPTAIN.

Brigade Major 17th Infantry Brigade

Issued to Sigs at
22.30 hours 18th
October 1918.

Copies to 8th Queens.
1st Royal Fusiliers.
3rd Rifle Brigade.
17th LzT.M.Battery
74th Field Ambulance.
24th Division 'G' (2)
183rd Infantry Brigade.
73rd Infantry Brigade.
Brigade Transport Officer.
Sigs.17th Infantry Brigade.
Staff Captain.
Intelligence Officer.
War Diary.
File.

Appendix XX

SECRET.

Copy No. 13

8th Bn. The Queen's Regt

OPERATION ORDER No. [illegible]

MAPS.

[illegible]

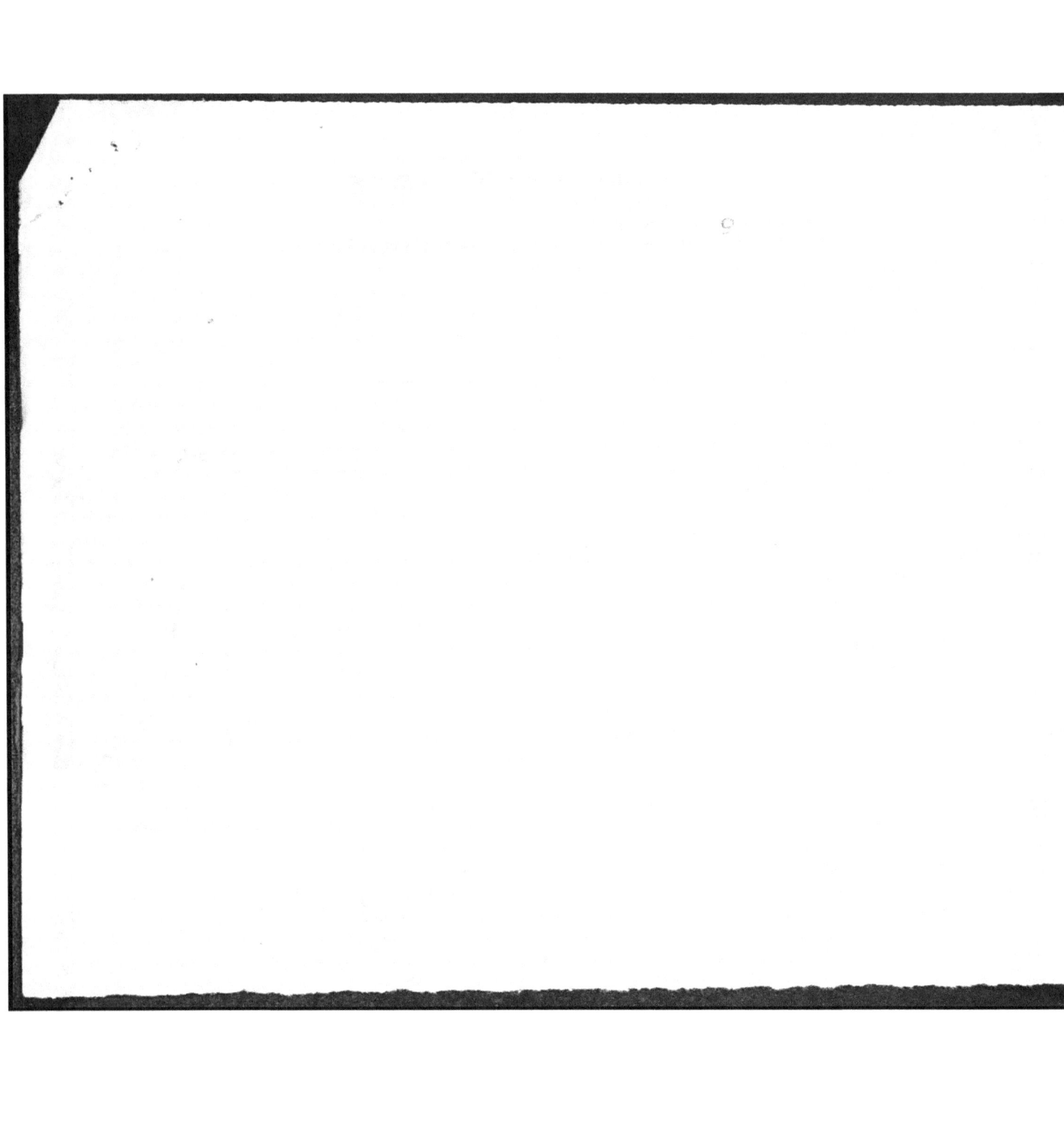

Appendix XXI

SECRET. Copy No. 12.

8th Bn. The Queen's. Regt.

OPERATION ORDER. No. A. 41.

Map Refs: 57c N.W. VALENCIENNES. 1/100.000. 23rd Oct. 1918.

1. The Battn will carry out a Tactical Scheme tomorrow in conjunction with 104 Coy. R.E. in accordance with General and Special ideas attached.

2. The Battn will be formed up in the street in which it is billeted ready to move off at 0820 hrs. Order of march - 'B', H.Q., 'C', 'D', 'A' Coys. Head of Column opposite 'B' Coys Officers Mess facing E. Dress - Fighting Order. The drums will not parade.

3. The Battn will march to its Assembly Position in the road running N.E. through N.5.d. (Sheet 57c N.W.).
Route. Road through M.16.d. & b. - PLACE D'ARMES - AVENUE DE VALENCIENNES.

4. Coy L.G. Limbers will march in rear of Coys, carrying full compliment of L.Gs & Magazines, etc. H.Q. Limber will not be required.

5. ACKNOWLEDGE.

Issued at 1415 hrs.
by RUNNER.

C. Tatham
Lieut & Asst Adjt.
8th Queens Regt.

Copies to:-

No 1. C.O.	No. 7. H.Q. 17 I.B.
2. o/c 'A' Coy	8. o/c 104. R.E.
3. " 'B' "	9. T.O.
4. " 'C' "	10. R.S.M.
5. " 'D' "	11. FILE
6. " H.Q. "	12. War Diary.

REF MAP:- VALENCIENNES. 1/100.000.

Scheme in conjunction with 104 Coy. R.E.

General Idea.

An enemy force has retired towards DOUAI in a N.W. direction from CAMBRAI having destroyed the Bridges over the CANAL DE L'ESCAUT.

This force has however left covering detachments to hinder our crossing the CANAL at various points.

8th Bn The Queens and 1 Section 104 Coy. R.E. forms part of the Advanced Guard to 24th Div. which has been ordered to cross at MORENCINES (immediately N. of CAMBRAI).

Special Idea.

Scouts have reported about ½ Coy. of the enemy holding HILL 80. near the "Y" of TILLOY.

O.C. 8th Queens decides to send 2. L. G. Sections across the CANAL by means of doors from houses and other expedients to cover the building of a light footbridge by the R.E. sufficient to enable 1 Coy to get across and drive the enemy off HILL 80.

As soon as this light footbridge is completed, the R.E. will build a pontoon bridge to enable the Bn and its 1st line Transport to cross.

23.10.18.

C. F. Tatham
Lieut & A/Adjt.
8th Bn Queens Regt.

Appendix XXII

Secret

17th INFANTRY BRIGADE ORDER No. 256.

1. March Table for the move of Brigade Group to CAGNONCLES this afternoon is attached.

2. The same billets as before will be taken over in CAGNONCLES.

3. 1 lorry for each battalion and one for Brigade H.Qrs and 17th L.T.M.Battery will report at Brigade H.Qrs after collecting supplies, time unknown.
Battalions will send a guide to Brigade H.Qr on leaving CAMBRAI to guide this lorry to Battalion dumps.

Ronald ...
Captain,
Brigade Major, 17th Inf: Bde.

Issued to Sigs.
at 15.00 hours.
25/10/18

Copies to
24th Division 'G' (2)
8th Queens.
1st Royal Fusiliers.
3rd Rifle Brigade.
17th L.T.M.Battery.
104th Field Coy. RE.
74th Field Ambce.
A.S.C.
Staff Captain.
I.O., 17th I. Bde.
Sigs. 17th Inf: Bde.
War Diary
File.

MARCH TABLE to accompany 17th Infantry Brigade Order No. 256.

Starting point - Cross Roads A.22.d.4.5 (57b. N.W)

Serial No.	Unit.	Time Head to pass S.P.
1.	Brigade H.Qrs.	16.00 hours.
2.	8th Queens.	16.02 "
3	1st Royal Fus.	16.08 "
4.	3rd Rifle Bde.	16.14 "
5.	17th L.T.M.Batty.	16.21 "
6.	Transport of all above Units in same order.	16.45 "

1. No transport will accompany Units. Companies will march closed up but 100 yards will be left in rear of Battalions and 20 yards in rear of Brigade H.Qrs.

2. 104th Field Coy RE. and 74th Field Ambce march independently not to start before 17.15.

****

Appendix XXIII

S E C R E T
****

17th INFANTRY BRIGADE ORDER No. 257.

Ref. Sheet 51A.
1/40,000

1. The Brigade Group will march to Billets in ST AUBERT tomorrow (26th instant) vacated by 56th Infantry Brigade.

2. Battalions will carry out a scheme in accordance with Table 'A' attached.

3. Remainder of Brigade Group will march in accordance with Table 'B' attached.

4. ACKNOWLEDGE ✓

Ronald McScobie
CAPTAIN.
Brigade Major 17th Infantry Brigade.

Issued to Sigs at
24.00 hours
25th Octr 1918

Copies to
24th Division 'G' (2)
8th Queens.
1st Royal Fusiliers.
3rd Rifle Brigade.
17th L.T.M.Batterys
104 Field Coy. R. E.
74th Field Ambulance.
195 Coy. A.S.C.
Brigade Transport Officer.
Sigs. 17th Inf.Brigade.
Staff Captain.
Intelligence Officers
War Diary.
File.

Recd 26/10/18
0035
CA

TABLE "A"

Ref. [illegible]
Sheet [illegible]

1. Line held by 24th Division on night 25/26th [illegible] through [illegible] immediately S. of NAVES and N. of CAGNONCLES.

2. Touch has been lost with enemy.

3. 8th Battalion Queens will act as advanced guard on 26th inst. to [illegible] Infantry Brigade in pursuit of enemy.
3rd Battalion The Rifle Brigade will be in support on the right
1st Battalion Royal Fusiliers will be in support on the left.

4. Brigade boundaries will be
Northern Main road NAVES-VILLERS-en-CAUCHIE (exclusive)
Southern CAGNONCLES (inclusive) - AVESNES (exclusive) -
ST. AUBERT (inclusive).

5. Leading platoon of 8th Battalion Queens will be clear of CAGNONCLES by 09.00 hours 26th instant.

6. 8th Battalion the Queens will secure the high ground N.W. of ST. AUBERT.

7. All Battalions will then reform and march to billets in ST. AUBERT on receipt of orders from Brigade H.Qrs.

8. C.Os. Battalions will attend a conference at 10.00 hours on 26th instant at Brigade H.Qrs ST. AUBERT.

TABLE "B"

Ref. Sheet.
57b. N.W.

Starting point B.4.b.6.2. (Fork Roads).

Serial No.	Unit.	Time head to pass starting point.
1.	104th Field Coy. RE.	09.00
2.	74th Field Ambce.	09.06
3.	Brigade H.Qrs.	09.12
4.	Brigade Transport.	09.14
5.	17th L.T.M.Battery.	09.34

ROUTE.

Main Road CAMBRAI - ST VAAST - AVESNES - LES AUBERT.

N.B.

ALL transport of Units will march under Brigade Transport Officers.

App XXIV

Operation Order. Ref map [illegible]

1. The Bde group will move to Billets in ST AUBERT to-day, vacated by 56 I.B.
2. Battalions will carry out a scheme as follows on the way.
3. Line held by 24th Div. on night of 25/26 runs through A of [illegible] immediately S of NAVES & N of CAGNONCLES.
4. Touch has been lost with enemy.
5. 5 Queens will act as Adv. gd. [illegible] on 26 & 17 [illegible] in pursuit of enemy, [illegible] M.B. will be in support on the right less R.F. in support on the left.
6. Brigade Boundaries will be :-
Northern - Road NAVES - VILLERS EN CAUCHIE (exclusive)
Southern - CAGNONCLES (inclusive) AVESNES (incl.) ST AUBERT (inclusive)
7. 5 Queens will secure the high ground N.W. of ST AUBERT.
8. All Battns will then reform & march to billets in ST AUBERT on receipt of orders from Bde HQ.
9. A I.D. Coy (Queens) will form the

Vanguard C Coy the Mainguard with D Coy in support. Messages to B.H.Q. at the head of B Coy.

10. Leading platoon of D Coy will be clear of [illegible] by 09.00 hrs. It will [illegible] off at 08.50.

11. Distance between Mainguard & Vanguard 500x between Mainguard & B.H.Q. 500x

12. [illegible] will march in rear of B Coy.

13. All Transport will march under Bde. Transport Officer. Starting Point & Time to be ascertained from him.

C F Ta[illegible]

Lieut & A/Adjt

11/11/18

07.10

Appendix XXV

17th Inf: Bde. No. G.7/11.

8th Queens.
1st Royal Fusiliers.
3rd Rifle Brigade.
17th L.T.M.Battery.

1. A Brigade scheme will be carried out tomorrow 29th instant in accordance with the attached General and Special Ideas.

2. Officer Commanding 3rd Battalion the Rifle Brigade will detail two Companies to act as the enemy.
These Company Commanders will meet the Brigade Major at 14.00 hours today at Brigade H.Qrs mounted in order to go over the ground.

3. DRESS:- Fighting Order except that the two companies detailed to act as the enemy will wear Service Caps. Great Coats, blankets and Jerkins will not be carried.

Ronald Nicol
Captain,
Brigade Major, 17th Inf: Bde.

28th October 1918.

Copies to 24th Division 'G' (2)
72nd Inf: Bde.
104th Field Coy. R.E.
24th Battn. M.G.C.

GENERAL IDEA

****

Refce. Sheet 51A. 1/40,000

1. 24th Division is advancing on a one Brigade front. Divisional boundaries are -

   NORTHERN CHAUSSE - BRUNEHAUT. (exclusive)

   SOUTHERN V.15.c.0.0.- Road fork V.18.c.4.8. (inclusive) - Road fork W.7.d.60.15. (inclusive)- Road fork W.3.d.3.1. (exclusive).

2. 73rd Infantry Brigade, leading Brigade on 28th instant has secured the high ground W. of HAUSSY and MONTRECOURT WOOD, but further advance down to the River was held up by heavy rifle and machine gun fire, from the direction of HAUSSY and MONTRECOURT.

3. 17th Infantry Brigade will advance through 73rd Infantry Brigade on the 29th instant and will secure the crossings of the SELLE River within the Divisional boundaries, mop up the villages of HAUSSY and MONTRECOURT, and push up to the high ground E. of the river in V.35. and about Maison Blanche.

****

SPECIAL IDEA

****

Ref. Sheet 51A
1/40,000

1. Line held by 73rd Infantry Brigade at 22.00 hours 28th inst, as follows -
V.17.c.2.7. - V.16.b.9.5. - V.10.d.2.0. - then a gap to V.3.d.2.0. - Corner of Wood V.3.d.2.3. - thence along N.E. corner of MONTRECOURT WOOD.

2. To secure the high ground MAISON BLANCE - P.29.c.0.0.
1st Battalion The Royal Fusiliers will attack on the Right, 8th Battalion The Queens on the Left, passing through the line held by 73rd Infantry Brigade at 10.30 hours on 29th instant.
3rd Battalion The Rifle Brigade, less two Companies will be in Brigade Reserve.

3. Inter- Battalion boundary will be :-

Main Road St AUBERT - MONTRECOURT as far as MONTRECOURT WOOD thence round S.E. corner of Wood to V.3.d.2.3. - Sand Pit in V.5.a. (exclusive to Right Battalion)- Road fork Q.31.b.95.00 (exclusive to Right Battalion).

4. O.C.17th L.T.M.Battery will detail two guns and teams to accompany each leading Battalion.

5. One section 104th Field Company R.E. will be detailed to accompany each leading Battalion if available.

6. Artillery will co-operate as follows :-

(i) Z to Z plus 30 — 2 Brigades F.A. on HAUSSY - SAULZOIR Rly.
(ii) Z to Z plus 60 — 2 Brigades F.A. on high ground P.35.a.& c, P.36.c. and around Maison Blanches.
(iii) Z plus 30 to Z plus 60 — The two Brigades F.A. in (1) above will lift to the targets in (2) above.
(iv) 6" Hows will fire on Eastern exits of HAUSSY and Sunken Road in P.34. and W.5. from Z to Z plus 30 then lifting to 1 line of Road in P.29.b.and d, P.30.b. & d. from Z plus 30 to Z plus 60.
(v) 60 Pounders will search Road V.5.d.6.0. - P.34.d.0.0. from Z to Z plus 30 lifting to Maison Blanche from Z plus 30 to Z plus 60.
(vi) Counter battery work will be carried out.

7. "A" Company 24th M.G. Battalion will support the attack from the river crossing by direct overhead fire.
O.C. 'A' Company M.G. Battalion will push sections across the river as soon as a crossing has been secured in order to assist the clearing of the remainder of the objective. He will make his Headquarters with O.C. 8th Batt.The Queens.

8. Brigade Headquarters will be established at 10.00 hours at the Solitary house V.13.b.3.5.

****

28/10/18.

937.

9/8 3/9

(6339) Wt. W160/M3016 1,500,000 10/17 McA & W Ltd (E 1898) Forms W3091.

Army Form W.3091.

Cover for Documents.

Nature of Enclosures.

8TH BN THE QUEEN'S (RWS REGT)

WAR DIARY

VOLUME XXXIX

NOVEMBER 1918

H. J. C. Peirs.

DEC 4TH 1918

Lieut Colonel
COMMANDING
8TH BN THE QUEENS RWS REGT

Notes, or Letters written.

Instructions regarding War Diaries and Intelligence Summaries are contained in F. S. Regs., Part II. and the Staff Manual respectively. Title Pages will be prepared in manuscript. November 1918

Army Form C. 2118

WAR DIARY
or
~~INTELLIGENCE SUMMARY~~
(Erase heading not required.)

Page 1

VOL XXXIX

Place	Date	Hour	Summary of Events and Information	Remarks and references to Appendices
ST AUBERT	1st		Batt^n engaged in training	
"	2nd		ditto One Brigade of the 19th Division came into the village during the day and one of the 61st Division during the night, making accommodation very crowded	
ST AUBERT – BERMERAIN	3rd		The Batt^n moved off at 03·00 hrs. and marched via HAUSSY to BERMERAIN, arriving there shortly after 06·00 hrs. Billets here too were very close, part of the 73rd Brigade and of a Brigade of the 61st Division being already in the village, but during the day these moved out and the men were able to rest in comfort. Plans had been laid some days before for an attack on a large scale on the 4th inst E of MARESCHES, the 73rd Brigade to carry out the preliminary attack under a barrage and the 17th Brigade then to pass through and capture the third objective, viz the villages of WARGNIES-LE-PETIT and WARGNIES-LE-GRAND. For this operation the 8th Queen's were to carry out the attack on the greater part of the Brigade front, with, however, one Company of the 1st Royal Fusiliers detailed to capture WARGNIES-LE-GRAND on the left. During the day news was received that the enemy was retiring and it seemed doubtful if the projected attack would develop in the way intended. Owing to casualties the Batt^n was still organized on a three-company basis, A and D Companies forming one Company under the command of Capt. J. BURRELL (D Coy)	App I O.O. A.42 App II 17 I B No G2/3 App III 17 I B Order 259
BERMERAIN – VILLERS POL	4th		The Brigade moved at 04·00 hrs. from BERMERAIN to SEPMERIES in close support to the 73rd Brigade who were then beginning to follow up the retreating enemy. During the morning the Batt^n moved to the E of MARESCHES and later to the N of VILLERS POL. During the afternoon it seemed likely that the 17th Brigade would	

CA

1875 Wt. W593/826 1,000,000 4/15 J.B.C. & A. A.D.S.S./Forms/C. 2118.

Army Form C. 2118

Instructions regarding War Diaries and Intelligence Summaries are contained in F. S. Regs., Part II. and the Staff Manual respectively. Title Pages will be prepared in manuscript.

NOVEMBER 1918

WAR DIARY or ~~INTELLIGENCE SUMMARY~~

(Erase heading not required.)

Page 2

VOL. XXXIX

Place	Date	Hour	Summary of Events and Information	Remarks and references to Appendices
VILLERS POL	4th	(Contd)	pass through the 73rd Brigade next morning and the front was reconnoitred. The situation at this time (16.00 hrs) was obscure: the 73rd Brigade had cleared the WARGNIES villages and were attacking the high ground E. of them. It was reported shortly afterwards that they had cleared this, but later it was found that they were still 300 yards short and that the enemy was holding this line in force. At night definite orders were received for the 17th Brigade to pass through the 73rd Brigade on the morning of the 5th with the 8th Queen's on the right, the 1st Royal Fusiliers on the left and the 3rd Rifle Brigade in reserve. C, D and A Coys were accordingly detailed to find the front line with B Coy in reserve. The Guards Division were advancing on the right, and a forward section of guns and two Stokes Mortars were working with the Battn, and a Coy of the 24th M G Battn was in close support	
VILLERS POL - LE PISSOTIAU	5th		The Battn started off ~~early~~ at 4 a.m and by 06.30 hrs. Battn H.Q were at the forked roads W. of WARGNIES-LE-PETIT and the river crossing was made ~~good~~ at once. By 07.00 hrs. the forward troops were well through the 73rd Brigade front line E. of WARGNIES and Battn H.Q. moved to the Cemetery. No touch had yet been found with the enemy or with the 1st Royal Fusiliers on the left. At 08.00 hrs. the Battn had cleared LA BOIS-CRETTE, taking 2 unwounded and 4 wounded prisoners, and a pause was made to allow the 1st Royal Fusiliers on the left to catch up. The advance was continued at 08.30 hrs. to LE PLAT-DE-BOIS and the high ground E. of it. The general	C.F.

1875 Wt. W593/826 1,000,000 4/15 J.B.C. & A. A.D.S.S./Forms/C. 2118.

Instructions regarding War Diaries and Intelligence Summaries are contained in F. S. Regs., Part II. and the Staff Manual respectively. Title Pages will be prepared in manuscript.

Army Form C. 2118

WAR DIARY
or
~~INTELLIGENCE SUMMARY~~
(Erase heading not required.)

NOVEMBER 1918

Page 3

VOL XXXIX

Place	Date	Hour	Summary of Events and Information	Remarks and references to Appendices
	5th	(cont'd)	idea was that the Battn should push on and overcome minor opposition or opposition from isolated posts, but that no attempt should be made to advance against a strongly held line until the artillery was in position to give support. At 10.00 hrs the Halte on the W. side of ST. WAAST had been gained, but we were held up by M.G. fire from the orchards and woods S. of ST. WAAST. and W. of the River de CAMBRON. A Company of the Grenadier Guards had also spread across our front from the right and had to be ejected. At 11.00 hrs the B.G.C. reconnoitred and decided to get the artillery directed on to the high ground N.E. of ST WAAST and W. of LE PISSOTIAU as soon as possible and that under cover of this fire the advance would continue. Arrangements were made at once, but meanwhile it was found that the forward Coys had managed to overcome the opposition and make some advance, but had again been held up by M.G. fire. It was also found ~~that~~ almost impossible to locate definite targets for the artillery owing to the thick rain. The B.G.C. accordingly decided to make an attack on the left in conjunction with the Division on the left early next morning under a barrage, but he required the 8th Queen's to capture the high ground W. of LE PISSOTIAU as a preliminary. The reserve Coy (B) were ordered to relieve D Coy and make the attack. This operation was not easy to organize as the shelling was fairly heavy, the ground was unknown, the night very dark, and the jumping-off place was across a river. However, it was carried out punctually and with complete success, as (according to civilians' statements) the enemy quitted the area directly the barrage began	App IV 17th I.B. Order 261

C.H.

1875 Wt. W593/826 1,000,000 4/15 J.B.C. & A. A.D.S.S./Forms/C. 2118.

Instructions regarding War Diaries and Intelligence Summaries are contained in F. S. Regs., Part II. and the Staff Manual respectively. Title Pages will be prepared in manuscript.

WAR DIARY or ~~INTELLIGENCE SUMMARY~~

(Erase heading not required.)

NOVEMBER 1918

Army Form C. 2118

Page 4

VOL. XXXIX

Place	Date	Hour	Summary of Events and Information	Remarks and references to Appendices
LE PISSOTIAU	5th	contd	and the M.G. fire from the flank ~~became intermittent~~ was not heavy. Meanwhile C Coy on the left had spread out and had also patrolled the River de CAMBRON which was reported as not difficult to cross. B Coy found LE PISSOTIAU clear of the enemy and accordingly marched in and occupied it, being enthusiastically received by the inhabitants. The enemy was however still holding the broken bridge on the road leading N. from the village and also had a post at the E. end of the village.	
"	6th		The 1st Royal Fusiliers attacked at dawn on the left, but were unable to get further than the River HOGNEAU. At 08.30 hrs. C Coy sent a patrol into ST. WAAST to endeavour to clear it and another patrol across the River de CAMBRON to gain the Railway Cutting N.E. of LE MAY, as the enemy had apparently gone back from this stream. C Coy were then ordered to follow up both these patrols and if possible push through ST. WAAST and up the railway to the Cemetery. At 09.00 Battn H.Q. were moved to COURTILFOI FARM. Meanwhile OC B Coy on the right had found himself close to a strong and commanding position of the enemy 300 yards from LE PISSOTIAU to the N. and N.E. on the other side of the River de MOULIN. The Liaison officer of the Guards on the right informed him that their line ran from the River de MOULIN to the factory at BAVAI station and that they were across the river at one point. On this information being reported to Brigade H.Q. orders were issued for the 3rd. Rifle Brigade to relieve the Guards	C.A.

Instructions regarding War Diaries and Intelligence Summaries are contained in F. S. Regs., Part II. and the Staff Manual respectively. Title Pages will be prepared in manuscript.

WAR DIARY
or
~~INTELLIGENCE SUMMARY~~
(Erase heading not required.)

NOVEMBER 1918

Page 5

VOL. XXXIX

Army Form C. 2118

Place	Date	Hour	Summary of Events and Information	Remarks and references to Appendices
LE PISSOTIAU	6th	Cont	and attack northwards. However, it was found that the river was the RIGOFOLIE, not the de MOULIN, and the Guards were facing E. and not N., the error being due to the misty weather and the difficulty of making reconnaissances owing to enemy M.G. fire. An officer was sent forward to reconnoitre the exact position and to intercept the 3rd. Rifle Brigade at BERMERIES and inform them of the situation. At 11.00 hrs. O.C. C Coy reported that he occupied the Railway Cutting N.E. of LE MAY but that the platoon sent to clear ST. WAAST had been held up and had suffered casualties, and he was withdrawing them. D Coy was thereupon ordered to relieve C Coy in ST WAAST and to try and push on. This relief was not complete till about 15.00 hrs owing to D Coy being caught in a heavy gas barrage on the way, and it was decided that their attack should be made at dusk with artillery to cover them. The platoon of C Coy in the Railway Cutting had meanwhile pushed on to the sunken road N. of the railway and W. of the River de MOULIN but could not get further and had to withdraw to the cutting. This information did not reach Battn. H.Q. till 21.30 hrs. An officer was at once sent down to re-establish if possible the position on the sunken road and to make sure there were no enemy in the area of the assembly positions of the 3rd Rifle Brigade who were to attack at dawn. He was also to report on the width and depth of the river. He reported at 01.00 hrs (7th) that the enemy had 3 posts on the W. side of the	

1875 Wt. W593/826 1,000,000 4/15 J.B.C. & A. A.D.S.S./Forms/C. 2118.

Instructions regarding War Diaries and Intelligence Summaries are contained in F. S. Regs., Part II. and the Staff Manual respectively. Title Pages will be prepared in manuscript.

Army Form C. 2118

WAR DIARY or ~~INTELLIGENCE SUMMARY~~

(Erase heading not required.)

NOVEMBER 1918

Page 6

VOL XXXIX

Place	Date	Hour	Summary of Events and Information	Remarks and references to Appendices
LE PISSOTIAU	6th	Cont^d	river and that the river was about 12 ft wide and 4 ft deep. D Coy had by this time cleared ST. WAAST village. This was reported to Brigade and it was decided to turn the artillery on to the enemy posts W. of the river, as there were no men then available to attack them. This and Lewis Gun fire had the desired effect and the enemy quitted their posts, and the R.E.'s were then enabled to bridge the stream at several points. B Coy had several minor encounters and incidents during the day in the course of which they had some casualties and took a few prisoners. During the day 2/Lt. W.T. EVERETT (C Coy) was killed and 2/Lt C.A. FIELD (A Coy) wounded (subsequently died of wounds). The award of M.C. to 2/Lts R.C. BROOKS and E. JENKINS was announced today.	
"	7th		The 3rd. Rifle Brigade attacked at dawn and captured the high ground N. of LE PISSOTIAU, the attack being entirely successful. On this objective being gained the 72nd Brigade passed through the 17th and the Batt^n was thereupon concentrated in billets in LE PISSOTIAU and spent the remainder of the day resting. The award of the Military Medal to the following was announced:- 68290 Pte. W. NEW, 68641 Pte. A YULE, 10592 Pte J.H BAYFIELD, 23173 Cpl. P.L ALLCROFT.	App. V 17 I.B. Order 262
LE PISSOTIAU - BAVAI	8th		The morning was spent in resting and cleaning up after the mud and wet of the preceding days. After dinners the Batt^n proceeded to march to BAVAI where it was accommodated in billets. On the way while passing Chateau de RAMETZ they came under shell fire from a long distance high velocity gun and	C.A.

Instructions regarding War Diaries and Intelligence Summaries are contained in F. S. Regs., Part II. and the Staff Manual respectively. Title Pages will be prepared in manuscript.

Army Form C. 2118

WAR DIARY
or
~~INTELLIGENCE SUMMARY~~
(Erase heading not required.)

NOVEMBER 1918

Page 7
VOL XXXIX

Place	Date	Hour	Summary of Events and Information	Remarks and references to Appendices
BAVAI	8th	Contd	a few casualties were suffered, including one officer (2/Lt E E PLOWMAN) wounded. Total casualties for the period 3 officers and 35 O.R's	
"	9th		The Brigade was under orders to move forward at an hour's notice and at one time during the morning orders were actually & received to proceed to BOIS DE CHÊNE, but before the Battn could get on the march the orders were cancelled and the Battn returned to billets in BAVAI. The 20th Division passed through the town going eastward and it was understood that they were relieving the Division in the front line.	
"	10th		A Church Parade Service was held, but otherwise no activity took place.	
"	11th		At 07 30 hrs. a message from Brigade H.Q. was received that the Armistice with Germany had been signed and that hostilities were to cease at 11.00 hrs, all troops remaining in their present positions until further orders. A considerable rearrangement of billets had to take place during the day owing to the incursion of XVII Corps H.Q. into the town and the consequent necessity of giving up billets to them	
"	12th		Nothing to report	
"	13th		ditto	

1875 Wt. W593/826 1,000,000 4/15 J.B.C. & A. A.D.S.S./Forms/C. 2118.

CAY

Instructions regarding War Diaries and Intelligence Summaries are contained in F. S. Regs., Part II. and the Staff Manual respectively. Title Pages will be prepared in manuscript.

WAR DIARY
or
~~INTELLIGENCE SUMMARY~~

(Erase heading not required.)

NOVEMBER 1918

Army-Form C. 2118

Page 8

VOL XXXIX

Place	Date	Hour	Summary of Events and Information	Remarks and references to Appendices
BAVAI	14th		Nothing to report	
"	15th		The following officers joined the Battn :- 2/Lieuts E.R SCRIVENER, W.H WILLIAMS, W.V. WRIGHT, E.S JENNER M.M., R BUTLER, G.H NASH, E.S TRAPPITT, H.S SELOUS and A CLARKE	
"	16th		Nothing to report.	
BAVAI - JENLAIN	17th		The Battn proceeded by march route from BAVAI to JENLAIN arriving in billets in the latter place about 11.30 hrs. Billets were on the whole crowded and draughty.	App. VI. O.O. A/43 " VII 17 I.B. Order 264 " VIII do. 265 " IX O.O. A/44
JENLAIN - AUBRY	18th		The Battn continued its march and proceeded via CURGIES, MARLY and the Southern outskirts of VALENCIENNES to AUBRY, arriving in the new area about 12.30 hrs. Billets again proved to be cold and draughty.	
AUBRY - SOMAIN	19th		The Battn proceeded again by march route via WALLERS, HELESMES and ERRE to SOMAIN, arriving there about 11.30 hrs. Billets here were much better, the town being practically untouched by shell-fire, and the men were for the most part fairly comfortably housed. The Division passed now from the Third to the First Army and from the XVII to the VIII Corps. Copy of congratulatory message from G.O.C Third Army is attached.	App X O.C. A/45 App XI
SOMAIN	20th		Nothing to report	
"	21st		2/Lieut ~~ditto~~ G. RAWES joined the Battn.	
"	22nd		Nothing to report	

C.F.T.

1875 Wt. W593/826 1,000,000 4/15 J.B.C. & A. A.D.S.S./Forms/C. 2118.

- Instructions regarding War Diaries and Intelligence Summaries are contained in F. S. Regs., Part II. and the Staff Manual respectively. Title Pages will be prepared in manuscript.

WAR DIARY
or
~~INTELLIGENCE~~ SUMMARY
(Erase heading not required.)

NOVEMBER 1918

Army Form C. 2118

Page 9

VOL. XXXIX

Place	Date	Hour	Summary of Events and Information	Remarks and references to Appendices
SOMAIN	23rd		Nothing to report	
"	24th		Capt E.A. MOORE and Lieut H.G. VEASEY rejoined the Battn from Sick leave to England	
"	25th		Part of the 12th Division, including the 6th Battn of The Queen's, marched through the town on the way to billets in AUBERCHICOURT. Capt C.E.S. BEADLE proceeded to Hospital	
SOMAIN – LECELLES	26th		The Battn moved from SOMAIN and proceeded via MARCHIENNES, TILLOY and ROSULT to LECELLES, taking over billets in the latter place from the 13th Middlesex Regiment. Accommodation on the whole was very bad, one Coy being billeted in huts in the middle of a German ammunition dump. This Coy was subsequently moved to better quarters. The Division now passed from the VIIIth into the Ist Corps. 2/Lieuts G.D. HONEY and E.V. TRAVERS joined the Battn.	App XIII O.O. A/46 XIII 17th I.B. Order 267
LECELLES	27th		Nothing to report	
"	28th		ditto	
"	29th		The award of the Military Medal to the following was announced:– 23013 Pte W.H. BURRIDGE, 2057 Cpl L SMITH, 3195 L/Sgt W.E. KENWARD.	
LECELLES – BAISIEUX	30th		The Battn moved by march route to its final destination at BAISIEUX, a distance of some 14 miles. Route via RUMEGIES, MOUCHIN, BACHY, WANNEHAIN	App XIV O.O. A/47 XV 17th I.B. Order 218 CA

1875 Wt. W593/826 1,000,000 4/15 J.B.C. & A. A.D.S.S./Forms/C. 2118.

Army Form C. 2118

Instructions regarding War Diaries and Intelligence Summaries are contained in F. S. Regs., Part II. and the Staff Manual respectively. Title Pages will be prepared in manuscript.

WAR DIARY
or
~~INTELLIGENCE SUMMARY~~
(Erase heading not required.)

NOVEMBER 1918

Page 10
VOL. XXXIX

Place	Date	Hour	Summary of Events and Information	Remarks and references to Appendices
BAISIEUX	30th	contd	and CAMPHIN. Billets were very crowded and in some cases very cold and draughty. The whole village had been allotted to the Battn as its billeting area, but it was found that the 15 Divisional Reception Camp and certain other elements of the IIIrd Corps were in possession of some 600 billets, but it was hoped that they would soon be moved out of the village and their billets rendered available for the Battn. Lieut. F.F.V. ROBERTS rejoined the Battn from the 17 L T M Battery.	

C F Tatham
Lieut. & Asst Adjt
8 Bn The Queen's (R.W. Surrey Regt.)

CA

App I

SECRET. Copy No. 14

8th Bn. The Queens Regt

OPERATION ORDER No. 22

Map Ref. [illegible] 8th Nov. [illegible]

1. The Battn will take to billets in BERMERAIN in the early morning of 9th inst.

2. The Transport will accompany the Bn on the march.

3. Starting Point — [illegible]
Route — V.19.a [illegible] — Maison Blanche? — Maison Bleue — BERMERAIN.

4. Order of march [illegible] Coys & [illegible].
The Battn will be [illegible] starting point ready to move off at 0300 hours.
Dress — [illegible]

5. The C.O. [illegible] H.Q. by [illegible] will [illegible].

6. Four Runners per Company will report to Bn H.Q. at [illegible] [illegible] [illegible].

7. [illegible]

8. [illegible]

9. Acknowledge.

Issued at 1205 [illegible]

App. II

17th Inf: Bde. No. G.2/3.

SECRET.

24th Division 'G'.

Reference 24th Divisional Order No. 262.

1. I attach a rough plan of attack.
Until I have more details as to the action of the 73rd Brigade it is impossible to make more detailed plans.

2. I have explained to Cs.C., 8th Queens and 1st Royal Fusiliers that their action forward from the GREEN line must be to push forward strong patrols boldly to feel the enemy's strength, find gaps and push through the gaps.
If however a continuous strong resistance is met, they must wait for organised artillery support.

3. I depend to a great extent on an advance by the 19th Division S.E. along the high ground N.E. & E. of WARGNIES-LE GRAND.
This advance by the 19th Division should not halt at the inter-Divisional boundary.

4. My present intention is to use the 3rd Rifle Brigade to pass through the two leading battalions on the 2nd day to continue the advance.

G Thorpe
1st November 18. 73rd Inf Bde B.G.C., 17th Inf: Bde.

Copies to 8th Queens.
1st Royal Fusiliers.
3rd Rifle Brigade.

ROUGH PLAN OF ATTACK.

1. DATE. To be notified later.

TIME. Shortly before dawn.

2. OBJECTIVES. First bound to be gained on first day is the RED Line explained to all concerned at to-day's Brigade conference.

When this line has been gained the advance will be continued eastwards. This further advance from the RED line will however only be carried out on the first day, on the initiative of Battalion Commanders by patrols to maintain touch with the enemy.

Any ground gained by patrols should be held.

3. The attack to gain the BLUE and GREEN lines is being carried out by the 73rd Infantry Brigade.

The 17th Infantry Brigade has orders to push through 73rd and gain the RED line as soon as the GREEN line has been captured.

4. This attack by 17th Inf.Brigade will be carried out as follows :-

(a) 8th Queens on the Right; will maintain close touch with the progress of the 73rd Brigade and push through on the front South of WARGNIES-LE GRAND

(b) 1st Royal Fusiliers on the left, will clear the village of WARGNIES-LE-GRAND.

(c) 3rd Rifle Brigade and one section 103rd Field Company R.E. will be in Brigade reserve.

NOTES

(1) The advance of both leading Battalions will be carried out by pushing forward strong patrols to test the enemys resistance and discover any gaps in his defences, reserves being then boldly pushed forward through these gaps to turn any portions which are holding out.

(2) This advance will be in conjunction with an advance by the 19th Division round the N.E. and E. sides of WARGNIES-LE-GRAND.

5. When the RED line has been gained the 1st Royal Fusiliers will immediately take over the Brigade front North of and including the VALENCENNES - BAVAY Railway. This railway (inclusive to 1st Royal Fusiliers) will then become the inter-battalion boundary for any further advance.

6. ASSEMBLY The Brigade will be assembled at Zero approximately as follows :-

8th Queens squares Q.6. c & d, Q.12. a & b,.
1st Royal Fus. " Q.5. c & d, and 11. a & b.
3rd Rifle Bde. East of the stream running through Q.18.central to Q.10.Central.

7. Details as to artillery co-operation are not yet available.

8. 17th L.T.M.Battery will attach two guns with teams and one half-limber to each forward Battalion.

9. HEADQUARTERS As far as possible the Headquarters existing at the time of Brigade and Battalions of 73rd Brigade will be taken over by 17th Brigade. If possible, Battalion Headqrs' of 8th Queens and 1st Royal Fusiliers will be at the same place for the advance from the GREEN line.

****

App. III 3

SECRET.

17th INFANTRY BRIGADE ORDER No. 259.

Ref: Map.
VALENCIENNES 1/100,000
51A.......... 1/40,000

1. The 24th Division is resuming the attack on the 4th instant, in conjunction with the Guards Division on the right and the 19th Division on the left.

2. Final objective of the first stage of the operations is the line of the main road BAVAY-BELLIGNIES.
This will be known as the BROWN LINE.

3. 73rd Infantry Brigade will capture the BLUE and GREEN LINES, as explained to all concerned at yesterday's Brigade conference.
17th Infantry Brigade will then pass through the 73rd Infantry Brigade and will capture the RED LINE.
When this line has been gained the advance will be continued Eastwards.
This further advance from the RED LINE will however only be carried out on the first day, on the initiative of Battalion Commanders, by patrols to maintain touch with the enemy.
Any ground gained by patrols should be held.

4. ASSEMBLY.
The Brigade Group will be assembled as under before dawn on the 4th instant :-

8th Queens, squares Q.6.c and d and Q.12.a and b.
1st Royal Fusiliers squares Q.5.c and d and Q.11.a and b.
3rd Rifle Brigade & 1 Section 103rd Field Coy R.E. } E. of stream running through Q.18.cent. and Q.10.cent.

5. PLAN OF ATTACK.
(a) 8th Queens on the right will maintain close touch with the progress of the 73rd Infantry Brigade and will push through the front S. of WARGNIES-LE GRAND.

(b) 1st Royal Fusiliers on the left, will clear the village of WARGNIES-LE GRAND.

(c) 3rd Rifle Brigade and 1 Section 103rd Field Coy. R.E. will be in Brigade Reserve.

NOTES.
(i) The advance of both leading battalions will be carried out by pushing forward strong patrols to test the enemy's resistance and discover any gaps in his defences, reserves being then boldly pushed forward through these gaps to turn any portions that are holding out.

(ii) The advance will be in conjunction with an advance by the 19th Division round the N.E. and E. sides of WARGNIES-LE GRAND.

(d) When the RED LINE has been gained the 1st Royal Fusiliers will immediately take over the Brigade front North of and including the VALENCIENNES-BAVAY Railway.

This...........

This railway (inclusive to 1st Royal Fusiliers) will then become the inter-battalion boundary for any further advance.

6. ARTILLERY ARRANGEMENTS.

(a) The attack of the 73rd Infantry Brigade will be carried out under a creeping barrage which will come down at zero on a line to be notified later and will lift at the rate of 100 yards in 4 minutes.

(b) There will be a halt of about 15 minutes on the BLUE LINE.

(c) The infantry, in conjunction with both flank Divisions, will advance from the BLUE LINE at Z plus 135 minutes under cover of the barrage.

(d) The barrage will continue as far as the GREEN LINE and will form a protective barrage 300 yards E. of the GREEN LINE, remaining for 15 minutes at a slow rate and then ceasing. The advance thereafter will be carried out without a definite barrage.

(e) 106 Brigade R.F.A. will accompany 17th Infantry Brigade from zero.
1 battery will be in close support of each leading battalion.

(f) One 6 inch Newton (mobile) will probably be attached to the Brigade and will be used to assist the advance of the 8th Queens.

N.B. Leading battalion Commanders will be responsible that their H.Q. are established close to those of the supporting batteries R.F.A. respectively.

7. MACHINE GUNS.
Arrangements as to machine gun co-operation will be notified later.

8. TRENCH MORTARS.
O.C., 17th L.T.M.Battery will attach 2 teams and guns (carried in half a limber) to each leading battalion at BERMERAIN.
During operations he will maintain his H.Q. near to Brigade H.Qrs.

9. AEROPLANES.

(a) O.C., 13th Squadron R.A.F. is arranging for Contact Aeroplanes to call for flares at the undermentioned times :-

Zero plus 2 hours.)
Zero plus 3 hours.)
Zero plus 4 hours.)

Flares

(b) For a counter-attack aeroplane to be in the air from daylight onwards.

(c) For artillery planes as required by the situation.

10. LIGHT SIGNALS.
White Very lights will be used within battalions to show the positions of advanced units and so enable reserves to be pushed through where the enemy has given way.
Green Very lights will be used as an S.O.S. signal by day and by night.

N.B. 73rd Infantry Brigade are using RED Very lights to denote points from which hostile resistance is coming.

SYNCHRONIZATION.......

11. **SYNCHRONIZATION.**
Watches will be synchronized at 17th Infantry Brigade H.Qrs BERMERAIN, Q.22.c.1.9 at 1900 hours on 3rd NOVEMBER.

12. Bill hooks and wire cutters will be carried forward tied on the man.

13. 17th Infantry Brigade H.Qrs. will close at ST. AUBERT and open at BERMERAIN (Q.22.c.1.9) at 00.01 hours on 3rd instant.
They will reopen at SEPTMERIES shortly before zero on the 4th instant.

14. **HEADQUARTERS.**
As far as possible the Headquarters existing at the time of Brigade and Battalions of the 73rd Brigade will be taken over by 17th Brigade.

15. Zero hour will be notified later.

16. **ACKNOWLEDGE.**

Ronald McKechie
Captain,
Brigade Major, 17th Inf: Bde.

Issued to Sigs.
at 2000 hours,
2nd November 18.

Copies to 24th Division 'G' (2)
73rd Infantry Brigade.
72nd Infantry Brigade.
8th Queens.
1st Royal Fusiliers.
3rd Rifle Brigade.
17th L.T.M.Battery.
103rd Field Coy. R.E.
74th Field Ambulance.
24th Divisional Artillery (2)
24th Battn. M.G.C.
Staff Captain.
B.T.O.
I.O.
17th Inf: Bde. Signals.
Brigade Major.
War Diary.
File.
Spares.

8th Queens

S E C R E T
****

Refce Sheet 51A
1/40,000

17th INFANTRY BRIGADE No 259/1

Reference 17th Infantry Brigade Order No 259 of 2nd NOVR 1918.

1. The Brigade will be assembled on 4th instant as in para 4 of above quoted order, but O.C. 8th Battalion The Queens will move his Battalion across the RHONELLE River into the valley in L.28.a., b and d. at the first opportunity after daylight.

2. 'B' Echelon Transport of Units will leave BERMERAIN at 06.00 hours 4th instant under arrangements to be notified by Brigade Transport Officer and will move to an assembly position in Q.5.d. clear of the road.

3. Brigade Headquarters will open at SEPMERIES (approx Q.6.b.6.7.) at 0530 hours 4th instant and will move on again to the Prison MARESCHES as soon as possible.
After this H.Q. will be established on the same line as 73rd Infantry Brigade are moving.

Ronald Scobie
CAPTAIN.
Brigade Major 17th Infantry Brigade.

Issued to Sigs
at 1930 hours
3rd Novr 18.

Issued to all recipients of
17th Infantry Brigade Order No 259.
****

objective

(c) 8th Queens will commence clearing houses between Railway and S. Bde boundary as far E. as Road and Railway junction H.30.a.9.4 as soon as 1st Royal Fusiliers have gained their objective

(d) When 3rd Rifle Bde has secured the high ground N of BAVAI it will mop up the town, establish a line on the Eastern side and attempt to gain touch with the Guards Division.

3/ Inter Battalion boundary for the above operations will be the BAVAY - WARGNIES LE GRAND railway inclusive to Right Battalion

4/ Artillery barrage will open on the line H.15.d.8.0 – H.15.a.8.0 for six minutes and will then advance at the rate of 100 yards in 3 minutes

5/ Machine Guns O/C 24th Batt M.G.C. to arrange to send 4 guns

forward with 1st Royal Fus:
to secure the left flank.
1 Coy less 1 section will
supplement the barrage by
overhead fire.
2 sections will take up a
position to support attack ~~from~~
of 1st Royal Fusiliers from
spur in H 28.c if attack of
8th Queens tonight is successful
6. Acknowledge.

Ronald McCabe
Captain
5/11/18 Brigade Major. 17th I.B.
21.25 hours.
Copies to 3 Battalions
17th L.T.M.B.
24th M.G.B
O.C. Adv. Group Artillery
24th Division "G"
Flank Brigades.

App V

5

SECRET.

17th Inf Bde Order No 262

1. 3rd Rifle Brigade will pass through 8th Queens tomorrow 7th instant. Final objective high ground LA BELLE HOTESSE H23 d 7 8 to corner of wood H 17 d 3 4.
2. The attack will be supported by an artillery and Machine gun barrages.
3. 19th Division on left and Guards Divn on right will be attacking at the same time.
4. When objective in para 1 has been secured troops of 72nd Inf Bde will pass through the 3rd Rifle Bde and continue the advance.
5. 8th Queens will then assemble in PISSOTIAU and 1st Royal Fus. in ST WAAST west of the river HOGNEAU.

App IV

SECRET

1st Inf Bde Order No 261

Ref. 51a 1/40,000

1/ 8th Queens are attacking at 22.00 hours tonight 5/6th in order to secure the high ground in H.28.

2/ Operations will be resumed on 6th inst. as under.

(a) 1st Royal Fusiliers will attack at 06.00 hours under an artillery barrage and will secure the high ground about BOIS LAPIETTE and wood in H.17.c and H.23.a.

Northern boundary will be line H.16. central H.17. central.

19th Division are advancing simultaneously to secure the high ground in H.15.b

(b) 3rd Rifle Bde will mop up ST. WAAST, and will then advance through 1st Royal Fusiliers and secure the high ground N of BAVAI as soon as 1st Royal Fusiliers have reached their

6. Should the 3rd Rifle Bde encounter little or no opposition they will push on to secure the high ground in H 24 A & B but will not advance beyond the line of the road BAVAI– BELLIGNIES

7. All details have already been issued.

8. Brigade HQ will be established at Zero hour at H 20 d 7. 8.

9 Zero hour will be 0600 hours November 7th.

10 ACKNOWLEDGE.

Rutcohe
Captain
Brigade Major 17th I B.

Issued at
2327.
6/11/18

Copies to

8th Queens	24th Div G
1st Royal Fus	24 M G C
3rd Rifle Bde	Adv Group Arty
17th LTMB	Flank Bdes.

App VI

6

SECRET. Copy No. 12

8th Bn. The Queens. Regt

OPERATION ORDER No [illegible]

Map Ref:- VALENCIENNES. 100.000 — 16. Nov. 1918.

1. The Battn. will march tomorrow Nov 17th to the [illegible] Area. The march will be resumed on the 18th inst. to the [illegible] Area under orders to be issued later.

2. Order of March, [illegible] the Battn. will be paraded in the Rue des [illegible] [illegible] [illegible] [illegible] at [illegible] hours.
Dress:- [illegible] [illegible] [illegible] [illegible] Respirators to be worn on the [illegible].

3. The Transport will [illegible] [illegible] of the Battn.

4. Blankets will be rolled in bundles of 10 and [illegible] labelled and dumped at the [illegible] [illegible] hours.
Officers' valises, [illegible] [illegible] and [illegible] will be dumped at the same place [illegible] [illegible] hours.
Officers' [illegible] will be [illegible] [illegible] [illegible] [illegible] will report at their respective [illegible] at [illegible] hours. [illegible] will report at [illegible] the same time.
The [illegible] will report at the [illegible] Room at [illegible] hours.

5. All Billets will be left in a clean and sanitary condition and all [illegible] [illegible] [illegible] [illegible] [illegible] by [illegible]. O.C. [illegible] will render a certificate [illegible] [illegible] on parading at [illegible] hours [illegible] [illegible] [illegible] [illegible] Officer [illegible] [illegible].

6. Details as to [illegible] [illegible] [illegible] [illegible].

7. Acknowledge.

Issued at 1945 hours
By runner

[illegible]
[illegible]

Copies to:-
No 1. C.O. [illegible]
2. [illegible]
3. [illegible]
4. [illegible]
5. [illegible]
6. [illegible]

App. VII

7

SECRET

17th Infantry Brigade Order No. 264.

1. The 17th Infantry Brigade Group, composed as under, will move to JENLAIN tomorrow 16th instant by march route.

Brigade H.Qrs	BAVAY.
8th Queens.	"
1st Royal Fus..........	"
3rd Rifle Bde	"
17th L.T.M.Batty........	"
104th Field Coy. RE......	FEIGNIES.
74th Field Ambce........	I.25.a.9.0
No.2. Coy Train	BOIS de CROTTE.

2. Advance parties on cycles will be sent off as soon as possible to the Town Major's office and will await the arrival of Captain H.BAIERLEY, M.C., 3rd Rifle Brigade who will allot billets in JENLAIN.

3. 104th Field Coy. R.E. will move to BISSOTIAU this afternoon. Billets for the night 16/17th will be allotted them by the 8th Bn. R.W.Kents (72nd Inf: Bde) ...

4. On arrival in JENLAIN area, S.A.A. in excess of 50 rounds per per man will be collected under Brigade arrangements and returned to SARRIFIES station.

5. ACKNOWLEDGE.

Captain,

Issued at
1330 hours.
16th October 18.

A/Brigade Major, 17th Inf: Bde.

Copies to 8th Queens.
1st Royal Fusiliers.
3rd Rifle Brigade.
17th L.T.M.Battery.
104th Field Coy. R.E.
74th Field Ambce.
No.2. Coy. Div Train.
8th Bn. R.W.Kents.
War Diary.
File.
Brigade Major,
Staff Captain.

App VIII

8

SECRET.

17th INFANTRY BRIGADE ORDER No. 265.

Ref: Map 1/40,000
Sheet 51 & 51a.

1. The Brigade Group will march tomorrow, November 17th, to the JENLAIN area. The march will be resumed on the 18th November to the DENAIN area, 8 I Corps, First Army, under orders to be issued later.

2. Units to pass the starting point, LA BELLE HOTESSE, H.23.d.70.70 at the following hours :-

17th Inf: Bde. H.Qrs..............0910 hours.
8th Queens........................0920 "
1st Royal Fusiliers...............0930 "
3rd Rifle Brigade.................0940 "
17th L.T.M. Battery...............0950 "
74th Field Ambulance..............0955 "

3. 104th Field Coy. RE. will be ready to join the column following 74th Field Ambce. at 1023 hours at H.22.a.50.10.

4. No. 2 Coy. Divisional Train will be ready to join the column following 104th Field Coy. RE. at road junction G.29.b.10.50 at 1115 hours.

5. Transport will move with units.

6. Details of administrative arrangements will be issued later.

7. ACKNOWLEDGE.

Captain,
A/Brigade Major, 17th Inf: Bde.

Issued to Sigs:
at 1800 hours,
16th Novr. 18.

Copies to 8th Queens
1st Royal Fusiliers.
3rd Rifle Brigade.
17th L.T.M. Battery.
74th Field Ambce.
104th Field Coy. RE.
No.2 Coy. 24th Div. Train.
24th Division 'G'
B.T.O.,
Signals, 17th Inf: Bde.
War Diary.
File.
Spares.

App IX 9

Secret. Copy No. 12

8th Bn. The Queens. Regt.

OPERATION ORDER No. 244

Map Ref. VALENCIENNES 1/40,000. 17th Nov: 1918

1. The Battn. will march tomorrow 18th inst to the AUBRY Area. The march will be continued on the 19th inst to the SOMMAIN Area.

2. On the 18th inst. Companies will be formed up in fours facing W. ready to move off at 1045 hours at the road junction at S of Rue de Lurens, as this is the Bde Starting point. Coys will leave room for the 1st Bn R. Fusiliers & 3rd Rifle Brigade to pass.
   Order of March. – "B" Coy, Drums, C.D. A Coy & H.Q. Coy
   O.C. "H" Coy will detail an Officer to act as i/c Stragglers.
   Transport will follow the Bn.
   Route. MARLY – Southern outskirts of VALENCIENNES – AUBRY

3. Dress – Full Marching Order. Shrapnel helmets and jerkins will be worn. Box Respirators will be carried at the Alert.

4. Advance parties as under will assemble at Bn H.Q. at 0700 hrs.
   1 N.C.O. per Coy.
   1 N.C.O. from the Transport.
   The Senior N.C.O. will take charge and will conduct the party to AUBRY where he will report to 2/Lt. TRAPPIT at the Church in AUBRY at 0930 hours.
   2/Lt. TRAPPIT will report to Bde. H.Q. [illegible] at 0816 hrs and will proceed to Aubry by ambulance car. He will report to a representative of [illegible] at the Church at AUBRY at 0900 hours.

5. Officers valises, [illegible] packs & rifles will be at the Q.M. Stores at 0930 hours.
   Blankets will be rolled in bundles of 10 and carefully labelled and dumped at the same place and time.
   Officers Mess kit will be collected by the Coy limbers at 0930 hours.
   The Maltese Cart will report to M.O. [illegible] at 0930 hours.
   The Mess Cart will proceed as already ordered.

6. All Billets must be left as clean as possible and in a sanitary condition. A certificate that billets have been inspected by an Officer and found satisfactory will be rendered by O.C. Coys to Orderly Room at 1025 hrs.

7. Details re lorries will be issued to Q.M. later.

8. Acknowledge.

[illegible]

Capt & Adjutant
8th Bn. The Queens Regt.

Issued at 2025 hrs.

Copies to:

No.		No.	
1.	C.O.	7.	T.O.
2.	O.C. A. Coy	8.	Q.M.
3.	" B. "	9.	I.O.
4.	" C. "	10.	L.G.O.
5.	" D. "	11.	File
6.	" H.Q. "	12.	War Diary

App X

Secret

Copy No. 12

8th Bn. The Queens Regt

OPERATION ORDER No. [illegible]

Map Ref. VALENCIENNES [illegible] 18th NOV 1918

1. The Battn will march tomorrow the 19th inst to the SOMMAIN area. Probable distance ... [illegible] miles.

2. Starting point [illegible] of [illegible]
TIME [illegible] to [illegible] 07.55 hours

ROUTE [illegible]

[illegible] — [illegible] will be carried between the [illegible]

3. Order of march [illegible] Coy, [illegible] "B" Coy, Qr Guard. The transport will follow the [illegible]
O.C. "B" Coy will detail an officer to [illegible] stragglers.

4. O.C. "A" Coy will detail [illegible] to act as [illegible]. They will report to the [illegible] officer at 07.[illegible] hours.

5. The [illegible] and [illegible] accompanied by a [illegible] will [illegible] at 07.00 [illegible]
The [illegible] will be [illegible]
Officers breakfast [illegible] will follow the Battalion. [illegible] must accompany this [illegible].

6. Billets must be left clean and [illegible] Certificate will be [illegible] before [illegible] moves off.

7. [illegible] blankets [illegible] in bundles of 10 [illegible] will be dumped at Q.M. Stores at 06.15 hours. Officers [illegible] will be at the same place at 06.45 hours.

8. [illegible] will report [illegible] as soon as they [illegible].

9. [illegible] will report [illegible] punctually.
1 N.C.O. [illegible] bicycles.
They will [illegible] 19th [illegible] at the [illegible] SOMMAIN at 23.00 hours.

10. ACKNOWLEDGE.

Issued at 2120 hours.

[illegible]
Capt & Adjutant
8th Queens Rgt

Copies to:

No 1	C.O.	No 7	T.O.
2	O.C. "A" Coy	8	Q.M.
3	" "B" "	9	M.O.
4	" "C" "	10	R.S.M.
5	" "D" "	11	[illegible]
6	[illegible]	12	[illegible]

App. XI

B.O

24th Division No. A. 196/71.

The following congratulatory message has been received by G.O.C., 24th Division from G.O.C., Third Army, and is published for the information of all ranks.

Third Army.

18th Novr. 1918.

"I cannot allow the 24th Division to leave the Third Army without expressing my appraciation of the part played by all ranks in the great battle which led to our victory and the probable termination of the war.

The Division has more than maintained the high opinion I formed of its qualities during the last time it served in this Army, and I feel nothing but regret at its departure to another Command.

I shall always remember with pride, the spirit, devotion and loyalty of all ranks by which the glorious result of the great battle was achieved.

(Signed) J. BYNG,
General."

- - - - - - - -

The Divisional Commander feels sure that all ranks will share his gratification in the praise conferred on the 24th Division, by so distinguished a soldier as General The Hon. Sir JULIAN BYNG, Commanding Third Army.

[signature]

H.Q., 24th Division.
19th November, 1918.

Lieut-Colonel.
General Staff.

App. XI

130

App. XIII

13

SECRET

17th INFANTRY BRIGADE ORDER NO 267.

Reference SHEET 44.
1/40,000

1. The 17th Infantry Brigade Group will move to the RUMEGIES area on the 26th instant in accordance with TABLE 'A' attached.
The move to final area will be made about the 30th instant.

2. 73rd Infantry Brigade Group will arrive in RUMEGIES area about 1400 hours on the 25th instant and will vacate that area about 1200 hours on the 26th instant.
Units will arrange to reconnoitre their areas on the morning of the 26th instant.

3. Lorries as under will be available and will report to Units at 1030 hours on the 26th instant.

Each Battalion........ 2 lorries.
Bde H.Q. & 17th L.T.M.B. 1 lorry.
104 Field Coy.R.E. and 74th Field Amblce. } 1 "

When loaded these lorries will rendezvous at the Church SOMAIN and proceed as a convoy in charge of 2/Lieut R.H.CLAY

4. 17th Infantry Brigade Headquarters will close at SOMAIN at 0730 hours on 26th instant and open at RUMEGIES at I.14.c.3.9. on arrival.

5. ACKNOWLEDGE

[signature]
CAPTAIN.
A/Brigade Major 17th Infantry Brigade.

Issued to Sigs
at 0830 hours
25th NOVR. 1918.

24th Division 'G'

8th Queens.	1st Royal Fusiliers.
3rd Rifle Brigade	17th L.T.M.Battery.
104 Field Coy.R.E.	195 Coy. A.S.C.
74th Field Ambce.	2/Lt R.H.Clay.
Sigs.17th Inf.Bde.	B.T.O.
Staff Captain.	
File.	

TABLE 'A' to accompany 17th Infantry Brigade Order No 267 dated 25/

Serial No.	Date	UNIT	from	to	Starting point.	Time head to pass starting point	ROUT
1	26th Nov.	Brigade H.Q.	SOMAIN	RUMEGIES	Cross Roads T.20.d.9.6.	0850 hours	MARCH
2	" "	8th Queens	"	LECHELLES	--do--	0855 "	- TIL BRILL SARS-
3.	" "	1st Roy.Fus.	"	RUMEGIES	--do--	0907 "	ROSIE X Roa
4.	" "	3rd Riflo Bde	"	RUMEGIES	--do--	0919 "	N.12. Queens
5.	" "	17th L.T.M.B.	"	RUMEGIES	--do--	0941 "	to LECH remaind
6.	" "	104th Field Coy.R.E.	"	RUMEGIES	--do--	0945 "	Brigade via
7.	" "	195 Coy. A.S.C	"	RUMEGIES	--do--	0955 "	SAMEO
8.	" "	74th Field Ambulance	"	RUMEGIES	--do--	1005 "	

NOTE. 1. Transport will accompany Units.

2. There will be no halt at 0850 first halt will be 0920 to 0930 after which the will march till 1050 hours in order to be clear of MARCHIENNES. After this h normal..

* * * * * * * * *

App XIV

14

Secret.

Copy No. 12

8th Bn. The Queen's Regt

Operation Order No. 147

Map Refs: Sheets [illegible] 1/40,000

Nov 2[illegible] 1918

1. The Bn. will move to its billet area in the vicinity of [illegible] [illegible] 30th inst.

2. The Bn. will be formed up [illegible] ready to move off at 0900 hours. [illegible] head of the Bn. will pass the starting point in I.20.a.5.0.
   Order of March: Drums, H.Q., [illegible] Coys, [illegible] Transport, [illegible] Coy [illegible] [illegible] Officers & [illegible].
   The following distances will be maintained throughout the march: 100 yds between Coys, 100 yds between [illegible] [illegible] the Transport.
   Dress: Full Marching Order. [illegible] [illegible] [illegible] [illegible] [illegible] [illegible] [illegible].
   [illegible] must [illegible] [illegible] [illegible] for [illegible].

3. Route: Fork Roads I.20.a.5.0. to [illegible] road I.17.b.6.0. – MOUCHIN – Road Junction [illegible] – [illegible] – [illegible] – BRILLON.
   [illegible] Distance: [illegible] miles.
   [illegible] will be [illegible] en route.

4. "A" Coy. will [illegible] [illegible] [illegible] [illegible] [illegible].

5. The Advance Parties will report to [illegible] [illegible] outside [illegible] at 0830 hours.
   [illegible] [illegible] [illegible] [illegible] [illegible]

6. [illegible] [illegible] [illegible] [illegible] [illegible] [illegible] [illegible] [illegible] [illegible].
   [illegible]
   [illegible]

7. [illegible]

8. [illegible]

9. [illegible]

[illegible]

Issued [illegible] 20.45 [illegible]

[illegible] Capt. [illegible]

Copies to: [illegible]

App XV

15

S E C R E T.

17th Infantry Brigade Order No. 268.

Ref. Sheets 37) 44) 1/40,000

1. The 17th Infantry Brigade Group, less 104th Field Coy, RE will move on the 30th instant to new area in accordance with Table 'A' overleaf.

2. Transport will accompany Units.

3. Units will send guides to the Church in RUMEGIES by 0900 hours on the 30th to pick up lorries as under :-

Each Battalion..........3 lorries.
Brigade H.Qrs...........2 "
Concert Party...........1 "
74th Field Ambce........1 "

These when loaded will rendezvous at the Church at RUMEGIES and proceed as a convoy under 2nd Lieut R.H.CLAY.

4. Brigade H.Qrs. will close at RUMEGIES at 0800 hours 30th inst. and reopen at CAMPHIN Chateau on arrival.

5. ACKNOWLEDGE.

Captain,
A/Brigade Major, 17th Inf: Bde.

Issued to Sigs.
at 1800 hours
29th Novr. 18.

Copies to 8th Queens.
1st Royal Fusiliers.
3rd Rifle Brigade.
104th Field Coy. RE.
74th Field Ambce.
O.C., 24th Div. Train.
195 Coy. ASC.
24th Division 'G'
24th Division 'Q'
B.T.O.
Signals, 17th Inf: Bde.
2nd Lieut R.H.CLAY.
2nd Lieut H.NICHOLSON, i/c Concert Party.
War Diary.
File.
Spares.

TABLE 'A' issued with 17th Inf: Bde. Order No. 268.

Serial No.	Unit.	From.	To.	Starting point.	Time of passing.
1.	17th Inf: Bde HQ.	RUMEGIES	CAMPHIN.	Fork Road I.7.b.6.0	0900 hrs
2.	1st Royal Fus.	RUMEGIES	CREPAINE.	-do-	0905 "
3.	3rd Rifle Bde.	RUMEGIES	CHERENG.	-do-	0917 "
4.	195 Coy. A.S.C.	-do-	GRUSON.	-do-	0930 "
5.	74th Field Ambce.	-do-	GRUSON.	-do-	0940 "
6.	8th Queens.	LESCELIES.	BAISIEUX.	-do-	(Not to pass (before 1000 (hours.

ROUTE via MOUCHIN to Road junction T.25.c.0.2 whence Serials 1, 2 & 6 via BACHY and WANNEHAIN, 3, 4 & 5 via BOURGHELIES and Cross Roads M.35.c.3.2

NOTE. Dinners on arrival for all units except 8th Queens who may make what arrangements they please.

(6392) Wt. W6192/P875 1,500,000 4/18 McA & W Ltd (E 2815) Forms W3091/4. Army Form W.3091.

G38/

Cover for Documents.

9 A 40

Nature of Enclosures.

8th BN THE QUEEN'S RWS REGT

WAR DIARY

VOLUME XXXV

DECEMBER 1918

1/1/19 H. J. C. Peirs, LIEUT COLONEL COMDG 8th QUEENS REGT

Notes, or Letters written.

Army Form C. 2118

Instructions regarding War Diaries and Intelligence Summaries are contained in F. S. Regs., Part II. and the Staff Manual respectively. Title Pages will be prepared in manuscript.

DECEMBER 1918

WAR DIARY
or
INTELLIGENCE SUMMARY

(Erase heading not required.)

PAGE 1.

VOL XXXX

Place	Date	Hour	Summary of Events and Information	Remarks and references to Appendices
BAISIEUX.	1.12.18.		The Battalion having now ~~moved~~ reached to its final destination, the day was spent in looking round the village with an eye to the eventual disposition of the Battalion. At the moment the village is very full the 15th Div Reception Camp and a Labour Company having a large number of billets. Interviews with both the C.Os of these units revealed the fact that neither knew when they were moving. The general idea however was fixed that the Battalion should centre round the BREWERY in which ~~were~~ are the Q.M. stores, the Canteen and will to which will be added two dining halls and the cookhouse for half the Battalion. The other two Company dining halls will be in the Weaving Mill a very large building about 300 yards from the BREWERY and NE of it. In this Mill also will be the Battalion Concert Hall and the Gymnasium. The men will be billeted as near as possible to their dining halls i.e. A & B Companies at the ~~E & F~~ East ~~& Eastern~~ Central portions of the Village and C & D Companies ~~at~~ in the West Central & Western portion of it.	

Army Form C. 2118

WAR DIARY
or
INTELLIGENCE SUMMARY
(Erase heading not required.)

Instructions regarding War Diaries and Intelligence Summaries are contained in F. S. Regs., Part II. and the Staff Manual respectively. Title Pages will be prepared in manuscript.

DECEMBER 1918

PAGE II
VOL XXXX

Place	Date	Hour	Summary of Events and Information	Remarks and references to Appendices
BAISIEUX.	2.12.18.		A conference was held at C. Company's HQ in the BREWERY which was attended by all officers at which the Time Table as shewn in Battalion Orders was discussed. Various methods of combining instruction + amusement were also discussed and various decisions were arrived at. As there appeared to be plenty of lorries running both to LILLE + TOURNAI it was decided to send 20 men per day to both these towns.	Bn orders of Dec 2nd. P.a.F.
"	3.12.18.		Such work as was possible on the lines decided on on 1st December was started. The transport was very busily engaged fetching wood from LECELLES and also from a Dump which we had established half way between LECELLES and BAISIEUX. Cookhouses were also started and two staircases leading to the Dining Halls were commenced. The work was necessarily slow in view of the great difficulty experienced in obtaining supplies of any sorts caused partly by a real shortage of material partly by lack of mechanical transport and partly due to Div HQ being 20 odd miles from us. On the whole the progress made during the first week was astonishing.	P.a.F.
"	7.12.18.		KING GEORGE Vth motored between TOURNAI + ROUBAIX. A party of officers + NCOs + men of the Battalion went to meet him. He did not inspect them.	P.a.F.

Instructions regarding War Diaries and Intelligence Summaries are contained in F. S. Regs., Part II. and the Staff Manual respectively. Title Pages will be prepared in manuscript.

DECEMBER 1918

WAR DIARY
or
INTELLIGENCE SUMMARY
(Erase heading not required.)

PAGE III
VOL XXXV

Army Form C. 2118

Place	Date	Hour	Summary of Events and Information	Remarks and references to Appendices
BAISIEUX.	8th DECEMBER – 18th DECEMBER.		Work on the before mentioned lines continued throughout this period. In addition a stage was commenced in the WEAVING MILL. The inhabitants have never experienced a large number of troops being billeted on them before and do not seem quite to understand the difficulties as yet. One or two are frankly obstructionists but in the main they are fairly allright. With regard to football grounds we have been lucky as we have four all of them rather damp however.	
	14th.		The Battalion played 1st Battn Royal Fusiliers at both Soccer & Rugger: at the former we drew 1 goal apiece, at the latter we won by a goal and a try (8 points) – NIL.	S.a.t.
			By the end of this period preparations for the Final dispositions were well advanced; and tables and chairs still however were very short the R.E. Workshops in TOURNAI not turning them out at the rate expected.	
	18th – 25th		On the 18th December the Labour Company moved to SINN and as the 15th Div Reception Camp had moved a few days previously the whole village was now at our disposal and Company's consequently moved to their final billeting areas. It was however still	

S.a.t.

Army Form C. 2118

Instructions regarding War Diaries and Intelligence Summaries are contained in F. S. Regs., Part II. and the Staff Manual respectively. Title Pages will be prepared in manuscript.

DECEMBER 1918

WAR DIARY
or
INTELLIGENCE SUMMARY
(Erase heading not required.)

PAGE IV
VOL XXXX

Place	Date	Hour	Summary of Events and Information	Remarks and references to Appendices
BAISIEUX	18/12/18 – 25/12/18		impossible to start the Dining Halls owing to lack of tables and forms. The cookhouses were however ready and as soon as the a/m articles arrive the halls can be started. A start has also been made with the Education Scheme and a certain number of classes are running under the general supervision of Lieut: R.W. ROSE.	
			The Orchestra had greatly improved and several Battalion Concerts had taken place, the hall being lighted with acetylene gas. In addition dances were started twice weekly for the men and proved very popular.	
	21st		The Battalion played 3rd Batt: The Rifle Brigade at Soccer on their ground and drew 2-2. The ground was very wet and the condition generally bad but despite this the game proved a good and exciting one.	R.A.
	25th & 26th		Unfortunately we had only enough tables and forms to dine two Companies at a time and accordingly the two rooms in the BREWERY were used. C & D Companies dined on Xmas Day & A & B on Boxing Day. Both lots of dinners went very well. B.G.C. 17th Inf Bde visited the dinners on both days.	
	27th – 31st		On the 27th C & D Companies assumed permanent use of their Dining Rooms. The Sgts had a dinner and a concert to follow it on the 27th but the Sgts mess cannot yet be started permanently. On 31st Major R.H. Rowland rejoined the Batt: from the Senior Officers School Aldershot. The main problem still left unsolved are tables & forms and the question of fuel which is still scarce and hard to obtain.	

1875 Wt. W593/826 1,000,000 4/15 J.B.C. & A. A.D.S.S./Forms/C. 2118.

R.A.

939.

(6392) Wt. W6192/P875 1,500,000 4/18 McA & W Ltd (E 2815) Forms W3091/4. Army Form W.3091.

1718/6

Cover for Documents.

Nature of Enclosures.

8th Bn. The Queens (R.W.S.) Regt

WAR DIARY

VOL. XLI

JANUARY 1919

24

ORDERLY ROOM
Q1230.
8th (S) QUEEN'S REGT.

R.J.H. Rowland Major
Commanding
8th Bn Queen's Regt.

5/2/19.

Notes, or Letters written.

14/3

Instructions regarding War Diaries and Intelligence Summaries are contained in F. S. Regs., Part II. and the Staff Manual respectively. Title Pages will be prepared in manuscript.

Army Form C. 2118

WAR DIARY
or
INTELLIGENCE SUMMARY
(Erase heading not required.)

January 1919 — Page 1

Place	Date	Hour	Summary of Events and Information	Remarks and references to Appendices
BAISIEUX	1st -31st		During this month substantially the same routine was followed as in December – parades and educational classes in the morning, football, cross country runs and other forms of sport in the afternoon, debates, concerts, whist drives and dances in the evening. Preparations were made for the presentation and consecration of a King's Colours and for subsequently trooping the same. The weather was damp for the first half of the month and then turned very cold with hard frosts and later several inches of snow, which interfered with outdoor parades and sports. The rate of demobilization increased considerably, until by the end of the month some 50 men per week were being sent to England either for final demobilization or for furlough on reenlistment. Events worth recording in detail are set out below	
	1st		The New Year's Honours Gazette contained the following awards:– D.S.O. – Major R.H. ROWLAND, D.C.M. – 60891 Sgt Drummer T P SHEPHERD, M.S.M. – 2631 R.Q.M.S. G.S. KERSWELL and 2469 C.S.M. W.J. TITE, Mentioned	

1875 Wt. W593/826 1,000,000 4/15 J.B.C. & A. A.D.S.S./Forms/C. 2118.

Instructions regarding War Diaries and Intelligence Summaries are contained in F. S. Regs., Part II. and the Staff Manual respectively. Title Pages will be prepared in manuscript.

January 1919

WAR DIARY
or
INTELLIGENCE SUMMARY
(Erase heading not required.)

Page 2

Army Form C. 2118

Place	Date	Hour	Summary of Events and Information	Remarks and references to Appendices
BAISIEUX	1st	(contd)	in Despatches – Lieut Col. H. J. C. PEIRS D.S.O., Major R. H. ROWLAND, 2/Lieut. C. E. LEWIN and 3021 R.S.M. L. G. TIPPEN.	
			The Battn played the 3rd Rifle Brigade at Rugby Football and beat them by 8 points to nil.	
	4th		The Battn played the 3rd Rifle Brigade at Association Football and beat them by 4 goals to 2.	
	11th		The Battn played the 13th Battn Middlesex Regiment at Association Football in the Divisional League and were beaten by 5 goals to 1	
"	14th		2/Lieut G. RAWES proceeded to U.K. for demobilization	
"	16th		The Battn played the 2nd Battn M.G.C. at Rugby Football ~~and were~~ in the Divisional League and were beaten by 17 points to nil	
"	19th		2/Lieut F. MITTON proceeded to U.K. for demobilization.	
	20th		The award of the M.C. to the following officers was announced:– Capt. J. BORRELL and Lieut H. P. BULLOCK. 2/Lieut J. B. HALL proceeded to	

1875 Wt. W593/826 1,000,000 4/15 J.B.C. & A. A.D.S.S./Forms/C. 2118.

CH

Army Form C. 2118

WAR DIARY
or
INTELLIGENCE SUMMARY
(Erase heading not required.)

Page 3

Instructions regarding War Diaries and Intelligence Summaries are contained in F. S. Regs., Part II. and the Staff Manual respectively. Title Pages will be prepared in manuscript. January 1919

Place	Date	Hour	Summary of Events and Information	Remarks and references to Appendices
BAISIEUX	20	(Contd)	U.K for demobilization.	
"	21st		Capt. J. BURRELL M.C. proceeded to U.K for demobilization	
			On the 20th 21st & 22nd performances of "Chu Chin Chow" were given by a troupe drawn from the Batt'n in the Theatre with great success.	

C F Latham
Lieut & Asst Adjt
5 Bn. The Queen's

1875 Wt. W593/826 1,000,000 4/15 J.B.C. & A. A.D.S.S./Forms/C. 2118.

VIII 42

940

(6392) Wt. W6192/P875 1,500,000 4/18 McA & W Ltd (E 2815) Forms W3091/4.

Army Form W.3091

Cover for Documents.

Nature of Enclosures.

8th BN THE QUEEN'S RWS REGT

WAR DIARY

VOLUME XLII

FEBRUARY 1919

MARCH 5th 1919

H. J. C. Peirs

LIEUT COLONEL
COMMANDING
8th QUEENS RWS REGT

Notes, or Letters written.

Army Form C. 2118

Instructions regarding War Diaries and Intelligence Summaries are contained in F. S. Regs., Part II. and the Staff Manual respectively. Title Pages will be prepared in manuscript.

February 1919

WAR DIARY
or
~~INTELLIGENCE SUMMARY~~
(Erase heading not required.)

Page 1

VOLUME XLIII

Place	Date	Hour	Summary of Events and Information	Remarks and references to Appendices
BAISIEUX	1–28 2/19		The Battalion continued in billets at BAISIEUX during the whole of the month, though towards the end part of the Brigade moved into TOURNAI. The weather throughout was against any form of sport, as the ground was covered with snow for more than half the month and after that the rain was frequent.	
			The chief event of the month took place on the 12th when the Corps Commander, Lieut General Sir Arthur Holland K.C.B., D.S.O., M.V.O., presented a King's Colour to the Battalion. Major General A.C. Daly C.B., Commanding 24th Division, was also present. The Battalion was by this time reduced by demobilization to between 350 and 400, but in spite of this and of the difficult conditions for a ceremonial parade caused by the snowy ground the consecration and presentation of the Colour proved a most impressive ceremony.	
			A few days prior to this orders had been received to	

1875 Wt. W593/826 1,000,000 4/15 J.B.C. & A. A.D.S.S./Forms/C. 2118.

Instructions regarding War Diaries and Intelligence Summaries are contained in F. S. Regs., Part II. and the Staff Manual respectively. Title Pages will be prepared in manuscript.

February 1919

WAR DIARY
or
INTELLIGENCE SUMMARY
(Erase heading not required.)

Army Form C. 2118

Page 2

Place	Date	Hour	Summary of Events and Information	Remarks and references to Appendices
BAISIEUX			have drafts of 15 Officers & 300 O.R's ready to proceed at short notice to the Army of Occupation, viz 10 Officers & 200 O.R's to the 10th Battalion The Queens, & 5 Officers & 100 O.R.'s to the 11th Battalion The Queens, both in the 41st Division. There seemed every prospect of the Battalion being shortly altogether dispersed, as these drafts would leave very few men beyond the number required for the Cadre.	
			Lieut Col H.J.C. PEIRS D.S.O returned from a months leave in the U.K on the 3rd and resumed command of the Battalion.	
			2/Lieuts. R.C. BROOKS M.C and H.S. SELOUS proceeded to the U.K on the 1st for demobilization	
			C.F. Latham Lieut & Asst Adjt 8th Bn The Queens	

1875 Wt. W593/826 1,000,000 4/15 J.B.C. & A. A.D.S.S./Forms/C. 2118.

(6392) Wt. W6192/P875 1,500,000 4/18 McA & W Ltd (E 2815) Forms W3091/4.

Army Form W.3091.

Cover for Documents.

Nature of Enclosures.

8th BN THE QUEEN'S R W S REGT

WAR DIARY

VOLUME XLIII

MARCH 1919

ORDERLY ROOM
Q 3644
8th (S) QUEEN'S REGT.

APRIL 1ST 1919

H. J. C. Peirs Lieut Colonel
Commanding
8th BN THE QUEENS REGt

Notes, or Letters written.

This map belongs to

8th Queens Diary

March 1918

Army Form C. 2118

Instructions regarding War Diaries and Intelligence Summaries are contained in F. S. Regs., Part II. and the Staff Manual respectively. Title Pages will be prepared in manuscript.

WAR DIARY
or
INTELLIGENCE SUMMARY
(Erase heading not required.)

Place	Date	Hour	Summary of Events and Information	Remarks and references to Appendices
BAISIEUX	1st MARCH – 31st MARCH		Throughout the whole month, the Battalion remained billeted at BAISIEUX gradually dwindling owing to demobilization and the sending of drafts to the Rhine. G.H.Q. permitted the release of officers who had joined or been commissioned in 1914 or 1915 amongst others the Battn lost Major R.H. Rowland DSO, Captain Riley & Lieut F.J. TATHAM the assistant adjutant. The Division is being rapidly reduced to CADRE & Div HQ ceased 26th March 1919. Returning inhabitants were a constant source of difficulty throughout the month as they naturally wanted to start making their houses habitable which they could not do while troops were still billeted on them. as much as possible was done to meet their wishes but it was not always convenient to move from houses at short notice.	E.a.J.

E.a. Fellows Captain & Adjutant.
8th Battn The Queen

1875 Wt. W593/826 1,000,000 4/15 J.B.C. & A. A.D.S.S./Forms/C. 2118.

(6392) Wt. W6192/P875 1,500,000 4/18 McA & W Ltd (E 2815) Forms W3091/4. Army Form W.3091.

1/24.

WO 44

Cover for Documents.

Nature of Enclosures.

~~8TH BN THE QUEENS RWS REGT~~

WAR DIARY

VOLUME XLIV

APRIL 1919

3/5/19

D C G Dickinson 2/ LIEUT
FOR OFF COMDG
8TH BN THE QUEENS
RWS REGT

Notes, or Letters written.

Army Form C. 2118

Instructions regarding War Diaries and Intelligence Summaries are contained in F. S. Regs., Part II. and the Staff Manual respectively. Title Pages will be prepared in manuscript.

WAR DIARY *or* INTELLIGENCE SUMMARY

(Erase heading not required.)

April 1919 — VOLUME XLIV

Place	Date	Hour	Summary of Events and Information	Remarks and references to Appendices
			The Battalion remained billeted in BAISIEUX the whole month and	
BAISIEUX	1ST		at the end was practically down to CADRE STRENGTH.	
	to		The following Officers left the Battalion on dates shewn as under:—	
	30th		2ND LIEUT E JENKINS M.C. To 11th Battn The Queens RWS Regt 16. 4-19	
			CAPTAIN E A MOORE To Command P OF W COY 19-4-19.	
			LIEUT W G CAMPBELL TO ENGLAND FOR DEMOB 21-4-19.	
			—"— R N ROSE ditto 21-4-19	
			2/LIEUT G H NASH To 2/4th QUEENS REGT 22 4-19	
			—"— E S TRAPPITT ditto 22. 4-19	
			Drafts proceeded to join Army of Occupation as follows:—	
			4 O Ranks to 11th Bn The Queens RWS Regt 11 4 19	
			21 O Ranks ditto 16. 4-19	

D.C.G. Dickinson 2/Lieut
for O C
8th Queens RWS Regt

1875 Wt. W593/826 1,000,000 4/15 J.B.C. & A. A.D.S.S./Forms/C. 2118.